Yes,
I Can
Say No

Also by Manuel J. Smith

WHEN I SAY NO, I FEEL GUILTY
KICKING THE FEAR HABIT

Yes, I Can Say No

A Parent's Guide to Assertiveness Training for Children

Manuel J. Smith, Ph.D.

ARBOR HOUSE
New York

Copyright © 1986 by the Institute for Systematic Assertiveness Training
and Human Development

Manufactured in the United States of America

10 9 8 7 6 5 4 3 2 1

Library of Congress Cataloging in Publication Data

Smith, Manuel J., 1934–
  Yes, I can say no.

  1. Child rearing.   2. Assertiveness in children.
3. Interpersonal relations in children.   4. Child
psychology.   I. Title.
HQ769.S5716   1986   649'.1   86–20602
ISBN: 0-87795-828-9

To the next generation,
always the more important one,
and its following members:

Kelli, Nikki, and Rich
Tracy and Phil
Joanne, Norine, and Mike
Garth, Tony, and Jonas
Cameron and Sean
and little Simon

Contents

CHAPTER TWO

How to Recognize When You Are Being Emotionally Manipulated: The Bill of Assertive Rights for You and Your Child

Manipulation: How people talk you and your child into doing what they want by making you feel guilty, ignorant, or foolish

CHAPTER THREE

Persistence: The Basic Foundation for Dealing with Peer Pressure and Other Social Manipulation

CHAPTER FOUR

Teaching Your Child to be Human: Coping With Errors, Faults, and Criticism   82

CHAPTER FIVE

Teaching Your Child to Assertively Cope with Other Children: Saying No, and Asking for What Is Wanted   111

Table of Dialogues

Preface

A bout four years ago I read an article in the *Los Angeles Times* and saw my name mentioned. It was in reference to the Irvine (California) Unified School District's research project STAR (Social Thinking and Reasoning), wherein children in the sixth through eighth grades were taught to be assertive with each other and with their teachers. My name was mentioned primarily because material in the course was taken from the national best-seller I had written on assertiveness training for adults, *When I Say No, I Feel Guilty*, and adapted to the needs of middle-school children.

The results of this training program were amazing. After the first year, the research staff found that for the hundreds of students in the original research group, the children taught to be assertive (as compared to those who were not) were ill less often, had a better attendance record at school, scored higher in math and reading (up to and above the national average on standardized achievement tests), had a better self-image, and showed a positive change in negative attitudes that would have predicted future drug abuse. A follow-up study three years later, with most of these students now in high school, showed that the children trained to be assertive were more resistant to peer pressure to use drugs, alcohol, or tobacco. Further, the assertiveness-trained students had achieved a higher overall grade point average (plus .45, meaning an increase of D+ to C, or C+ to B, or B+ to A) than the students not trained to be assertive.

These startling increases in positive coping, as well as in academic achievement, are reliable, with younger students (including those trained after the original group) showing the same positive increases as they move through high school. The long-term increase in overall grade point average as the children move through high school—a half-point advantage over the nonassertive pupils—can make the difference between going to college and not going to college for many of these students. And the even longer-term implications are staggering: It would be more than fair to say that the assertive students had been given not only an academic and personal advantage over their untrained peers during their school years, but perhaps even a lifetime advantage.

I know of no school training program with results like these. And the most astonishing thing of all is the fact that these very positive results were not derived from special courses in math or reading, or the dangers of drugs and alcohol, but from a simple, systematic course on how to relate to other people in a more mature and assertive way. This course achieved these results by giving the children who took it a set of realistic and practical social skills to cope with the ways their environment and their peers really operate.

In the last few years, thousands of students in California have been trained to be more assertive by teachers using STAR materials. These methods and techniques have been used to teach younger children, in grades three through five, how to respond more effectively in social conflict. STAR has also been adapted to the needs of high-school students with the same good results and renamed PLUS (Promoting Learning and Understanding of Self).

Having spent a number of years working on these methods and developing them into a systematic training package, I was pleased to learn they were being used by educational researchers to help children cope better. Needless to say, I contacted the people of the STAR research project in the Irvine Unified School District and have worked with them since, providing input into their excellent educational research and development program.

Initially working without this input, the Irvine researchers had confirmed systematically what I had experienced clinically in teaching thousands of people to be more assertive. The skills I developed and taught were not my personal skills, effective only if *I* used them or if *I* taught them to people in my own special way; dozens (and later, many hundreds) of my colleagues demonstrated in the early years of the assertiveness-training movement that the verbal skills in the training package could be successfully taught by virtually anyone, and are simple enough for even mentally handicapped students to learn quickly and benefit from. Therefore, you needn't worry that you may not be able to do a good job teaching your child because you are not a teacher.

It's a sad fact of life that there are those who are advantaged and those who are not, and that those who are advantaged are going to lead happier and more successful lives than those who are not. Given a choice—and now you do have that choice—it's up to you as a parent to see that your child has the type of training necessary to gain that advantage. No one else is going to do it. Unless there is a radical change, I predict it will take at least twenty years for the material in this book and the Irvine STAR program to be routinely available in school districts nationwide to teach young children how to be assertive. Practically speaking, it isn't available now except in a relatively small number of schools in California. My hope is that the publication of this book will not only enable you to teach your own children but will speed up the adoption of assertiveness training in schools across the country, so that we will not have to mark time for another generation before all our children have a lifetime advantage.

Acknowledgments

T he material in this book is not the result of one person's effort but one end result of the work of many professionals in clinical and educational psychology and teaching. A list of all who have contributed would number in the hundreds. I thank them first, even though anonymously.

Next, congratulations and thanks go to the staff and administration of the STAR research project of the Irvine Unified School District, Irvine, California, for successfully developing, field-testing, evaluating, supporting, and then teaching teachers about the STAR curriculum program. Special recognition is due Bruce Givner, Ph.D., deputy superintendent, whose personal concern and support was felt from the boardroom to the teaching laboratory; Anne Foster, M.S.; Margaret ("Bunny") Nurick, B.A.; and Judy Sumner Brown, M.S.—all three of whom participated in the writing and/or testing of STAR; Nancy Richards, M.S.; Christine Honeyman, M.S.; and Debbie Krumpholtz, M.S. —the three people who translated STAR into PLUS, the high-school version, and evaluated it as well as doing the long-term follow-up on STAR students; and the many others who contributed their share to STAR.

The work of William Benn, M.S., research director of the STAR project, in conceiving of STAR and then making it a reality, must be specially noted. Without Bill's brilliant foresight, ideas, writing, sweat, and tenacity in assertively and genially solving problem after problem, STAR and this manuscript would not exist.

I would also like to thank Bill, Nancy, Debbie, and Chris, as well as my friend and colleague Joseph B. Sidowski, Ph.D., professor of psychology and former chairman of the psychology department at the University of South Florida in Tampa, for their review of this manuscript. Joe's enthusiasm for this project and constant prompting for more output helped greatly.

Very special thanks are due Jesse Kant, Ed.D., and Harold S. Kant, M.S., J.D., Olympic Village, Lake Tahoe, California, for their ideas, critiques, and contributions, as well as their encouragement and support over the past five years. Without the efforts of Hal and Jesse, the follow-up research on STAR and PLUS might not have been possible.

Although the reviewers of this manuscript have improved it, I myself must be responsible for any errors or inaccuracies that remain.

I and the staff of the Irvine Unified School District wish to acknowledge partial support of the STAR project by the California Department of Education (ESEA Title IVC) and the Children Assistance Trust, which made it possible to help so many children, and potentially many more.

I also wish to acknowledge the technical help given by Zenith Data Systems Corporation, especially Susanne Sultan of the Zenith Educational Division, Torrance, California, in the preparation of the manuscript and in expediting and furthering the research goals of the STAR project.

Special thanks go also to Jennifer Patten Smith for her unflagging support and her criticism of the manuscript as it was written; and to Philippa ("Flip") Brophy of the Sterling Lord Agency for her counsel and good work. Without either of these two morale boosters, this book might not have been written.

One final acknowledgment does not have to be made for anyone with knowledge of the publishing industry, but I want to make it anyway. The hard work of Ann Harris, editor in chief of Arbor House, made this manuscript much more than what I wrote. God must have smiled on this project for Ann to collaborate with me.

Yes,
I Can
Say No

CHAPTER ONE

Teaching Your Child How to Become a Successful Adult

The Good Child

Mary was shy, self-conscious, and eight years old. Her brother's idea of having a conversation with Mary was to tease her unmercifully. Her second-grade classmates often did the same thing. Socially, young kids sometimes behave like sharks. Sensing another child's vulnerability, as sharks sense blood, they attack that child verbally. Often the attack is vicious and cruel, making children like Mary even more self-conscious and shy. There was nothing really wrong with Mary, other than her inability to deal with cruel teasing, or even constructive criticism by her friends. She had a poor self-image and lacked self-confidence, but the basic reason she couldn't cope with teasing was because she was a good child.

All of us know what a good child is. A good child is a people pleaser —more specifically, an authority pleaser. A good child is obedient and patient, willing to accept what we grown-ups think is important without fighting us, and usually causes very little trouble, especially in the younger years. A good child thinks highly of other people, especially those who seem to know what they are doing, and very little of him- or herself. A good child expects other people to take care of him or her, and when others expose the good child's imperfections, the good child is defenseless.

Because Mary was basically a good child, she was very susceptible to peer pressure and easily teased into believing that she was inferior. In teaching her to be a good child, her parents did not teach her how to handle social conflicts—such as disagreements, arguments, criticism, or teasing—because a good child is not supposed to engage in any of these things (especially with mom or dad) nor be the victim of such things. A good child is taught that children who do these things are bad and should be avoided.

Advice like this wasn't much help to Mary. How could she avoid her brother, who lived in the same house, or the classmates she spent every day with? And if she ignored most of her classmates, whom could she relate to? Children want to belong, not be loners. This advice on how to cope properly could not work.

Mary began to experience three emotional consequences—the same three that all of us experience when something we've been taught should work doesn't: alternating periods of anxiety, depression, and resentment (or smoldering anger). In addition to these, there is usually a sneaking suspicion that in some way we have been conned, though we are unable to put a finger on how. Mary had a psychological problem she could not solve, so she turned to the primary primitive coping mechanism available to her: She withdrew from the conflict situation.

When you and I see a child like Mary treated this way, our hearts go out to that unfortunate little soul. First, we identify strongly with the youngster because of our own childhood experiences. Next, our sense of human dignity and fair play is outraged that things like this can happen to a defenseless child, even at the hands of other, supposedly innocent children. Our immediate impulse is to tell those kids in no uncertain terms to shut up. But even when they do, we still feel impotent and helpless, because what will happen later when we are not there?

This dilemma over what to do about the pressures youngsters put on one another when adults are not around extends far beyond childhood teasing. Good children like Mary, who want to belong but have low self-esteem, can be readily talked into misbehaving, neglecting their schoolwork, truancy, delinquency, cheating, and—later—into premature sexual experiences, smoking, drinking, and drug use. Because we don't know how to handle the problem, it is usually left to the child to figure out how to solve it. Sadly, the child tries to do this the same way we did in our own childhood—and, like us, does not succeed. What can be done about this emotional dilemma that seems to have no practical answer? One approach, rarely used until a few years ago, is to systematically teach the child how to cope psychologically and behaviorally with cruel teasing and other pressures to conform to whatever the child's peer group wants. Luckily, little Mary was taught to do this by an expert.

Assertive Behavior: Adult Communication, Problem Solving, and Self-Assurance

When Mary began staying home from school more and more, and her grades started to fall, she came to the attention of Chris, my colleague and a psychologist on the staff of the Irvine project STAR (Social Thinking and Reasoning), a course being used with middle-school children. After sizing up what was happening to Mary, Mary's teacher and Chris announced to the second grade that they were going to give a demonstration of something the children would all find useful and helpful: how to cope assertively with their fellow students, especially when being criticized or teased. Chris first explained the assertive technique to the children and described its effects. Its main effect is to make the person who learns and practices it less emotionally vulnerable to teasing or criticism. Its second effect is to exhaust the tormentor, not by denying what has been said or remaining silent, but by asking for an explanation or by deliberately inviting more of it, thereby giving the teaser or critic no payoff in seeing the other person squirm. As Chris pointed out to the children, it's no fun to criticize or tease someone when the person doesn't get upset.

Chris then asked for volunteers to demonstrate how to cope with teasing. A few students raised their hands, but not Mary. After these children finished their demonstration of assertiveness, Chris asked if there was anyone else who was particularly sensitive to teasing and would like to learn how to be less sensitive. Holding their breaths, Chris and the teacher waited for Mary to volunteer. Mary, looking around and seeing no one else wanting to practice, raised her hand shyly. The rest of the class was instructed to tease and criticize her. Standing at the head of the class for twenty minutes, with Chris at her side coaching her, Mary learned how to respond assertively to teasing and criticism from her classmates. At the end of the demonstration, having seen Mary change from a frightened little girl into someone who handled their criticism and teasing with a smile, her classmates gave her a loud round of applause. During the following weeks, Chris and the second-grade teacher observed Mary use her newly learned skill repeatedly, without prompting or coaching, on the playground with other children when they began to tease.

Parents and teachers also become very concerned when good children turn out to be overly aggressive and explosively angry, instead of passive and withdrawn, when being good doesn't work for them. Greg, an eleven-year-old boy in the sixth grade, demonstrated this behavior, the opposite of Mary's but deriving from the same conflict—trying to be a good child in a less than perfect world whose inhabitants didn't respond as they were supposed to.

Greg was a below-average student with behavior and discipline problems. He was sent to the vice-principal two to three times a week, usually for getting into fights with other students. He was being considered for suspension and transfer to a special school for emotionally handicapped children just before he was selected for enrollment in the STAR program at his school. STAR is designed to teach good children how to be assertive with each other and with their teachers. In the course, Greg learned that he was too emotional and aggressive—unnecessarily so—in trying to cope with social conflicts. His teacher taught him to be assertively persistent, calm, firm, and friendly with other students, staff, teachers, and other adults, instead of being aggressive and angry.

Halfway through the course, Greg's parents showed up at school unexpectedly to talk to his teacher. They reported that Greg's behavior and ways of coping had changed so radically that they hardly recognized him as the same boy. His actions the previous weekend had prompted them to find out what Greg was being taught. Prior to his learning to be assertive, they had stopped taking him out to dinner with them because his behavior was so unpredictable. He was likely to have an emotional outburst in the restaurant, insulting the waiter or waitress, or walking out if anything went wrong. Having seen him begin to behave more calmly in other situations, they had decided to take another chance, and the three of them had dinner out. As can happen, the dinner was both a disaster and a God-sent test of Greg's newfound coping skills. The waitress fouled everything up, even forgetting to order Greg's dinner. But Greg's parents were thrilled because he took charge and dealt with the waitress persistently, firmly, and amiably until she got everything right.

In the course of that year, Greg's grades shot up, the number of times he was disciplined went back to normal, and Greg began to offer to teach his assertive skills to his friends. Greg summed up this positive change and maturity with "I just never knew!"

Teaching children to be good children leaves them little room for independent judgment. Since dependence induces a poor self-image and little ego strength, good children strive to at least appear perfect—and in a perfect environment they succeed. But the world is not composed of perfect environments, inside or outside the classroom, and that's where these children run into trouble. If the good child does not understand the material presented by the teacher, he or she will rarely admit this by raising a hand and asking the teacher to explain further. Both academic achievement and grades are therefore lower than what the good child's natural ability and intelligence should produce.

STAR allowed those children trained in its social skills to fulfill more of their academic potential because, first, it allowed them to be less defensive and secretive about their difficulties in understanding the material they had to learn in school. It also enabled them to deal with peer pressure that would have diverted them from studying, and helped them gain self-confidence by giving them a way to cope with humiliating peer criticism. The resulting boost in self-image and ego (a typical result of assertiveness training) encouraged the youngsters to rely increasingly on their own abilities and accomplishments for feeling good about themselves, rather than depending on mood-altering substances to relieve their anxieties and give them good feelings.

Ideally, teaching your child to cope assertively with social pressure and conflict should begin as early as possible, starting at about age seven. But even if your child is older, this training is very worthwhile. If your child learns to be assertive in the elementary-school period, from about age seven to ten, he or she will be better able to cope in the coming middle-school years, when pubertal and prepubertal social pressures and awakening sexuality usually cause a significant drop in academic performance. If your child is already in the middle-school years—about eleven to thirteen—learning to be more assertive will provide better ways of coping with the enormous pressure to conform that lie ahead during the high-school years: pressure to gain social acceptance at the expense of academic interest, performance, and potential. If your child is a teenager between fourteen and seventeen, learning to be assertive during this period will enable him or her to handle the larger, unsupervised environment of college, especially during the first two years, when as many as 50 percent of entering freshmen drop out. Thus, there are positive payoffs for your child in learning how to assertively cope with the pressures of living with other human beings at any point during the ten-year span between seven and seventeen.

This book will not tell you how to control your child or teenager and get him or her to do what you want. Such a goal is hopeless and foolish —you cannot control anyone to that degree. Trying to do so is impractical, like substituting a verbal harness for the leather one that restrained the child as an infant. Unfortunately, some parents feel they cannot cope with their children unless they control almost everything a child can possibly do. If you sincerely feel that is the only way you can keep your child out of trouble, off drugs, or away from premature sexual experience, this book is not for you. It is not a quick fix to straighten out a teenager already in deep trouble.

You *can* control young children, but this kind of control diminishes when your child enters school, and after ten to twelve years of age it is effectively over. Just telling them what's right—that is, what you as a parent want—doesn't work anymore. A wiser course is to begin giving children the permission and ability to think for themselves—they will need to do this anyway sooner or later—and avoid the nasty side effects of parental overcontrol: rebellion, troublesome behavior, alcohol and drug abuse, promiscuity. Parental overcontrol leaves a child with a negative sense of identity: "If I have to be controlled all the time, with mom or dad always telling me what to do and what I'm doing wrong, I must be really stupid and certainly not competent. If I can't be trusted to do things properly myself, even if I make a few dumb mistakes while I learn, then I certainly can't respect myself."

One typical result of this type of child rearing is that the child looks away from mom and dad for approval and toward peers to boost his or her ego. When that happens, other children can talk this child into just about anything. A second result of overcontrol is that the child begins to resent mom and dad and to deliberately do things that upset them as a way of getting back at them for always treating him or her as a second-class person.

Teaching children how to think for themselves, feel confident about themselves, and to carry out decisions in the face of peer pressure is the purpose of this book. One of its objectives is to give a child the thinking and verbal ability, as well as the self-respect, to say no—and mean it— to alcohol, drugs, misbehavior, or premature sex. Giving children these abilities is not a simple matter of telling them about the dangers of drugs or alcohol and how to say no to them, but teaching them how to say no to lots of things that damage self-respect and positive self-image, thereby minimizing a chronic need for peer approval and chemical ego boosts. When you teach your children to be assertive—and as you will see, this can be taught systematically as early as age seven—you help foster a positive self-image that will stand them in good stead not only during their school years but later on in life.

At this point you may be asking yourself, "What is assertiveness?" It's a very good question. If we were to assemble a blue-ribbon panel of the top ten clinical diagnostic experts in psychology and psychiatry from prestigious hospitals all around the country—Bellevue, Walter Reed, Langley-Porter, Mass. General, and others—and parade a group of people in front of them, our panel would easily agree as to which ones would benefit from assertiveness training and which ones would not. But if you asked these same ten experts to *define* what they were diagnosing— *assertiveness* versus *nonassertiveness*—they would give you ten different definitions.

Assertiveness has not been very well defined or thought through, even in expert clinical circles. One common definition is "Standing up for your rights, while respecting the rights of others." These are grand words but they are tossed around without the specifics that tell you what people's "rights" are in any situation. Another frequently used definition is a negative one: "Assertiveness is not being aggressive." But aggression is also poorly defined. Depending on circumstances, aggression can be angry, childish impulsive behavior, or mature, determined, and motivated behavior. You will also often hear, "Assertiveness is being different from everyone else, being an individual." This definition suffers when you decide that you like what other people do and how they live.

All these commonly used and superficial definitions of assertiveness fail to mention the two elements of being assertive; making one's own decisions about what to do, and carrying out those decisions in the face of social pressure or opposition. This, basically, is what the STAR program, my earlier book *When I Say No, I Feel Guilty*, PLUS (the high-school version of STAR), and this book are all about.

If we can't rely on a clear clinical definition of what assertiveness is, at least we can start with the working definition—and it's not a bad one —offered by my edition of Webster's Dictionary. It says that to assert oneself is to set forth and defend an argument, claim, or position self-confidently. Essentially, our assertiveness is based on the faith we have in our own judgment, even if it runs counter to what is popular, faddish, or "in." When we assert ourselves, we don't have to have a whole battery of Supreme Court lawyers (or the court itself) standing behind us, telling everyone that we are right. Using this definition, one can see that competent, mature, and successful adults will have at least a modicum of assertiveness, simply because they have had a lot of experience in thinking for themselves.

A little over a decade ago, transactional analysis (TA) became very popular because it offered a useful way of looking at how we routinely, automatically, and unthinkingly behave toward other people: as a critical parent (usually punishing), as an insignificant child (usually good, but also naughty), or as an adult (always straightforward). According to TA, your problems in dealing with another person come about because you interact with him or her as if you were a critical parent dealing with an insignificant child, or vice versa. To correct these problems, TA states that you need to deal with other people on an adult-to-adult level instead of a parent-child level. If you behave like an adult while the other person behaves as a parent or child, you will feel better about yourself because the critical parent can't make you feel rotten, and you will leave him or her no option except to deal with you as another adult.

According to the tenets of TA, eight-year-old Mary had problems in school because the other children interacted with her as if they were critical parents (teasing and criticizing her), and Mary responded on the child level. In transactional-analysis terms, Chris's demonstration of assertively coping with criticism worked for Mary because it taught her how to respond in an adult way to a bunch of critical parents she had not been able to handle. In TA terms, assertiveness in fact *is* adult behavior.

The Socially Competent Adult and the Good Child: As Different as Apples and Oranges

You know what an adult is and so do I: someone we can rely on when we have to. We could make a long list of the fine points of being an adult, but it would be worthless unless we included the one fundamental upon which all the other points depend: An adult is a socially competent, independently functioning person, able to think for him- or herself, cope with life's problems, and take care of all day-to-day decisions that have to be made, without depending on someone else to do this. By "socially competent," I do not mean being witty, pleasant, and charming, but having the ability to solve the problems other people present us with, including their attempts to talk us into things that are really not in our own best interests.

When we rear a child with the goal of producing a socially competent person, we often make the mistake of training the child to be a good child, like Mary, and assume that the good child will automatically mature into a socially competent adult. Unfortunately that assumption is not valid. A good child lives by fixed rules laid down by its parents, which usually begin with "Always . . ." and "Never. . . ." A good child is obedient, deferential, and dependent, accepting a parent's (or someone else's) judgment of what is right and wrong. A good child rarely if ever says no to someone and means it. All parents train their offspring to be good children, as we will see, but few train them in the skills they will need to be effective adults. Teenagers often have to learn these skills on their own, and are handicapped if they do not or cannot learn them.

The personal skills required to live a satisfying and productive adult life are often the opposite of the skills required to be a good child. A socially competent adult uses independent judgment in determining how to behave and what is right or wrong in a particular situation. Competent adults occasionally take chances and must deal with personal mistakes in shaping their lives into what they want them to be. The adult has to know when to be cooperative and when—patiently and, if necessary, stubbornly—to resist the influence and pressure of others. A socially competent adult is rarely deferential to other people, and uses the word *no* very often.

The Parent's Conflicting Goals: Rearing a Good Child and a Future Adult

The very young child, of course, must be taught to be a good child if family life is to be harmonious. You have to make most of the decisions for a very young child, and your child needs to obey you without much backchat to ensure a stable family routine and to ensure the child's very survival during the early years.

In rearing your child, you have two goals that are in conflict: producing a good child now, and producing a socially competent adult later. While training your child to be a good child is an absolute necessity, that early training is ultimately secondary to training the child to be a competent adult. Your child is only a child for a few quickly passing years. He or she will be an adult and face adult problems for a lifetime. This conflict can complicate things. The childhood years are trying for most parents, especially for the mother. The parent in charge has to figure out how to make the family process work, and at the same time ensure that the kids are neither turned into robots in order to make communal family life easier, nor allowed so much freedom that the family home is transformed into a twenty-four-hour fast-food franchise located in a hot-sheet motel. Neither of these extremes of rigidity or permissiveness is good childrearing, because neither resembles the conditions the child will likely live under as an adult. Parents need to find solutions that will achieve both goals: preserving the family as a working unit, and rearing their children in the best practical way possible to be independent, socially functional adults.

The Removable Plaster Cast of the Good Child

Thus teaching a young child to be a good child is a temporary, though essential, expedient. To keep in mind this indoctrination's practical and only purpose, think of it as the equivalent of putting a plaster cast on a broken leg. The purpose of the cast is to provide support while the weak leg grows stronger; it will not be kept on indefinitely. The same thing can be said for the training you have to give to make your child a good child during the early years. The psychological plaster cast should be removed as the child matures so he or she will have the freedom to learn, gradually, how to be a functioning adult. In practice, the best way of doing this is to remove the cast layer by layer, as the child grows up, rather than all at once at the end of high school, when he or she is now supposed to be an adult.

The Young Child's Restricted Environment

You can successfully train a younger child to be a good child and to behave like a good child around you because the younger child's environment is fairly restricted and simple. You plan and regulate most of the child's activities, and the child does almost everything with you or under your direction. You and the rest of your family exert the greatest influence on your child's thinking and behavior. This arrangement of directive parent and good child works well until the child goes to school. After that, you will never again have as great an influence on your child, simply because you are no longer the only important part of his or her total environment. In school the child begins to behave and believe in accordance with the expectations of peers, teachers, and other adults.

The Preteen's Expanded Environment

Twenty-five or thirty years ago, the environment in which a child grew up was much more restricted and therefore much less complex than it is now. We had a great many social rules that directed children or teenagers away from making important decisions. We were not supposed to be sexually active, or take drugs, or drink booze. Males were supposed to behave in certain "masculine" ways—to be strong and tough—and their primary goal in life was to succeed outside the home. Females were supposed to behave in other specific ways—to be kind, caring, and nurturing—and their primary goal in life was to get married and rear children.

But today, children approaching puberty and entering the middle-school years find themselves in a literally explosive environment. Most of the absolute rules about good and bad that they learned earlier are no help in coping with this new world and its challenges. The ideas and behaviors that children are exposed to are not the simple and stereotyped ones of thirty years ago, but are varied, contradictory, and complex. "When is sex okay?" "What am I going to grow up to be?" "Do I want to be a career person like my father, or a relationship person like my mother? If so, do I really need to learn this stuff?" "When is it okay to start drinking?" "What kind of person takes drugs?" "Is it okay for me to use drugs?" "If my friends are doing it, why shouldn't I?"

All of these are questions that children approaching or in their teens have to answer. There will be hordes of people, including your child's peers, who are quite willing to tell your child what to do, and the good child is usually talked into believing what they say. Good children who have not learned to think for themselves *before* this period of transition are like the disadvantaged souls in the old joke: "The meek will inherit the earth." "Yes," says a cynic, "but the pushy ones will take it back in the first twenty-four hours!"

During this time, your child has to learn to deal with his or her changing body, new sensations and interests, and sociosexual role, as well as what is right and wrong for an almost-adult. Amid all this uncertainty and confusion, he or she will be faced with formidable peer pressures and criticism. Your inexperienced child has to work out ways to deal with this confusing and sometimes frightening environment.

The typical preteen has to reevaluate most of what was taught him or her previously as a good child. The old lessons must be placed in a new perspective, especially those beginning with "Always . . ." or "Never . . ." whose intention was to prescribe how the good child should behave to please others. During this period of rapid change, your child will need to start thinking independently, to make decisions without you, and to take responsibility for the outcome of these decisions. In short, preteens have to begin thinking as adults do and assert themselves on a regular basis. Many parents, unfortunately, encourage their almost-teenagers to hold on to childish assumptions that life is orderly, that people are fair, and that virtue will prevail. These parents fail to tell their children between the ages of ten and thirteen, "Remember all those good things we taught you up to now on how to behave and what to believe? Well, they won't work anymore. Everything is going to change and you will have to work out the new rule book by yourself. We can help, but you have to do it."

If you have not taught your child to be socially competent in the early years, there will be a great deal of catching up to do, when the child's environment becomes more complex. Ideally, you should start to teach your child how to handle more complicated situations before the child experiences them. As Vince Lombardi, the late great coach of the Green Bay Packers, said, "Football games are won Thursday afternoons on the practice field, not Sunday afternoons on the playing field." If you begin early, as soon as children are capable of understanding what you are teaching them, they will come to see assertiveness as a natural attribute, and assertive behavior will gradually become automatic.

Are Assertive Children More Difficult to Handle?

Teachers and parents are often uneasy with the concept of children asserting themselves. They feel that kids are hard enough to control without giving them license to make adults' lives more difficult. This is a mistaken impression. The three-year follow-up of the STAR project found that kids trained to be assertive caused no more disciplinary problems than the untrained students. Teaching them to be assertive is not handing them a loaded verbal gun that will allow them to run amok. Even more important to understand, if you as a parent or as a teacher tell a child to do something, and it routinely doesn't get done, it is never the child's assertive qualities that are causing the problem. In fact, teaching a child to be assertive eliminates many of the ineffective coping behaviors that children use to try to get out of doing things, or to deny that they are at fault. I doubt that there is a teacher or parent who has not heard a child say "I didn't do that," right after seeing the child do it! When kids learn to cope assertively with some of the dumb things they do, instead of denying that they did them, they typically make fewer dumb mistakes. Moreover, the mistakes they do make are corrected quickly because time isn't wasted in arguments.

The Key to Getting Your Children to Do What You Ask: Communication, then Consequences

Parents who are frustrated by disobedient or unmotivated children are often the cause of the problem because they either don't tell their children straightforwardly what is wanted or they don't back up what they say. The key to understanding most of the interactive behavior between two human beings and the problems we all experience with this behavior is described by two words: *communication* and *consequences*. The psychological concepts these two words represent account for so much in understanding what we do and what we see in other people that five of the chapters in this book concentrate on straightforward assertive communication, while the last chapter is devoted solely to the way consequences back up communications and make them work. As you will see in the last chapter, making judgments about behavior payoffs is so important in human interaction that I think of benign everyday consequences as the "silent assertive message."

When you teach your child to assert him- or herself, you can also expect that the child will try to use that assertiveness to get out of things you want done. This, as we say in the trade, "goes with the territory," is harmless, and is good practice for your child. After all, if he or she can't say no to you (a safe person to learn from), to whom can your child say no? Asserting him- or herself to you is no great problem. As long as neither of you takes away the other's dignity and self-respect, this assertiveness does not mean that you are no longer the parent with parental authority or that your child is no longer the child. With experience, your child learns that you really do mean what you say, because he or she can't con you out of what you want done.

This book is written to help you to teach your child to be more assertive and reap the benefits thereof. It will first teach you, as a parent, how to be assertive yourself (even to your child), and then show you how to teach assertiveness to your child. This way you will understand what each element of assertiveness is before you teach it to your child. Further, your first learning how to be assertive results in one of the most effective teaching methods known, behavior modeling. If you behave more assertively, without even trying to teach it to your child, in the long run your child will learn to be assertive, using you as a model, by copying your behavior in "monkey see, monkey do" fashion.

Simple modeling of assertive behavior was the method used in the first successful attempt I am aware of to teach young children to be more assertive. This was done by my colleague Martin Willins at the Laguna Unified School District in southern California about ten years ago. Marty held weekly therapy "rap" sessions with a group of children having mild emotional and behavioral problems. Whenever he was with them, Marty modeled being assertive. During the sixth meeting, he wanted to make a point, but broke the rules of the group. The seven-year-old boy who had the floor said, "Marty, when you set up the group, you made a rule that if anybody wants to speak to the group, he gets in the center and speaks to everybody."

Marty answered, "Give me a break. I've been driving for hours to get down here to Laguna. I'm beat. You don't know how hard it is on me. I kill myself for you guys, and what do I get?"

The boy replied calmly, "I understand how you feel, Marty, but the rules of the group are that you take center floor."

Marty, of course, then took center floor because this was exactly the type of persistent, assertive verbal behavior he wanted these kids to adopt. He was demonstrating to them, as STAR does, that in solving social conflicts with their peers or teachers, they could be much more effective by being assertive than by getting angry and then physically acting out their angry feelings, or by giving in and lowering their self-esteem even more. Marty and STAR both paraphrase that old saying "Don't get angry, just get assertive [even]!"

The response of the seven-year-old (who had adopted the assertive verbal style Marty had modeled for dealing with disagreements and arguments) seems both humorous and appealing, at least in part because it doesn't sound as if it came from a seven-year-old. It sounds more like the response of a socially competent adult, because it reflects a thought-out position usually taken only by an adult. Assertiveness, in fact, can be thought of as socially competent adult behavior at its best, whereby one uses one's brains and experience to resolve problems between human beings instead of making them worse.

Teaching your child how to become mature by communicating like a socially competent person and by learning to think and make judgments about the consequences of his or her choices are discussed in detail later. But before we discuss assertiveness, we need to face its lack. Let's turn to the next chapter, where we will examine the prime factor causing you and your child to be nonassertive; the manipulation of your feelings of guilt, ignorance, and foolishness by other people.

CHAPTER TWO

How to Recognize When You Are Being Emotionally Manipulated: The Bill of Assertive Rights for You and Your Child

A s you have seen, it is important to view teaching your very young child to be a "good child" as a necessary but temporary expedient. A good child does what you tell him or her to do with little resistance, accepting that mom and dad know best. Any problems that may arise are handled either by you or by another adult you have selected to supervise the child. You assume that when your child grows older, he or she will begin to think independently. Unfortunately, however, this early training has a negative side effect: Your child grows up thinking that it is always others—even peers—who know best. And this is where serious problems can begin.

To counteract this negative side effect, we have to teach children to discriminate—to think for themselves. We don't want them to throw out the good things we have spent years teaching them; rather, we want them to modify the rules appropriately as they mature. As children become more and more competent at making decisions for themselves, they become able to take on more responsibility for their own well-being, the ultimate practical goal of child rearing.

This chapter is about teaching children to think for themselves as they mature, so that they are not intimidated by other people into doing things that are really not in their own best interests.

Manipulation: How People Talk You and Your Child into Doing What They Want by Making You Feel Guilty, Ignorant, or Foolish

To understand how your child can be talked into doing all sorts of things by friends and schoolmates, even if he or she doesn't want to— such as neglecting schoolwork, playing hooky, cutting classes, or abusing drugs or alcohol—we have to first look at how you yourself can be talked into doing things against your own better judgment. Your own response in such circumstances is a fairly reliable indicator of how your child will respond, since your child has learned to behave this way from you.

Think about the last time you swore you would never agree to do something again, either because you really didn't want to, or it was such a pain that it wasn't worth it. Perhaps last year you served as secretary for a committee of your social club, church or temple, PTA, etc., and kept all its records, or made cookies for its bake sale, or used your house for meetings. Deciding to be firm, you have let the organization know that you are not going to do the same thing again this year.

DIALOGUE 1

How You Get Conned into Something after You Swore, "Never Again!"
Setting: Just before the first meeting, bake sale, etc., the committee chairperson calls you, and the conversation goes something like this.

CHAIR: You know, we are really lost without you.
YOU: That's nonsense—anybody can do what I did.
CHAIR: No, really. We can't get anyone to volunteer her house after everyone saw how nice yours is [or: No one can make those cookies for the bake sale like you].

You: Well, I'm just not going to get involved again. It was too much of a hassle.

CHAIR: What can we do? We have no place to meet.

You: (Getting sucked into providing a solution that is really not your responsibility) How about Charlie's place?

CHAIR: He has relatives staying with him.

You: Mary has a nice big house.

CHAIR: Her husband is sick.

You: How about your place?

CHAIR: My wife is visiting her mother on the Riviera.

You: I don't know what to say.

CHAIR: I never thought you would let us down like this. Tell you what. Let's go on as before for just a couple of meetings until we get out of this jam, okay?

You: (Grasping at straws) But my house is a mess. We're cleaning and painting.

CHAIR: Don't worry about it. We'll understand. Without you there's no place to meet.

You: (Grudgingly) Okay, but just for a couple of times.

CHAIR: Of course.

Those couple of times, of course, stretch out into another year because the chair asks you to handle setting up the meetings somewhere else and one crisis after another prevents everyone else from volunteering his or her home for the next meeting.

Now why, you might ask yourself, do you get into such a mess time after time, bruising your self-respect in the process, when you know exactly what you want to do—or not do? As is very clear, you know how to say no. You do it all the time. The problem is coping with all the confusing verbal garbage that is dumped on you after you say no. The real reason why this happens to you, even when you swear it won't ever again, is that you are *emotionally manipulated* into feeling guilty about not doing what other people want. A good working definition of psychological manipulation: *Manipulation is whatever anyone else does to reduce your ability to think and your right to judge for yourself what is best for you.*

Although manipulation can take many different verbal forms, it invariably involves making you feel ignorant, foolish, or guilty. You can always recognize manipulation, no matter what its form, by remembering how you felt as a child when you got into trouble. Manipulation makes you feel like a small, dumb kid again, as if mom had just said to you, "Look! If you don't care about cleaning up your room properly, neither do I. I'm just the representative of four thousand years of civilized thought and culture, which somehow, dummy, you missed out on!" Obviously these aren't mom's exact words, but the effect of such words is the point: You feel guilty. So remember, as a rule of thumb, that when people make you feel as if mom just said to you, "I'm just the representative of four thousand years of civilized thought and culture," they are trying to manipulate you emotionally.

You allow yourself to be manipulated—without even knowing that you are being manipulated—because as a child you were taught, in the most well-meaning way, that things like logic, reasoning, criticism, caring, responsibility, understanding, goodwill, and intellectual give-and-take are noble and always to be respected. You were taught that you should always be logical, reasonable, and open to criticism, for instance, because these behaviors are what keep all of us from sinking to the level of animal aggression to resolve conflict. You were not taught, however, that these noble concepts can be used for less than noble purposes, such as conning you into doing something you really don't want to do.

When your children do something with their friends that upsets you, typically it is because they are behaving in the same way you did in that first dialogue—i.e., their friends emotionally manipulate them into feeling guilty, anxious, or dumb whenever they don't do what their friends want. If your son obeys you because you have taught him to feel guilty, anxious, or dumb when he disobeys you (just as you were taught by your parents), he will behave in that same way with his friends. This is the only way he knows how to behave under these circumstances. For example, the last time your son was supposed to do a chore, and didn't, something like the following manipulative dialogue between him and a friend could have taken place.

DIALOGUE 2

How a Son Gets Talked Out of Doing What Mom or Dad Wants
Setting: Your son has promised to clean out the garage after
school on Friday afternoon so you can have your garage sale there
Saturday morning. He begins the job, and a friend of his walks in.

FRIEND: What are you doing?
SON: Cleaning out the garage.
FRIEND: You can do that later. Let's bike down to the park.
SON: I can't.
FRIEND: Why can't you?
SON: My mom will kill me if I don't clean this place up.
FRIEND: Tell her you're done and let's go.
SON: I can't do that.
FRIEND: Why not? I tell my mom that all the time.
SON: But what if she finds out?
FRIEND: So she finds out! Big deal! She gives you a bad time. So what?
  Hasn't she chewed you out before?
SON: Yes, but—
FRIEND: What are you—a momma's boy?
SON: No.
FRIEND: Don't be a jerk. The rest of the guys are down at the park. You
  want me to tell them that you can't come because your mother said
  you can't?
SON: No.
FRIEND: Then let's go.
SON: Oh . . . okay.

Before your son can learn to say no to friends like this one, and mean
it, he has to learn how to say no to you. Learning how to say no to you
really means learning how other people—including you, who love him
—manipulate him by making him feel guilty or foolish in order to
control his behavior, even when there is nothing really important to feel
guilty about.

Parents (including your own, and you yourself) do not get up in the morning and say something like, "I wonder how I can screw up my kid today?" Yet though they mean well, most parents end up training their children to be easily manipulated. They do this, usually unconsciously, because, first, they were reared that way themselves by their own parents, and second, because training a child to be emotionally manipulable is, as discussed earlier, an effective way of controlling a child's behavior in the short run.

But if you can manipulate your child, so can others. And while your manipulation is generally benign, to protect the child and the family unit, there is no guaranty that others, either peers or adults, will have the same concern for your child's well-being. A manipulable child, who has little or no understanding that he or she is being emotionally played upon, is a likely candidate to be talked into doing all sorts of things by others. What a manipulable child can be talked into is limited only by the wants of the manipulator. You may feel that it will most often take the comparatively benign form of playing with friends instead of studying or completing chores, but there is no guarantee that manipulators will not eventually talk your manipulable child into trying drugs or alcohol, or a premature sexual experience.

As a parent, you will also face the problem of your child's manipulating *you* as soon as he or she becomes a sophisticated teenager. By then, children are slick as smelts in using the manipulation you have taught them. That's when you will hear your daughter tell you that she is "worried about those premature wrinkles and lines you are getting around your eyes" (I care about you!) as a result of too much work. She adds, "Don't you think you should take a break—like a vacation— soon?" (It makes logical sense—taking her along, of course, without her saying this.) "After all," she tells you, "Sally's mom cares about what she looks like." (Don't you care?) "They go to Hawaii at least once a year, and she makes less money than you!" (Are you too cheap?)

To enable your child to say no effectively to peers, you have to teach him or her about emotional manipulation. You can do this by pointing out what manipulation is, with examples like the one above, and how this takes away your child's own ability to judge what is best to do in any situation. The whole purpose of this book can be simply put: We have a lot of automatic habits that allow us to be manipulated almost involuntarily. By learning to be assertive, we can change those almost involuntary habits into voluntary choices, in which we decide for ourselves what is best for us to do.

The Prime Assertive Right

The teaching format of this book is based on one principle: *Give an idea, then practice on an example.* This is the method I have found most effective in teaching people to become more assertive. It combines both rote practice, to become familiar with assertive skills, and thinking about the concept to be learned. Teaching your children how to think for themselves, by helping them practice using their own judgment as to whether they should feel guilty, foolish, or ignorant, is the key to dealing with manipulation. It is so important an idea that I call it the *prime assertive right.*

Assertive Right I (The Prime Assertive Right) *You have the right to be your own ultimate judge of your emotions, thinking, and behavior, and are responsible for the initiation and consequences of what you feel, think, and do.*

What does this really mean to you and your child in a practical, non-philosophical sense? It means you and your child have the ability to recognize when you are being psychologically manipulated, and that you have the right not to accept automatically the negative feelings of guilt, anxiety, or ignorance that the manipulator tries to induce in you.

If the idea of being your own judge of what you do sounds strange to you, don't reject it out of hand without first examining what it means. Many people get upset when first thinking about it, yet can see its relevance and worth through examples. For instance, are you your own judge when you see a physician? If you are like most of us, you know very little about medicine and almost automatically defer to anything the physician says when you don't feel good or are worried about your health. Whether we are sick or not, most of us are as much at ease talking to a physician as we would be in consulting Hippocrates upon his descent from Mount Olympus after a chat with Zeus about golf, real estate, and tax shelters over a three-martini lunch. In that situation, however, you *are* your own judge, even if you don't feel that you are.

To help you see this, take away the intimidating title of "doctor" and replace it with "auto mechanic." Is your auto mechanic your personal judge simply because he knows more about your automatic transmission than you do? Of course not, and neither is your physician. Both are simply technical experts whom you hire to advise you on the best course of action. *You* still have to make the decisions on what to do, and you have to take responsibility for those decisions. Must you replace the whole carburetor in your car because your mechanic says "Terrible, terrible—the carburetor is shot. This car has been abused"? (This is guilt induction.) Or can you just have it tuned up? Should you feel guilty because there is some moral mandate that you maintain your car to your mechanic's personal standards—and thereby run up a repair bill limited only by his estimate of your ability to pay it? With respect to your physician's advice, there is no real difference between dealing with your doctor and dealing with your mechanic. You are still responsible for making your own decisions about your state of health. A technical expert —any technical expert—can only advise you on the best course to take.

If you accept your doctor's advice, this does not mean you have been manipulated. When we are intimidated by physicians and allow them to be the judges of what is best for us, it is not because they ask for that responsibility. We give it to them. I have worked closely with many doctors and I have not known one who did not encourage his or her patients to be collaborators in the treatment of illness, or who resented any questioning about the wisest treatment. If you feel that your physician is a domineering and intimidating exception, or likes playing God, your own judgment of the inappropriateness of his behavior toward you is the only justification you need to find yourself another physician.

Okay, you may say, but how can you be your own judge when you are in front of a real one in municipal court for a traffic ticket? You may be convinced that your ticket was unfair because the boob in uniform testifying that you broke the law was only trying to fill his quota for the day, yet the municipal judge believes the policeman, fines you, and then admonishes you to be a better driver in the future.

In this situation, too, you are still your own emotional, intellectual, and behavioral judge. You can make your own decision as to whether the municipal judge's fining you, and then trying to make you feel guilty, was appropriate or not. However, telling the judge that he doesn't know what in hell he is talking about may not be very wise. If you decide to exercise your prime assertive right and be your own emotional judge, that does not mean you leave your intelligence outside the courtroom door. Your prime assertive right does not say that you have to shout your decisions from the rooftops so that everyone will know them. On the other hand, if you really want to tell the court off, and are willing to take the consequences, you can do so. That decision is no different from telling your auto mechanic that you don't want your carburetor replaced, and then later being in a pickle because it poops out when you need your car. It's up to you.

As you can see, deciding to be your own emotional judge does not always mean you will make the appropriate, correct, or wise decision. But it will be your decision and linked to how you feel about yourself, not someone else's and linked to how he or she has tried to make you feel about yourself. Happily, most of the time if you make a dumb decision, you have the option to correct it later.

You may be asking yourself at this point, "But how can I apply this to my kids? Where do I draw the line with them? They are not ready to make certain judgments and take responsibility for them, because they don't know the consequences. And there are some things we should always feel guilty about."

With respect to the first part of that question, you are right: Young children don't always know what is best to do, so you will have to tell them. But you can do so without taking away their assertive rights and dignity by inducing guilt. If your son decides that he doesn't like a chore you assign him, you don't have to insist he like it, just that he do it. Most of us have to do things in life that we don't like, yet we do them because they enable us to do other things we do like. In this situation your parental authority is all you need. You are still the boss.

As for there being some things we should all feel guilty about, if you assume that to be true, you get onto very shaky ground about which even legal, religious, philosophical, and psychological experts can't agree. Even in such extreme cases as killing someone, we often can't agree that one should feel guilty. There are too many exceptions to hard-and-fast rules: self-defense, unavoidable accident, protecting one's country in wartime, and so forth. If we can't agree on life-and-death issues, what's the sense of insisting that your son should feel guilty about not liking to clean up the garage? Why should any of us feel guilty just because we don't like to do certain things? What we do is what counts, not how we feel about it.

Furthermore, if your son promises to clean up the garage today because you need to use it for a sale tomorrow, and then forgets to do it, he will very likely feel quite guilty, anxious, and foolish on his own. He doesn't need you to induce these reactions. As we shall see later, no matter how angry you may be—wanting to strangle him with your bare hands in the heat of the moment—teaching him to be assertive will help him acknowledge realistic and valid guilt, and then get over it as soon as possible, so he can be comfortable with you again instead of withdrawing from you emotionally as a way to cope with that guilt.

How to Tell When You're Being Manipulated: Your Everyday Assertive Rights

In order to show your child how to take on more and more responsibility for being his or her own judge, you first need to understand, in very practical terms, how other people routinely manipulate *you*. It's usually an hour or so after you are conned into doing something, while you are still stewing over the incident, that you begin to see the manipulative ploys that sucked you in—and come up with good answers to them. "Why didn't I think of that?" you complain. Yet the next time you are manipulated, all the good answers you thought of after the fact desert you. And it wouldn't be much help to remind yourself during a conflict with someone that you are your own ultimate judge. That statement is fine philosophically, but not much help in your daily dealings with the people around you. To understand and recognize everyday manipulation for what it is, and then teach your child how to recognize it too, let's take a look at the most common ways in which you are psychologically manipulated as spelled out in your Everyday Bill of Assertive Rights. These rights overlap and have a common theme, since they all derive from your prime assertive right to be your own ultimate judge.

STAR teaches children these same everyday assertive rights, but in a simplified, behaviorally focused form that will enable children to handle such situations as making or refusing requests, accepting or rejecting criticism, and expressing their individual needs, wants, or interests. In this listing of your and your child's everyday assertive rights, each right is stated in two ways: first for the adult (or almost-adult) and then for the youngster. Both versions say the same thing, even though different words and a different approach are used.

In teaching your child to be assertive, remember that your child's assertive rights are rights that preserve and protect his or her dignity and self-respect. They are not a license to do whatever one wants and get off scot free, but they do free your children from external manipulation of their personal feelings, including artificially induced feelings of guilt, foolishness, and ignorance. Just as you are responsible for the consequences of being your own judge and asserting yourself, as well as for everything else you do, when your children learn to be assertive, they will also learn what goes along with being assertive: personal responsibility for making their own decisions, and for the consequences of these decisions.

Assertive Right II Adult: *You have the right to offer no reasons to other people to justify your behavior.*

Child: *You don't have to make excuses to everybody for what you do.*

When you get into a social conflict (a fancy term we psychologists use for things like arguments, disputes, discussions, and disagreements), as opposed to a legal conflict (with police or judges) or physical conflict (with muggers, assailants, etc.) and you say either that you want or don't want to do something, what is the first thing you are likely to hear from the other person? It doesn't matter whether you are turning down someone else's request, such as lending your house for the PTA meeting, or asking for something you want, such as telling your spouse that you want to go somewhere different this year on vacation—Bermuda, perhaps, instead of visiting your mother-in-law in Springfield again. Unless you are dealing with an assertive person, you will get one of the standard manipulative responses, with "Why?" as the most likely.

When the other person asks why, we don't answer that we simply feel uncomfortable about hosting the PTA meeting this month. We foolishly try to prove that it is impossible or will be a disaster. That shifting of responsibility for our decisions onto external circumstances over which we have no control (it will rain; my house is too hard to find; there isn't enough room; etc.) is what sets us up for the manipulator. The other person pooh-poohs our excuses and dispenses with them one by one, demonstrating that we really have no valid reasons for refusing. Consequently, we wind up doing what we really don't want to do.

Similarly, there is no commonsense rationale for allowing someone who wants to borrow your car, to start asking you to explain why you won't let him or her borrow it. It's your car, not the other person's, yet you wind up feeling that you have to explain why you can't—or, more accurately, won't—lend it.

In situations like these, relying upon external circumstances—reasons over which you have no personal control—is about as effective as telling the manipulator, "I would like to help out, but God handcuffed me this morning and I can't reach into my pocket to give you the car keys." The manipulator will simply reply, "No problem! I just talked to God and He gave me the keys to the handcuffs."

This automatic "reasoning" response on your part suits the manipulator to a tee, as the following manipulative dialogue illustrates.

DIALOGUE 3

How You Get Manipulated into Loaning Your Car Because You Believe Reasoning Will Resolve Conflicts
Setting: You and I are friends and co-workers who live near each other. I jog up to your home on Saturday morning, where you are watering the lawn while your car sits in the driveway.

ME: Hi! Busy?
YOU: Sort of.
ME: Good. Then you wouldn't mind if I borrowed your car this morning, would you?
YOU: (Really not wanting to lend your car) Well . . . I have some errands to run.

ME: When will you be back?

YOU: Not until late this afternoon.

ME: Terrific. That would be fine with me.

YOU: Well . . . I have to go quite a distance and may not get back in time for you.

ME: Are you going downtown?

YOU: No.

ME: I'm not going there either. Where are you going?

YOU: Uh . . . to Malibu.

ME: Terrific. That's exactly where I have to go. Tell you what. I'll drive us both there, let you off, and pick you up when I'm done.

YOU: I just can't lend you my car.

ME: Why not?

YOU: My insurance doesn't cover anyone else but me. (God just handcuffed me.)

ME: No problem. My insurance covers everything from a semitractor to a Boeing 707. (I just talked to God and He said it's okay.)

YOU: But my brakes are bad. (God handcuffs.)

ME: No sweat. My brakes are lousy too. I'm used to that. (God unhandcuffs.)

YOU: I forgot . . . the spare is flat. We can't use the car. (God taketh away.)

ME: No problem. I'll take it down to the service station now and get it fixed. On me! (God giveth back.)

YOU: Look, why don't you just take the car, do what you need to do, and leave it in the driveway for me when you're done?

ME: Oh? . . . .Okay. But I'd be happy to drive you to Malibu. . . .

YOU: No, you take it (grumble, grump, moan).

You were *trained* to automatically feel and respond this way—and up to now, very likely you have trained your children to do the same thing —because we all assume that reasoning is a good way to solve mutual problems. That assumption is true as long as the parties in the conflict have mutual goals—e.g., the best way to get the upright piano out of the moving van and into the upstairs sitting room. But when the parties have different goals—e.g., you want the least damage to your home in moving the piano, while the driver of the van wants to make another delivery in the next forty-five minutes—reasoning becomes manipulative. With these different goals, you will say what route you want to take, the driver will ask you why you want to do it that way, and then he will give you "better" reasons for doing it his way—which is to shoot it in through the upstairs front window with the furniture catapult he mounted on the back of the moving van and wants to try out.

When you were a child and your parents disagreed with you, it would have been much easier and better for you if they had simply asserted their parental authority, said that you couldn't do what you wanted, and stuck to their guns when you gave them backchat. Instead, you were asked *why* you wanted to do such and such, and then your reasons were shot down by them with "better" reasons why you shouldn't do what you wanted. It's much more efficient in the long run (as we shall see in the next chapter) to tell your children they cannot do something simply because you don't want them to do it. After several assertive discussions with your kids, an amazing thing happens. They start to listen to you. They realize that you mean what you say, and also learn that they can't countermanipulate you into giving in.

Assertive Right III Adult: *You have the right to judge whether you are responsible for finding solutions to other people's problems.*

Child: *It's not necessarily your fault when things go wrong.*

As a child, you were trained to be responsible, and that's admirable. But in training you to be responsible, your parents didn't follow through and also teach you that when things go wrong, or a problem exists, you're not necessarily at fault. Try to remember: As a child, how many times did you respond to mom or dad with "Gee, too bad. But that's not my problem," and get away with it?

Because we were trained never to duck out of responsibility, other people very often use this desirable characteristic to manipulate us. The word *we* is a tip-off to this manipulation. At the office, for example, a co-worker may say to you, "*We* decided that everybody has to take a turn answering the phone during lunch. Do you want Mondays, Tuesdays, Wednesdays, and Thursdays, or Tuesdays, Wednesdays, Thursdays, and Fridays?" When this happens, it may be in your own best interest to ask, "Who's *we?* I didn't decide that." Or at home, when your next-door neighbor says "We have a problem with our fence," you can usually assume that your neighbor wants to do something to your perfectly good but ordinary fence, for which he wants you to share the cost. In this type of situation, you may find it wise to say, "Gee, I don't have a problem with the fence. What problem do you have with it?" As you will see in later chapters, you can then prompt the manipulator to spell out what is bothering him or her so you can decide if there really is a problem with the fence.

In the following dialogue, you can see how your child will respond to manipulation that makes him feel responsible for someone else's problem.

DIALOGUE 4

How a Son Is Manipulated by a Friend out of Studying Because Mom and Dad Have Taught Him to Be Responsible
Setting: Your son is studying and his friend wants him to go to the beach.

FRIEND: Let's go to the beach.
SON: I can't go to the beach today.
FRIEND: Why not?
SON: I have a math test tomorrow morning and I have to study for it.
FRIEND: You're good in math. You don't need to study!
SON: I'm not that good.
FRIEND: Sure you are!
SON: You think so?
FRIEND: Sure!
SON: I'd like to get a good grade in math.
FRIEND: What for? Only nerds worry about math. You want to be like them?
SON: I'm not a nerd.
FRIEND: Then what are you studying so hard for when you could be playing volleyball with the rest of the guys?
SON: If I don't study, I'm afraid I might not get a good grade tomorrow.
FRIEND: You got nothing to worry about! I told everybody we'd be there at two. We have to go to the beach.

SON: Why?
FRIEND: If we don't show up, the rest of the guys can't play as a regular team.
SON: But I have to study.
FRIEND: If you don't come, what am I going to tell them?
SON: Oh . . . okay.

Assertive Right IV Adult: *You have the right to change your mind.*

Child: *You can change your mind if you feel uncomfortable.*

Very few of us like it when someone else changes his or her mind and screws up what we want or have planned to do. Thus when you find out you have made a poor decision and it is not in your own best interest to carry out an agreement, you can count on the other person's trying to manipulate you into not changing your mind. This manipulation is based on the assumption that if you want to change your mind, something must be wrong. If there is nothing wrong with the agreement that you now want to change, that means there must be something wrong with you personally.

Most of us feel guilty in this situation simply because we have been indoctrinated in this assumption all our lives. As adults, however, we often *should* change our minds, not necessarily because of hard, demonstrable evidence, which we rarely have, but based on our personal experience of how such things tend to work out. Usually, it is our prior experience that gives us an uncomfortable feeling about our initial decision, and in many cases the uneasy feeling turns out to be a good predictor of what will happen.

Yet, when we get this feeling that things are not right, we are likely to put it down to irrational anxiety or our own personality weakness. Thus, when we want to change our minds and the other person asks why, we avoid saying that we simply feel uncomfortable about our initial decision. Instead, we fall into the trap of trying to justify our change with external, rational reasons. When this effort fails, as it will, we sometimes admit reluctantly that we feel very uncomfortable about what was agreed to. The manipulator then tells us we shouldn't feel that way—e.g., "You really have a problem. You need professional help because what you want to do is sick [neurotic, flaky, weird, etc.)." You can see this manipulation work in the following dialogue.

DIALOGUE 5

How You Are Manipulated into Taking a Friend Shopping Because You Believe You Should Not Change Your Mind
Setting: You call a friend when you decide to change your mind.

You: I've decided not to go shopping this Friday night.
Friend: Why not?
You: Well, my daughter is going out on her first date Friday and I think I should be home waiting for her.
Friend: That's silly! You're just being a neurotic mother!
You: I am not! I'm a concerned parent.
Friend: And what good is sitting home worrying about her going to do?
You: I'm not going to worry. She can take care of herself.
Friend: Then why do you want to stay home?
You: I think I should be there in case something happens.
Friend: Nothing's going to happen.
You: The boy she's going out with may turn out to be a creep.
Friend: Who's that?
You: Jimmy.
Friend: Jimmy's the sweetest kid on the block. If anything happens on that date, it would be because your daughter inherited her father's sex drive.
You: How can you say something like that?
Friend: Only to point out how silly you sound. Nothing's going to happen.
You: I guess I am a little worried about her.
Friend: That's sick! You should see a shrink! You're acting just the way you said your mother did, and you hated that.
You: No I'm not. That was different!
Friend: No it's not. Your daughter is a better kid now than you were then. You're just being silly, and that's all there is to it! So let's go

shopping Friday and forget all this nonsense of being neurotically overprotective.

YOU: You really think so?

FRIEND: Of course! There's no reason for you not to go shopping on Friday. I thought you were one of the most reliable people I know. Once you said something, you meant it.

YOU: I am!

FRIEND: That sale is for Friday night only, and you said you'd drive me there.

YOU: You can get someone else to go with you, can't you?

FRIEND: Who?

YOU: Someone you work with.

FRIEND: Yuck!

YOU: There's nobody else you can go with?

FRIEND: Nobody. You'll pick me up at seven?

YOU: Oh . . . okay.

In this manipulative dialogue, your friend seems quite level-headed, commonsensical, and reasonable, while you seem like a neurotic wimp. That perception is a result of the manipulator's setting things up to seem that way. That perception is also totally irrelevant. You have concerns that worry you, even if they are irrational. When we worry about something, the most common mistake others make is to try to get us to cover up our worries and ignore them. If, for instance, you have an appointment with a physician for an examination next week and express your worry about it to someone else, the most likely response you will get is "Don't worry! Everything will be all right."

That response is well intentioned but useless. The best way to cope with—and, ideally, get over—worries (irrational or not) is to talk with someone who will really listen to you about what causes them. If your friend in the shopping dialogue had been less self-concerned and manipulative, and had allowed you to talk about your worries, you might even have decided that going shopping was a better idea than staying home. But it would have been your decision, not your friend's, with much happier results than still being worried, inhibited from honestly saying so, and feeling like a fool to boot.

When your children try to change their minds, they are subject to this same manipulation by their peers, as the following dialogue illustrates.

DIALOGUE 6

*How a Daughter Is Manipulated by a Girlfriend into Premature
Sexual Activity Because She Was Taught by Mom and Dad to
Honor Her Agreements*
*Setting: Your fourteen-year-old daughter is talking to her friend
Bimbo about dating.*

DAUGHTER: I've changed my mind about going out on another double
date with you and Bobby and Fred this weekend.

FRIEND: Why?

DAUGHTER: Last time it wasn't any fun. Bobby and Fred are creeps!

FRIEND: We talked about this before! Bobby and Fred are not creeps.
You just were a real drag on Friday, and you agreed to get with it.

DAUGHTER: I was not. Bobby was real pushy and grabby!

FRIEND: You were a drag. It's no fun having an audience that doesn't
do anything but sit there and watch.

DAUGHTER: That's not my fault!

FRIEND: It certainly is! Is there something wrong with you? Do you have
a hang-up or something?

DAUGHTER: No . . . I just feel uncomfortable about it.

FRIEND: You shouldn't feel that way. It's unnatural.

DAUGHTER: Well, I worry.

FRIEND: About what?

DAUGHTER: You know . . . about how old we are.

FRIEND: You are a real dimwit. If you're big enough, you're old enough.
You're not as developed as I am, but you're big enough.

DAUGHTER: I know, but I'm upset about it.

FRIEND: You probably have an immature hang-up about it. It's really
nothing. Anybody can do it.

DAUGHTER: I don't know . . .

FRIEND: All you have to do is try. Fake it.

DAUGHTER: Are you sure?

FRIEND: Trust me. You're not going to be a drag again this Friday, are
you?

DAUGHTER: No . . .

Assertive Right V Adult: *You have the right to make mistakes, and be responsible for them.*

Child: *When you make a mistake, you can admit it, and you don't have to fall apart.*

Most of us behave as though erasers for correcting errors do not exist, as if making mistakes is not part of living. When we make a mistake, we do one or all of the following three things. We deny that the mistake was important: "I know that when I leaned on the Empire State Building it fell over, but it wasn't the tallest building in the world anymore, and it was really old anyway! It would have had to come down sometime! Or we deny responsibility for the mistake: "It wasn't my fault—someone shoved me!" Or we deny that a mistake even occurred: "George told me to do it. It must be part of urban renewal for this area of Manhattan."

The source of this consistent, maladaptive pattern of responding to mistakes is clear. When you were a child and did something wrong, your father very likely said something like "Who did this?" and you innocently said, "Me." Your father then did or said things that made you feel stupid, careless, or irresponsible. As a fast learner, the next time your father asked "Who did this?" you probably said, "Not me!" Your father then said, "Oh? Okay," and walked off looking for someone else to blame.

In teaching adults how to cope assertively with their mistakes, I tell them that they can freely admit to errors, and then correct them, if possible. I ask them to do this without the traditional "I'm sorry" added on. "I'm sorry" is so overused that it does nothing to calm down the person who is irritated by your mistake. I remember once lecturing to a class, bumping into something behind me, then turning and automatically saying "I'm sorry" to the air-conditioner. If you use "I'm sorry" as routinely and as meaninglessly as the rest of us, and if you really do want to apologize, you will get a much more positive reaction from other people if you tell them how you truly feel: "I really feel bad about this."

We continue to deny responsibility even after we mature, because we feel that if we make a mistake, we owe someone something. The person who tries to manipulate you into doing that something will agree with you and automatically use your guilt feelings against you. The following dialogue illustrates how you can be manipulated into never quite making up for a foolish mistake, no matter how much you do to make amends.

DIALOGUE 7

How You Are Manipulated by a Friend into Bending over Backward to Make Up for a Dumb Mistake
Setting: You and I are old friends and co-workers. You were supposed to pick me up at work and drive me to a dental appointment at noon. It's one o'clock when you finally show up.

ME: Where the hell were you?

YOU: What do you mean, where was I?

ME: You were supposed to pick me up at noon, and now it's one o'clock!

YOU: Pete, you expect too much of me. I've been busy all morning— doing some of your work, I might add—and you're upset about my forgetting to pick you up. Big deal!

ME: Big deal? My tooth is killing me and it's no big deal? I could have made my own arrangements to get my tooth fixed, but you said you would make an emergency appointment with your brother, the dentist—who also needs the business.

YOU: Oh! . . . I'm so sorry—I forgot all about that!

ME: You're sorry. That does me a lot of good!

YOU: Please, let me see what I can do. Let's go in and I'll fix it so you can see him at five. I'm sure he'll do that for me.

ME: Okay. But how can I get there? You were supposed to pick me up because my car is at the mechanic's getting fixed.

YOU: No problem. I'll take you there at five.

ME: Can you wait for me? I'll need a ride to the garage afterward.

YOU: Sure, I'll wait for you. Then I'll drive you to the garage.

ME: Well, that makes up for some of the problem you caused with your forgetfulness.

YOU: Good. I feel much better now. Where's the garage?

ME: Nutley [70 miles west of the dentist's office].

YOU: Nutley? Where's that?

ME: Just a stone's throw across the river. We'll be there in no time.

YOU: Oh . . . okay.

Assertive Right VI Adult: *You have the right to say "I don't know."*

Child: *You are not supposed to know everything. You can say "I don't know" without feeling bad.*

There are two correct answers to every question. Suppose I ask you to tell me the square root of 4.362. One correct answer is 2.0885. The other, equally correct and truthful, is "I don't know." In my doctoral oral exam, I was pleasantly surprised to find out that the *only* correct answer for speculative questions outside my trained field of competence was "I don't know."

As a child, unfortunately, whenever you were asked a question and said "I don't know," you were made to feel like a fool, as if you were supposed to know the answer to anything asked of you. In school this continued, to see if you remembered what you were taught. When you said "I don't know" to the teacher, you were given a zero on that question, as though it were an incorrect answer. While this may sometimes be useful in the limited area of school performance and memory testing, it is a very distorted viewpoint with respect to the rest of your life. There is nothing to be embarrassed about when you don't know something. If it's important, you can always find out the answer.

As a result of your childhood experiences, if you are like most of us, you learned an automatic emotional response that prompts you to feel dumb, anxious, and guilty whenever someone asks you something you don't know. Even though we realize intellectually that we don't have to know everything, we still feel uncomfortable when we are asked for an answer we do not have.

We are likely to be asked all sorts of things we don't know when other people try to manipulate us: "What would happen if every Tom, Dick, and Harry did . . . ?" "Don't you know that . . . ?" "What kind of person does . . . ?" and so forth. Very often the manipulator will try to set you up in order to "sandbag" you, asking a question to which he or she already knows the answer. The intent is to make you feel stupid, thereby compelling you to go along with the manipulator's way of doing things.

In dealing with questions other people throw at us, we usually do not discriminate between questions that have factual answers and those based upon the arbitrary judgment and motives of the person asking the question. Most of the time we automatically let the questioner be the judge of what the appropriate answer is, and we try to give an answer that will fit the manipulator's "reasoning" to show him or her that we are not dumb. Very few of us feel comfortable simply saying "I don't know," though that answer avoids the whole manipulative-counter-manipulative sequence intended to talk us into conforming to the other person's wishes.

As the following dialogue shows, our learned belief that we always have to know the answer to every question can be used to emotionally maneuver us into doing what a manipulator wants.

DIALOGUE 8

How You Are Manipulated into Not Returning Merchandise
Because You Don't Have All the Answers
Setting: A colleague and I demonstrate this type of manipulation
to a group of novices learning to be assertive. My colleague comes
into my boutique, Pierre of Bev Hills, on Rodeo Drive, to
complain about a purchase.

ME: Why, Ms. Vanity! How good to see you again! What brings you into Pierre of Bev Hills again so soon?

COLLEAGUE: Pierre, this outfit I got from you on Friday just isn't right.

ME: Oh? What's the problem?

COLLEAGUE: (Giving a slew of answers to that question) It's too outré. And too loose around the tush. The color doesn't work. It's just not me.

ME: Do you know that this outfit has been judged by haute couture experts around the country as likely to set off a new wave in clothes?

COLLEAGUE: (Getting intimidated) Well . . . I thought I heard something like that. . . .

ME: I'll bet you haven't seen the issue of *Vogue* with Ali MacGraw on the cover.

COLLEAGUE: (Still intimidated) I think so. . . .

ME: Obviously you haven't! Otherwise you would know that she's wearing the same outfit you have on. The same color and accessories.

COLLEAGUE: Really?

ME: Of course! Within two months there will be hundreds of women wearing it. Right now you are at the cutting edge of high fashion. You're weeks ahead of everyone else.

COLLEAGUE: Really?

ME: Where do you live?

COLLEAGUE: Manhattan Beach.

ME: You're six months ahead of everyone else.

COLLEAGUE: Gee, Pierre, I don't think it will work for me.

ME: You have been asking your husband what he thinks about it, haven't you?

COLLEAGUE: Well . . . only sort of.

ME: Who knows more about high fashion—your husband or Pierre of Bev Hills?

COLLEAGUE: You?

ME: Of course I do! This is the twentieth century. Get with it! You can't go along with everything he tells you. You have to learn to assert yourself. If he said you should jump off a cliff, would you?

COLLEAGUE: No. . . .

ME: Well, there you are.

COLLEAGUE: But, Pierre, it's too loose below the waist.

ME: If you wore it any tighter, you would get gangrene! Do you know why it was designed that way?

COLLEAGUE: Uh . . . (Trying to think of an answer)

ME: I thought so. This is to get away from the trend of trying to look like a hooker advertising her wares. Not even a high-class hooker. A cheap one!

COLLEAGUE: Oh.

ME: Tell you what you should do. Don't give up on being fashionable and avant-garde. Wait for a while until you see how popular this style becomes. Then come back and I'll tell you what I think.

COLLEAGUE: You think it will be popular in two months?

ME: Without a doubt! But you will have to wait longer for Manhattan Beach to get with it.

COLLEAGUE: Okay.

ME: Splendid. You will be way ahead of the rest of the moos out there.

To be successful and happy, you don't have to know everything or every consequence of every action you take in life. In fact, you can't. So when you or your child are questioned manipulatively, each of you can say "I don't know" and, with practice, feel quite comfortable about it.

Assertive Right VII Adult: *You have the right to decide if you need the goodwill of others in order to cope.*

Child: *You don't have to be friends with everyone, and you don't have to like what everyone does.*

All of us like to be liked. We like people to feel friendly toward us. It makes us feel good about ourselves and other people. But while having other people like us—having their friendship and goodwill—is important in life, in most situations it is not essential to our well-being or success. In reality you can probably count on the fingers of one hand (both hands if you are really lucky) the number of people who sincerely care whether you are happy and successful. Since we do want to be liked, we tend to confuse this desire with the *necessity* of being liked. Consequently, if anyone threatens to remove his or her goodwill, that threat, even if subtle, makes us anxious.

You can recognize this way of manipulating you when the other person says things like "I thought we were friends . . . I could count on you . . . things would never come to this," or by doors slamming, pots banging, frowns and dirty looks, even unusually prolonged silences. If you act as the manipulator wants, then goodwill is restored. In short, this type of manipulation is crass emotional extortion. If you give in to it, you guarantee that person will use it again on you in the future. If you do not respond to it, the manipulator will use it less and less with you, because there is no payoff for doing so.

Women are particularly vulnerable to—and, ironically, also adept at —this type of emotional manipulation. They are vulnerable because traditionally women have been trained to focus on relationships, and therefore are caring-oriented. The vast majority of women feel that it is their responsibility to generate caring relationships with other people, particularly with family and spouse. A woman consequently sees the possible removal of caring as a threat to her own image and success as a person. Women are also adept at this manipulation because of their sensitivity to the importance of caring.

As you can see in the following dialogue, the withdrawal of goodwill and its reinstatement in reward for compliance can be used on you or your child in almost any situation.

DIALOGUE 9

How You Are Manipulated Out of Asking for a Salary Raise Because You Need Other People's Goodwill
Setting: You go into your boss's office to ask for a raise.

You: (Knocking on the door) Can I talk with you for a minute?

Boss: (Smiling and getting up with arms outstretched in "friendship") Of course! My door is always open for you. Come on in and make yourself comfortable. By the way, my family wanted me to say how impressed we were with your kids at the barbecue over at my place last weekend. I think they are just great. You should be proud of them.

You: (Beaming from ear to ear) Thanks, I am. We all enjoyed your hospitality very much.

Boss: What can I do for you?

You: Well, I've been with this company for five years now, and I think I deserve a raise.

Boss: (Frowning, withdrawing behind the desk, and dropping the friendly attitude) A raise?

You: Yes. I have really worked hard for this outfit and I think I deserve one.

Boss: (In a very serious and stern tone, like a parent talking to a naughty child) Look, I like you. And the reason why is that you're not like the rest of the hustlers around here. You know what I'm talking about. They are only looking for an angle, the fast buck! You're not like them. You're a company person. That's what makes you so terrific to work with.

You: Yes . . . but I think I deserve a raise.

Boss: (Looking at you with shaded eyes) Don't worry about a raise, or even think about it. (Slyly glancing to either side to see if anyone's around, and whispering) We have plans for you in this company.

You: Really?

Boss: (Smiling and friendly again, while leading you to the door) Wait and see. Oh—and listen, we're having another barbecue at our place next month. We want you and your family to join us again.

You: Gee, thanks.

Boss: Don't mention it—especially to them out there.

You: Okay.

Boss: Swell. And remember, my door is always open to company people like you.

Assertive Right VIII Adult: *You have the right to be illogical in making decisions.*

Child: *You don't always have to prove you are right to everyone else.*

Our Western culture teaches us from childhood to use logic as a basis for deciding things. The noble intent of this education is to increase our percentage of good decisions by basing them on something more substantial and reliable than whim, guesswork, superstition, or luck. Unfortunately, despite all this fine training in logical thinking, few of us realize that logic is also routinely used to manipulate us by "proving" that we are wrong and the other person is right, and that therefore we should do what the other person wants.

The logical system we are trained to use is called Boolean or binary logic, a fancy name for yes—no, 1-0, up-down, in-out, black-white, left-right, etc.: If something's not up, it has to be down; if it's right, it can't be left. This binary logic does not allow for shades of gray. But human beings, even though we respect logic in our lives, and rightly so, don't fit nicely into neat binary, yes-no categories. We often have conflicting motivations that logic can't handle, like planning to lose three pounds this week, yet still wanting a fat burger with all the trimmings for today's lunch. What makes matters even more complex is that we're smart enough to arrange things so we get away with it—having our fat burger and still losing three pounds.

Logic says that since weight loss is based on less intake of fatty, salty, and starchy food, one should not eat a fat burger and expect to lose weight. But we can. Thus, reality shows us that this simple logic is not infallible. Yet, when we get into conflict with another person over an issue and that person uses logic selectively to convince us we are wrong, we buy it because of our ingrained respect for logic. It's as if the manipulator is moving along in front of a huge smorgasbord of facts making a selection of things for us: "Fact one . . . That's a terrific argument," he says, placing it on the logical plate he intends to feed us. "Fact two . . . No way! Forget that! Fact three? . . . Hmm . . . maybe. Fact four . . . right on! Fact five . . . Can't hurt. Fact six . . . Nooo . . . not really," and so on. The following dialogue points out this manipulative use of logic.

DIALOGUE 10

How Mom Logically Manipulates Daughter into Studying Instead of Going on a Date, and How Anyone Else Can Logically Manipulate Daughter into Going on a Date Instead of Studying Setting: Teenage daughter wants to go out on a date tonight but has a test tomorrow morning. In a conversation with mom, her intention not to study tonight comes up.

MOM: You're going out tonight?
DAUGHTER: Yes. Animal is picking me up at eight.
MOM: That could be a mistake.
DAUGHTER: Why?
MOM: Look at it this way. You want to go to college, don't you?
DAUGHTER: Sure.
MOM: The better your grade point average, the better chance you have to get into Vassar, right?
DAUGHTER: Right.
MOM: That means you want your grade point average to be as high as possible, right?
DAUGHTER: Right.

MOM: I won't even mention that disastrous B-minus you got in nuclear physics last year. So, it's only logical you have to concentrate your efforts in classes where you have a good chance to make high marks, right?

DAUGHTER: Right.

MOM: Therefore, you have to concentrate on differential calculus this year, right?

DAUGHTER: But I'm fine in calculus!

MOM: That's what you said about quantum mechanics last year. If I remember correctly, you only got a B on your last calculus test, right?

DAUGHTER: Right.

MOM: Therefore you could do better, right?

DAUGHTER: Right.

MOM: To do better, it's only logical that you study calculus tonight instead of going out with Animal, right?

DAUGHTER: I guess so. . . .

MOM: It's not me who's telling you this, but plain old logic. You decide what's best for you by being logical.

DAUGHTER: Okay, mom. You win.

MOM: It's not me. It's only logical that you should study.

Now mom's intent in this manipulative dialogue seems noble: to help her daughter get better grades and be successful and happy. It also may be that she doesn't like her daughter going out with Animal. Her intent is irrelevant. She has still manipulated her daughter's decision-making process using selective logic. It may be that her daughter has an overall A-minus average, which means upping her grade point average would be like trying to gild the lily. Or her average could be so low that trying to improve it would be as meaningful as rearranging the deck chairs on the *Titanic*. Again, this is unimportant. What is most important here is that mom was able to manipulate daughter into studying, whether she needs to or not.

If mom can easily and logically manipulate daughter into studying, then someone else just as easily and logically, can manipulate her into not studying, whether she needs to or not. One of the major findings of project STAR was that the students trained to be assertive had significantly higher overall grade point averages, and fewer attempts by peers to pressure them. These results indicate that if youngsters are allowed to make up their own minds after they have been taught how to resist manipulation, they will decide what is important themselves, and most will choose to study and improve their grades.

Assertive Right IX Adult: *You have the right to say "I don't understand."*

Child: *You don't always have to understand everything and can say "I don't understand" without feeling bad.*

As children, you and I exasperated adults because we were often slow in learning things—which is to say we didn't learn things as fast as adults wanted us to. I'll bet that as a child you could count on one hand the number of times an adult responded to your confession of "I don't understand" with "That's okay. Don't worry about it. You'll catch on eventually." Exasperation was shown when we made mistakes in learning anything: our homework, chores, and things in general, but especially when learning complicated and subtle social customs. We were expected to know how to behave appropriately toward adults without having this behavior spelled out to us.

This common experience as children trained us to be psychologically sensitive to the expectations and wants of our parents, family, relatives, teachers, and friends without their having to tell us what their expectations were. We were supposed to be able to read minds and give people what they wanted to see or hear, even if they denied having such expectations. In other words, we were supposed to understand intuitively (without being told) the real meaning behind the classic guilt-inducing denial supposedly favored by the stereotypical Jewish mother: "Don't worry about me. Enjoy yourself. I'll get by somehow."

Now that we are adults, other people expect us to read their minds when they are not assertive enough to tell us what is bothering them about us. You are supposed to understand when something is wrong without the other person's having to tell you, and then understand how you are supposed to make up for upsetting him or her.

For example, many of us have experienced the situation of welcoming an older relative into our home on an extended visit. Things go swimmingly for a few days. Then, as you are doing something in the kitchen, chatting away with your relative, you turn around to find he or she has disappeared. Puzzled, you search the house and finally locate the person sitting rigidly in the guest room, staring off into space. You ask, "What's wrong?" and you invariably get the reply "Nothing. Nothing at all!" But it's clear that something is definitely wrong, and you are supposed to be sensitive enough to know what it is.

Who knows what upset that relative, who is now trying to manipulate you into making up for upsetting him or her? You may have been chatting about taking your child to parents' night at school next Friday, while your relative wants to go with you and your spouse to see a new play opening that same night, but is too unassertive to tell you exactly what is wanted. Or you may have been preparing Southeast Asian pot luc muc for dinner because it's your spouse's favorite, and you should have known that your relative wouldn't like it.

Now recognizing this emotional manipulation for what it is, you might feel like saying sarcastically: "Thank God! I thought you were going senile." A better response for coping with this chilling silent manipulation is "I don't understand. You look very upset. Did I do something to cause it?" If that doesn't get straightforward communications going again, then try "Okay, when you feel better, come back to the kitchen and we'll pick up where we left off." This response gives the manipulator no payoff for the manipulation, yet does not start a fight.

Unhappily, instead of this more assertive response, the typical behavior sequence usually includes one or more of the following: (1) pleading with the relative to let you know what's bothering him or her; (2) getting into a fight while not being exactly sure what's being fought about; (3) making up to the relative while not knowing how to, or what is being made up for; and/or (4) getting silently angry and resentful and vowing never to have this person in your home again.

This oversensitivity to the wants and expectations of others can have a seriously negative effect on your children's academic performance as they go through school. All children know what any teacher would like from them, even if this is unrealistic and the teacher knows it: Teachers like to see instant or at least very rapid understanding of the material taught. This desire is not entirely altruistic: When pupils do not understand their teacher, it may mean that the teacher is not a very good teacher. I have yet to meet a teacher who is not sensitive to how well or badly he or she communicates with students, though teachers who are not very good are likely to keep this self-awareness to themselves. Because children have been indoctrinated to develop this sensitivity to what the teacher really wants, they can feel helpless when they don't immediately understand new ideas and concepts given to them. When the teacher asks the class, "Is there anyone who doesn't understand this?" the typical child gives the teacher what he or she really would like to hear—dead silence. At the same time, the child is hoping that someone else will raise his or her hand and ask the teacher to explain it again. Unfortunately, this rarely happens, since children have also learned that when they confess ignorance, the rest of the class mimics the usual adult reaction: exasperated disdain. Your children recognize that they face negative feedback from other children when they admit they are less than perfect.

Dealing publicly with their academic imperfections in class can be a real problem for your children. I know that as a youngster I went through eleven years of formal schooling before I asked any of my teachers a question with any intelligence behind it. During that time I don't remember any of my peers behaving any differently. Perhaps that's one of the reasons we were called the silent generation. When I finally got fed up with being given things to memorize, and began asking why these things were important, the whole class groaned, giving me clear feedback about my stupidity and lack of sensitivity to what they perceived our teacher really wanted: quiet acceptance of dogma without ever questioning it. I endured my classmates' disdain and kept asking questions during that semester because I was tired of listening passively and not learning much more from lectures than I could from reading a book. The next semester I quit high school and got a job because I needed the money. Later, that teacher said that she missed me and my questions, because I had sparked up the class for her. Her reaction was one of the reasons I went back to school after a year and a half to finish up and then go on to college.

In the worst case, trying to learn without comprehending what is taught generates a negative cycle in which one tries one's best and falls behind, tries harder and still falls behind, and then coasts or gives up. Even in the best case, children labor under a constant handicap that prevents them from living up to their academic potential.

The purpose behind this kind of manipulation is to make you feel ignorant for not being able to read minds. No long dialogue is needed to explain it—the following minidialogue says it all. During a lecture to my clinical colleagues and their graduate students at Long Beach State

College a few years ago, one of the graduate students asked me a question:

GRAD STUDENT: Dr. Smith, what exactly do you mean by the "feeling of ignorance" that is induced by manipulation?

ME: (Being manipulative) Do you mean to tell me that with all your clinical graduate training and after an hour of my describing manipulation, you don't know what a feeling of ignorance is?
GRAD STUDENT: I do now.

Both you and your child can learn to say comfortably, "I don't understand," and, in conjunction with the assertive verbal skills covered in later chapters, to cope with manipulation as well as with your irrational feelings of ignorance when confronted with something new.

Assertive Right X Adult: *You have the right to say "I don't care."*

Child: *You don't have to be perfect, and you don't have to feel bad when you are just you.*

From childhood, most of us have been taught that we should try to improve ourselves whenever we can. This is a noble motive and it's easy to understand why we were taught this. Unfortunately, however, there is no platinum bar with deep marks on it in the National Bureau of Standards that tells us what is improvement and what is not. Neither are there absolutes on which to base judgments of what is good (and will therefore make us better) and what is bad (and will therefore hinder us).

Each of us is as convinced that we really know what is good and bad as we are that we should improve ourselves. But we need only look at the radical changes that have occurred over the last thirty years to realize the extent to which society's ideas of good and bad have altered. People who talked about sex in public then were socially ostracized or even jailed. Nowadays we talk about sex at cocktail parties and watch TV programs about how to have good sex. What was scandalous behavior then is widely accepted now. Values that were thought to have been fixed in stone have given way to values that completely reverse what we believed back then. Throughout history, in fact, as our society, circumstances, and environment changed, our labels of "good" and "bad" have changed with them.

Given that our notions of good and bad are arbitrary and changeable, though at any one time we may see them as infallible and permanent, we are very susceptible to manipulation based on our respect for self-improvement. All manipulators need do is point out that we should care more—ostensibly about ourselves, but really about them—and in so doing improve ourselves by doing things their way. As irrational as this guilt induction is, we feel guilty as hell if we don't care and try to improve. We feel this way because we irrationally believe that we have to be perfect, and since we know we aren't, we strive to at least appear perfect.

This belief that we should always try to be better and to do better makes us vulnerable to emotional manipulation. Other people point out that we could be better workers, parents, dentists, housepainters, CIA agents, lovers, nurses, tennis players, etc., if we would strive to meet *their* standards. Their standards of improvement, however, are often impossibly high and arbitrarily set, based on their personal wants. For example, a co-worker might try to get you to do part of his or her work by saying, "A really good secretary [or file clerk, salesperson, manager, CIA agent, etc.] would want to grow and improve by helping out with the typing [or Xeroxing, sales meeting, United Way campaign, cover-up, etc.]."

You can often see this manipulation in action when what you are doing is more desirable than what someone else is doing—for instance, during the preparations for the annual office party. As you enjoy yourself decorating the office, invariably someone will come up and point out that you could improve the festive effect by doing it differently. When this happens you usually end up as an assistant, cutting, stapling, and gluing, while that person takes over the creative and fun part of the job. People are always ready to show us how to improve something that is fun to do, but I have yet to have anyone come up to me and say, "Hey, hold on there! You can improve the way you clean up that toilet. Watch me and I'll show you how to do it better."

This kind of manipulation can be, and is, applied to anything you do, and even how you feel—especially how you "should" feel about important things and about those around you. Other people will commonly point out that not only should you want to improve yourself, but if you really were a good person, you would care more about them—about their feelings, comfort, and convenience. At home, for example, it's very likely that family members have manipulated you into doing something with the words "If you really cared about me, you would . . ." The implication, of course, is that what you are doing now is not what a really good spouse, mother, or father would do, and that you can improve the way you care about that person and his or her specific wants.

The key to dealing with this manipulation is to recognize it as manipulative guilt induction, and then remind yourself that you cannot be everything to everybody. You will never be perfect, and why should you even want to be? You have to accept who you are, and you have to set your own priorities. Your kids may push you to take them to Disney World this Saturday by complaining that you don't care enough about them. But it may also be that you have to finish an important job this weekend, and you can't do both. The only practical way you can deal with these two pressures is to realize that while you do care about your kids' enjoyment, right now you care more about getting that job done. You don't have to automatically feel guilty because they imply that you are not as good a parent as you could be. You will never be as good a parent as they want you to be, because their notion of a good parent is that the sky is the limit for their demands upon you. In short, this weekend the kids are right—you are not perfect and you don't care as much about them as you could, so everybody stays home until you finish that work. Next weekend is a different story, since your priorities about what you care about most can change.

If you can be manipulated because you believe that you should always care, your child can be manipulated in the same way, as the following dialogue points out.

DIALOGUE 11

How Daughter Is Conned by a Friend into Stealing Dad's Vodka Because She Was Taught to Always Care
Setting: Your daughter is talking with one of her friends about a party to be held at the friend's home.

FRIEND: You've got to help me out.
DAUGHTER: How?

FRIEND: Bimbo said she was going to bring the booze for the punch, but her mother caught her taking it and now she's grounded.

DAUGHTER: So?

FRIEND: So you've got to get a bottle of vodka from your father's supply.

DAUGHTER: I can't do that!

FRIEND: Why not?

DAUGHTER: If my dad caught me, he'd do a lot more than ground me.

FRIEND: Don't talk like a child! You're a lot smarter than Bimbo. You won't get caught. Besides, you and your father are real close. If he caught you, you could sweet-talk him out of anything.

DAUGHTER: I can't do that to my father.

FRIEND: Why not?

DAUGHTER: It just wouldn't be right.

FRIEND: I thought we were good friends.

DAUGHTER: We are!

FRIEND: It doesn't sound like it. You don't care enough to help me out. At least Bimbo tried! She's a real friend who cares.

DAUGHTER: I do lots of things for you!

FRIEND: Like what?

DAUGHTER: Like helping you with your homework, for instance!

FRIEND: Homework! Anybody can do that. But when I really need a friend, what happens? You fink out on me!

DAUGHTER: I am not finking out!

FRIEND: If you cared more about me than about getting caught taking some stupid vodka, you'd do it!

DAUGHTER: I do care about you!

FRIEND: Not much, it seems.

DAUGHTER: I do!

FRIEND: Then prove it.

DAUGHTER: Ohhh . . . okay. But this is the only time!

FRIEND: Sure. I knew you were a good friend.

The Bill of Assertive Rights calls your attention to the most common types of manipulation, but your children can be emotionally manipulated in many other ways. To cope with manipulation, children have to first recognize that they are being manipulated. You can teach them how to recognize manipulation by using similar dialogues in which you play the role of the manipulator. As you do this, point out how what you say makes them feel guilty, foolish, or ignorant, and then point out that they are likely to do what the manipulator wants in order to avoid these feelings. Talk to your children, as teachers guided by STAR and PLUS do, about why and how their assertive rights are important in helping them feel good about themselves rather than irrationally guilty, ignorant, or foolish.

Your Child's Personal Interests and Goals

Nowhere in this book will you find a statement on what you or your child should always do. The Bill of Assertive Rights is not a fancy new scientific set of shoulds that replaces an old-fashioned set you were taught in childhood. It does not tell you what your goals or your child's should be. It has no dogmatic statements, such as telling you, for example, that everyone should do his own thing. Sometimes you may want to do someone else's thing, and assertiveness helps you do that, too. It does not tell you how to behave and why—e.g., "Sex is good for you, will improve your mental health, and restraint will lead to neurosis." You have to decide yourself when sex is appropriate and when it is not, according to your own value system; assertiveness only helps you to back up that decision.

Nor does the Bill of Assertive Rights present you with a belief system, such as claiming that faith in science is better than faith in religion and making the assumption that religion is only for the troubled or personally insecure who need a strong external structure to tell them what to do. While religion can be used in that way, so can science. Having known as many personally insecure scientific zealots as I have religious ones, I can't see any difference. If you are religious—or an atheist—and you want your child to be able to cope with social pressure to follow beliefs that are more popular than those that you value, assertiveness can back up your and your child's beliefs. What is more fitting to back up your faith in your beliefs than faith in yourself? Assertiveness does not make a saint out of a sinner or vice versa. It only makes one a much more efficient and capable saint or a much more efficient and capable sinner. The material in this book is a guideline for becoming very effective in achieving your goals. It makes no presumption as to what those goals should be.

This book doesn't even tell you that you or your child should be assertive. It only points out how to be assertive and what the typical results of learning to be assertive are. You and your child still have to decide whether, when, and where to be assertive in order to achieve a goal.

In summary, before going on, make sure you are satisfied that your children can recognize the most common forms of emotional manipulation that interfere with their own personal goals, as well as with their personal judgments of what is right and what is wrong.

In the next chapter, we begin to look at the verbal assertive skills that your children can use to actively cope with manipulation, and to increase their self-respect, confidence, and maturity.

CHAPTER THREE

Persistence: The Basic Foundation for Dealing with Peer Pressure and Other Social Manipulation

How Involuntary, Unthinking Responses to Manipulation Can Become Voluntary, Thinking Ones

A fter you and your child learn to recognize manipulation, what then? It doesn't make much sense just to say to the person who tries to make you feel guilty, ignorant, or foolish, "Stop manipulating me!" That person won't have the slightest idea of what you're talking about. Your assertive rights are concepts, ideas that free you from automatically accepting artificial guilt. They only make you aware of manipulation and the way you have automatically responded to it. To back up your assertive rights and keep other people from violating them, you will need a set of assertive verbal skills. These are not ideas but specific behaviors that you and your child can use to deal with manipulation. The whole point of learning these assertive verbal skills is to change your behavior pattern and your child's from an involuntary, automatic response to a voluntary, thinking response. In other words, if you want to go along with the manipulator, that's fine, but this will be a decision you make, not one that you, or your child, are conned into.

The Three Characteristic Behaviors of Nonassertive People

If we again called in those top ten clinical diagnostic experts from the first chapter and asked them what they paid most attention to in determining whether or not a person is assertive, they would list a number of self-defeating behaviors that cause a nonassertive person problems. The three most common negative behavioral characteristics of the typical nonassertive person are (1) lack of persistence in sticking to one's goal in the face of opposition, (2) excessive emotional sensitivity and/or behavioral overreaction to criticism, whether constructive or destructive, and (3) an overreaction of anxiety and guilt when a mistake is made. The assertive verbal skills given here, in *When I Say No, I Feel Guilty,* in STAR, and in PLUS are specifically designed to help correct these problems. This chapter will discuss the first of these negative characteristics and offer a simple assertive verbal skill to deal with it.

As adults, you and I can easily see the worth of learning something new to solve old problems. We motivate ourselves. With younger children, motivation to learn is not likely to be a problem either, because they will readily learn almost anything you teach them, and their problems in comprehension will be overcome with patience on your part and repeated practice. Children older than ten, however, may need some motivation to learn the assertive verbal skills. They need to see how these skills apply to problems they face every day. So before you start to teach your children the basic assertive skills for coping with social conflict, it is wise to pique their interest by showing them that being assertive is fun to learn and useful to them in everyday activities with others of their own age group.

Getting Your Child Interested in Learning to be Assertive

You want certain positive things to happen to your children over the next ten years: That is your motivation in teaching them to be assertive. But children are much more concerned with the here and now; they want to know how things will immediately help or hinder them. The best way to get them interested in learning something new is to show that it has an immediate positive payoff. The way I get adults interested in learning to be assertive is to first give them a simple, general tool that is immediately perceived as useful and valuable; assertive social conversation. I do this even before I tell them about assertiveness, assertive rights, and emotional manipulation, in order to get their attention and interest.

If your children are like other children, they can do with at least two or three more friends. But they often get tongue-tied in talking to children they don't know well. By teaching your children the basic components of social conversation before anything else, they can immediately put the skills of Free Information and Self-Disclosure into practice outside your home, thereby getting a positive payoff that is personally important to them. With this practical demonstration, you show your children that assertiveness is something that will help now, not something they will have to wait a long time to see results of (though it *will* have big payoffs down the road). Starting off this way will get them interested in finding out how the other assertive skills can help them. With the skills of Free Information and Self-Disclosure, we are setting the bait, so to speak.

Free Information and Self-Disclosure: The Basis of Social Conversation for Shy Kids

Assertive Self-Disclosure in conjunction with Free Information can help your child stop being shy with other children and make new friends. Free information is what someone gives you for free when you are talking with him or her. It's whatever you get in addition to what you ask for. For example, when I ask "Do you live here?" and you reply either "Yes" or "No," you have given me no free information—nothing more than what I asked. On the other hand, if you reply, "No, I used to live in here but I moved to Del Mar last year with my spouse, three kids, and two Labradors because my kids love to swim in the ocean," you have given me a wealth of free information on which I can follow up and find out more about you, your interests, your family, and your dogs.

Unless we simply do not want to communicate, we usually give free information about whatever is important to us just then to the person we are talking to. Around the middle of April, people are likely to tell you about their income-tax problems. In late spring you will learn about upcoming vacations. If a child is born, you will hear about it. If a promotion is due, you will find out. If a person is worried or distressed, you will hear about those concerns also. Your children will hear about the same things from their peers: vacations, baby siblings, gifts, worries about school, and problems with other kids.

Recognizing and following up on freely given information helps you to avoid awkward silences with new people, since you (and your child) will always have something interesting to say: feelings, thoughts, and follow-up questions about the other person's concerns, plans, happenings, and interests. To master social conversation in this way, you and your child can practice how to recognize and follow up on the free information that other people give in their conversations. The following demonstration dialogue is one I always use in teaching adults to recognize free information, or the lack of it, in assertiveness seminars.

DIALOGUE 12

A Female Colleague and I Demonstrate the Use of Free Information
Setting: We are supposedly waiting for an elevator in the lobby of an office building. I turn to her and introduce myself.

ME: Hi. I've seen you in the building many times before, but I've never taken the time to introduce myself. I'm Pete Smith.
COLLEAGUE: Hello.
ME: Do you work in the building?
COLLEAGUE: Yes.
ME: On the second floor?
COLLEAGUE: No.
ME: On the third floor?
COLLEAGUE: No.
ME: The fifth floor?
COLLEAGUE: No.
ME: Sixth?
COLLEAGUE: Yes.
ME: Nice meeting you.

As you can see, my colleague gave me no free information at all. Now we will replay it, with her giving me lots of free information.

ME: Hi. I've seen you in the building many times before but I've never taken the time to introduce myself. I'm Pete Smith.

COLLEAGUE: Hello. I'm Marion. Nice to meet you.

ME: Do you work in the building?

COLLEAGUE: Yes. I work on the sixth floor in a legal office. [FREE INFORMATION]

ME: Oh. Are you a lawyer? [Follow-up on FREE INFORMATION]

COLLEAGUE: No. I work there part-time as a legal secretary. I'm really a student at UCLA working for my M.B.A. [FREE INFORMATION]

ME: No kidding! I'm at UCLA too. [SELF-DISCLOSURE]

COLLEAGUE: Really? What department?

ME: Psychology.

COLLEAGUE: Well, it's a small world! My boyfriend, Igor, is the senior fullback in football, assistant coach of the weight-lifting team, and does anatomical research in kinesiology in the subbasement of the psychology department at UCLA. [FREE INFORMATION] Do you know him?

ME: Nice meeting you.

As you can see, upon meeting new people you may get all sorts of free information that can be important to you. To teach your child to make social conversation with new people easily, practice together on how to recognize and then follow up on free information, with you role-playing a new friend. Have your child pretend not to know you, and with each question give the child some free information to follow up on. In the first part of the exercise, make it easy, giving bits of free information that no one could miss. Then gradually reduce the amount of free information until your child has to pay close attention to everything you say in order to recognize it. This teaches your child to be a good listener. You can make up a fantasy story as you go along. If your child doesn't follow up on what you give for free, but asks something else, stop and make sure that he or she recognized your free information but decided not to pick up on it. By learning to identify and follow up on free information, your child will never be stuck for something interesting to say.

In the previous dialogue, self-disclosure was also used. Even though free information and self-disclosure are very similar, there is an important distinction between them. Free information can almost always be thought of as something people give us without having to be prompted and without much thought about what they are saying. Self-disclosure, on the other hand, requires some deliberation. Self-disclosure is important because it makes it much easier for the other person to talk to you. He or she can get involved by following up on your personal statements, making the conversation two-way. If you do not disclose any information about yourself, the conversation will begin to sound like that of a prosecuting attorney questioning a witness, and the other person will soon stop sharing personal information.

After you are confident that your child can recognize free information, have him or her comment to you about the free information before following it up with self-disclosure. The child's disclosure may be as simple as "I don't know anything about field hockey. Is it hard to play?" or "My sister likes that game. Have you ever played with her?"

Other children are also often shy and have a difficult time talking about themselves, so your child may want to ask a new friend questions that can't be answered with a simple yes or no. This will prompt the other child to give more substantial information that can be followed up. Have your child practice using questions that start with the five W's —who, what, where, when, or why—as in the following dialogue. If your child is older, use the following practice dialogue as a model for learning Free Information and Self-Disclosure, but change the context to one giving and following up on information about classes, extracurricular activities, sports, automobiles, hobbies, girlfriends, boyfriends, and other interests of teens and almost-teens.

DIALOGUE 13

Son Makes a New Friend Using the Assertive Skills of Free Information and Self-Disclosure
Age level: Ten to seventeen.
Setting: A young boy is unchaining his bike from the rack after school and another one is watching him.

Boy 1: Hi.
Boy 2: Hi.
Boy 1: This is my new bike. I just got it last weekend. [FREE INFORMATION given to prompt the other child to talk] Do you like it?

BOY 2: That's a really neat Zumimoto.

BOY 1: It feels nifty riding it. [SELF-DISCLOSURE] Where's your bike?

BOY 2: At home. My dad won't let me ride it to school. [FREE INFORMATION]

BOY 1: I'll bet you don't feel good about that. I wouldn't. [SELF-DISCLOSURE] Why can't you ride it to school? [Follow-up on FREE INFORMATION]

BOY 2: He said I'm not old enough yet to take my bike.

BOY 1: Yeah. My mother says that too, but dad lets me. [SELF-DIS-CLOSURE] How old are you? [Follow-up on FREE INFORMA-TION]

BOY 2: Eleven, but I wish I was thirteen, or lived closer to school. [FREE INFORMATION]

BOY 1: My birthday was on Saturday. I'm eleven too. [SELF-DISCLO-SURE] Where do you live? [Follow-up on FREE INFORMATION]

BOY 2: On Yale Loop near the corner of Barranca. I like to go to the Minimart for ice cream on the way home. [FREE INFORMATION]

BOY 1: That's only four blocks from where I live. [SELF-DISCLO-SURE] Let's go there.

BOY 2: Okay. Can I try out your bike?

BOY 1: Sure. You ride it one block and I'll ride it the next.

BOY 2: Okay!

BOY 1: What kind of bike do you have?

BOY 2: A black, ten-speed Fishimuzo with whitewall racing wheels and a whip antenna.

BOY 1: Gee, what a bike! I'd really like to try it out. [SELF-DISCLO-SURE] No wonder your dad doesn't want you to take it to school. Do you think someone might rip it off? [Follow-up on FREE IN-FORMATION]

BOY 2: Maybe, but I'd still like my old bike with balloon tires to ride to school. [FREE INFORMATION]

BOY 1: What happened to it? [Follow-up on FREE INFORMATION]

BOY 2: Dad gave it to my sister, and she won't let me ride it. [FREE INFORMATION]

BOY 1: My sister acts like that too. [SELF-DISCLOSURE] How old is yours? [Follow-up on FREE INFORMATION]

BOY 2: Nine, and she's starting to act like mom. A real pain! [FREE INFORMATION]

BOY 1: No kidding. My sister does the same thing. [SELF-DISCLOSURE]

With practice in assertively using Free Information and Self-Disclosure, your children will not only feel comfortable in talking to new friends but can help another shy child make conversation. Your child will learn how Free Information and Self-Disclosure make social conversation with peers so much easier (especially for children in puberty or close to it) and make creating new friendships a snap. You will see, as I have, that this success in finding an answer to the almost universal problem of social conversation with new people will motivate your child to see what else you have in your bag of assertive skills. You can take advantage of this eagerness by beginning to teach the child the basics of being assertive in social conflict situations, starting with being more persistent in the face of social opposition and emotional manipulation.

Does Anger Help or Hurt in Being Assertive?

You may ask, "Why do I need to learn any of these skills? When I get angry, I can blow anyone who messes with me out of the water!"

It's true that anger allows you to assert yourself at times by overriding all other emotions—including induced guilt, foolishness, and ignorance—that at other times may inhibit you from asserting yourself. In fact, without training, most of us assert ourselves only when we get angry. But when you do get angry and assert yourself, you do so in an emotional fashion, and you typically pay the price of feeling uncomfortable afterward because you lost your "cool."

Your anger also has a negative side effect on the clarity and effectiveness of your communication with other people: They pay more attention to your anger and less attention to what you are trying to communicate. When you are furious with your child, for example, you can say things like "You want to go outside again so you can come in and get some more muddy tracks on my nice clean rugs! Ha! You are going to spend the rest of your life in your room!" Now your child, having had experience with your anger, knows that you are angry and don't mean what you say.

The same applies to your work situation. If you are a man, you might get angry and say, "I don't give a damn! I've had it up to here with the crappy way things are done here!" Then you tell others what you want done, but they discount what you say by telling each other, "Don't worry about Harry. Nicest guy in the world, but every once in a while he flips his lid. Wait until Monday morning and everything will be fine." As predicted, when Monday morning comes, you have calmed down, and you also feel a bit sheepish, so the disputed issues usually aren't raised again.

If you are a woman and you get angry at work, the same thing happens, but your co-workers dismiss your anger with slightly different words: "Don't pay any attention to what Harriet just said. She's a great person—she just freaks out at that time of the month. Wait a week and everything will be cool again."

Moreover, you can't always rely upon anger to motivate yourself to be assertive. You will often need to be assertive under circumstances that do not provoke anger. A manipulator may not act in a way that angers you. He or she may conceal the self centeredness that shows itself by irritating, pushy, pompous, condescending, or transparently devious behavior. I have known hundreds of very effective manipulators who are always reasonable, logical, pleasant, and even charming. They do not arouse anger in other people, but they still make others feel guilty, foolish, or ignorant when something is wanted.

In short, using anger to motivate yourself to be assertive has two problems. First, people you care for, or see and work with regularly, pay attention to your anger and not to why you are angry. (The same thing will happen to your children when they feel themselves manipulated, except that they are not supposed to show anger or act it out. So your children will just drag their feet in doing what you or their teacher wants, using passive aggression—a way of acting out silent anger—that will also be ineffective.) Second, anger is an unreliable approach in dealing with people you interact with rarely. You just can't count on anger to motivate you and make you impervious to manipulation when you have only one chance to straighten something out.

In the long run—and that's what counts—anger doesn't help you assert yourself effectively. You need something better than raw emotion for dealing with social conflict. Ideally, this should be a verbal skill that is simple to understand and use even in the face of very clever manipulation. Ideally, it also should be simple to learn, so your child can use it too. A basic verbal assertive skill, Broken Record, which is used to learn to be more persistent in the face of emotional manipulation, has all three of these attributes. Let's look at Broken Record in some detail so that you can understand and use it effectively, and then teach it to your child with later dialogues.

The Verbal Assertive Skill of Broken Record

Broken Record involves speaking as if you were a broken record, saying what you want to say over and over again until the manipulator realizes that manipulation gets him or her nowhere in dealing with you. My colleague and good friend Dr. Zev Wanderer, a master clinician, gave this simple way of communicating directly and assertively its descriptive title as a means of explaining to very nonassertive people how to stick to their goals. Broken Record is a basic way of communicating assertively, and is very effective—a kind of subtle brick being thrown at a window. I tell adults that in teaching them ways to cope effectively in social conflict I am going to begin by using persistence. Demonstrating Broken Record, I show them how to be a functional Bella Abzug or Marlon Brando. I also point out that later, practicing the use of other verbal skills, they can also learn to become assertively sophisticated and unflappable—a kind of functional Gloria Steinem or Rex Harrison. But I emphasize that learning to be persistent via Broken Record is a prerequisite to learning these other valuable skills.

Each of the verbal assertive skills you and your children will learn is valuable in itself. Individually they may sound a bit odd or unnatural. Even so, the best way to learn them is one at a time, as building blocks that are later combined into a very effective and complete coping style. When you do this, your assertive speech pattern will not sound very different from normal, but the assertive components that make the difference will have become part of your speech habits.

Broken Record may sound like a very mechanical way of communicating, because it is deliberately designed to exclude all nonessential elements. In some situations this method of communication will be the only effective one. No matter what the other person says, you repeat what you want, and that's all! In situations where the lines are drawn and you have to stick to your guns, using Broken Record does not necessarily make you sound rude, abrasive, or unfriendly. You can even smile at the other person and still be persistent in getting your message across. To help learners sound more humane and less mechanical in a situation where Broken Record is the only skill that can be used, I have them preface whatever they are going to repeatedly say with "I understand what you're saying, but . . . [BROKEN RECORD]" Most often, however, Broken Record is used in conjunction with other verbal skills, so your assertive communications, even when psychological push comes to shove, sound like normal communications.

While at first glance you may think that using Broken Record consistently must be a snap, it takes practice and experience to overcome your automatic, nonthinking responses to manipulative tactics, as the next dialogue points out. This dialogue is one I always use to introduce novices to the skill of Broken Record. In it, one learner is at home and another learner role-playing a manipulator from the same neighborhood knocks on the door to solicit contributions to send Boy or Girl Scouts from the local troop, as well as the organizers of the charity drive, on a month's vacation in Tahiti or on a grand tour of Europe. The learner may well want to contribute something to this organization, but for learning purposes he or she is instructed not to give anything, using Broken Record to refuse the request.

DIALOGUE 14

How You Can Be Manipulated by a Door-to-Door Solicitor
Setting: You answer a knock on your door, and a person soliciting for a charity talks to you.

SOLICITOR: Hi. I represent the local Scout Chapter. We are collecting donations to send our socially awkward Scouts for a month to Club Carib in Tahiti.
YOU: I understand what you want, but I'm not interested. [BROKEN RECORD]
SOLICITOR: You have children, don't you?

You: (Immediately and automatically getting sucked in by a manipulative ploy) Yes, but I wouldn't give any money to send them to Tahiti.

Solicitor: Are they Scouts? They aren't, are they?

You: No.

Solicitor: That's my point! Don't you care about children other than your own?

You: Of course I do, but to send them to Tahiti . . .?

Solicitor: Experience is everything in life. These kids will not feel so socially awkward after a month at Club Carib. It will give them the social confidence they need to make it in life as a lawyer or doctor or used-car dealer. It will motivate them to achieve those goals.

You: But Tahiti . . . Couldn't you send them to the mountains or to Catalina?

Solicitor: It's not the same thing. These kids need to learn how to be social in posh circumstances. They have to learn to eat quiche and seviche with aplomb. It's essential for their future development as middle-class achievers and yuppies.

You: But I'd like *my* kids to go to Tahiti!

Solicitor: Would you wish these socially awkward Scouts any less?

You: No, but—

Solicitor: If you had a socially awkward Scout for a kid, you wouldn't be so hardhearted. One of my nephews is a Scout. He's seventeen and so inept that he doesn't know his ear from his elbow! He has never been anywhere special. Without this charity drive, he won't know what the posh life we should all aspire to is like! Don't you care about a kid in your own neighborhood?

At this point I tend to step in and stop the dialogue because half of the learners usually get bogged down by manipulation, as this one does. As you can see, this learner starts to use Broken Record as instructed, but gets sidetracked into a manipulative argument immediately. This happens because one of the prime bases for psychological manipulation is our reflexive acceptance of the adversary model used for discovering "truth" and resolving conflict in our society. In other words, whenever there is a disagreement between two people, each assumes that he or she is right, and therefore the other person has to be wrong. Consequently, most of us, adults and children, are unthinkingly sucked into defending what we think or want to do by having to prove the other person wrong.

In Being Assertive, Do You Have to Be Right and the Other Person Wrong?

In a social conflict, neither party is right or wrong. Those labels are superfluous and do nothing to resolve a conflict; they only complicate it. The most productive way to resolve any disagreement is simply to view it as a situation in which one side wants something the other doesn't. Yet this adversary behavior pattern is so ingrained that we tend to fall into it even after it is pointed out to us, and after we are specifically instructed not to view others as adversaries in order to learn a new technique for dealing with social conflict.

We become particularly susceptible to this automatic way of behaving when the manipulator starts to ask us questions and we feel we have to answer him or her (as pointed out in your Bill of Everyday Assertive Rights). This learned response is so strong in most of us that we become very uncomfortable when we first try to change this habit. So the main effect of practicing Broken Record is to reemphasize and strengthen the voluntary link between your thinking brain and your tongue during social conflict. With only a little practice, you will feel very comfortable in repeatedly saying what you want in order to get your point across without being sidetracked by the manipulator.

Let's replay that last dialogue with you as the person being solicited, using Broken Record to cope with me, the manipulator. I will try to get you into an argument, which, if you don't lose (consequently feeling that you have to contribute), will at least make you feel very uncomfortable.

DIALOGUE 15

How to Avoid Getting Baited into Not Sticking to Your Point
Setting: The same as before.

ME: Hi. I'm the representative of the local Scout chapter. We are conducting a charity drive to send socially awkward middle-class Scouts to Tahiti for a month to correct their social inadequacies. You will want to contribute to this worthy cause, won't you?

You: I understand how you feel about this cause, but I'm not interested in it.

Me: How can you say that? I can see that you're a concerned parent. You are one, aren't you?

You: I understand, but I'm not interested. [BROKEN RECORD]

Me: How can you say you're not interested? If you're not interested, you obviously don't understand how important this is to these kids.

You: I understand, but I'm not interested. [BROKEN RECORD]

Me: You are not one of those people without kids who vote down education bonds, are you?

You: I understand, but I'm not interested. [BROKEN RECORD]

Me: That's cold. Really cold! Don't you care about kids who are less socially adept than your own?

You: I understand, but I'm not interested. [BROKEN RECORD]

Me: Maybe your spouse would be more interested than you are. What time is he [or she] due home? I can call back then.

You: I understand, but I'm not interested. [BROKEN RECORD]

Me: You keep saying you understand. If you understand, what did I just say?

You: I understand, but I'm not interested. [BROKEN RECORD]

Me: Okay . . . Maybe you don't care about the kids in the neighborhood, but your next-door neighbors will. Can you give me their names?

You: I understand, but I'm not interested. [BROKEN RECORD]

Me: You won't even give me their names?

You: I understand, but I'm not interested. [BROKEN RECORD]

Me: I have a lot of homes to call at. What time is it now?

You: I understand, but I'm not interested. [BROKEN RECORD]

Me: You won't even give me the time of day!

You: I understand, but I'm not interested. [BROKEN RECORD]

Me: (Recovering some of my composure) Well, thank you. Have a nice day.

If you are like most learners, you may well be asking, "Why can't I deal with these people the way I always do—just shut the door on them?"

The answer is, yes, you can always shut the door on a salesperson, but you are going to need the skill of Broken Record to deal with manipulation in the world outside of your home, when closing the door is not possible.

Long dialogues, like the last one, are useful because they give you and your children lots of practice in dealing with manipulation. It's like getting in shape with hundred-pound barbells when in real life you will routinely need the strength to lift only fifty-pound objects. After learning verbal assertive skills through long practice dialogues utilizing all sorts of manipulative examples, you will find that manipulators in the real world rarely surprise you with something you haven't encountered before.

In learning how to be comfortable using Broken Record, you can go back to the dialogues in the previous chapter that show how you are manipulated, and substitute a Broken Record response for any nonassertive response. The following replay of the first manipulative dialogue points this out.

DIALOGUE 16

Saying No to the PTA Chairperson Who Wants to Use Your Home for Meetings
Setting: The chairperson of the PTA (or some other organization) wants you to help out again.

CHAIR: You know, we are really lost without you.
YOU: That's a nice compliment. Thank you.
CHAIR: No, I really mean that! We can't get anyone to volunteer their house after everyone saw how nice yours is.
YOU: Well, I'm just not going to get involved again. It was too much of a hassle.
CHAIR: What can we do? We have no place to meet.
YOU: I don't know. [ASSERTIVE RIGHTS III AND VI]
CHAIR: We can't meet without a place like yours!
YOU: I understand your problem, but I don't want to get involved again. [BROKEN RECORD]
CHAIR: Could you see if Mary would let us use her place? She's a good friend of yours.

You: I understand your problem, but I don't want to get involved again.
[BROKEN RECORD]

CHAIR: My place would be okay, but my wife is visiting her mother on the Riviera.

You: (Not being asked for anything, there is no response to make.)

CHAIR: I never thought you would let us down like this. Tell you what —let's go on as before for just a couple of meetings until we get out of this jam, okay?

You: I understand your problem, but I don't want to get involved again.[BROKEN RECORD]

CHAIR: Humph . . . (Looking at you with a different perspective) Well . . . Don't worry about it. We'll find somebody who cares enough to help out.

You: (Ignoring the gross guilt induction) Swell. How's about a cup of coffee for old times' sake?

CHAIR: (Always the politician) Of course.

I recommend that you first practice using Broken Record with another adult. There is nothing better to prepare you for facing real manipulation than to hear it directed at you in practice, and to respond assertively. Have the other person read the dialogue once, silently. You will be surprised at how infrequently during your dialogue that person will have to refer to the script again in order to manipulate you.

When you feel comfortable and competent in using Broken Record with an adult, let your child practice it. First have your child play the manipulator, trying to get you to do something the child chooses, while you use Broken Record as a response to your child's manipulation. In doing this, you are making sure that your child understands what manipulation is, so he or she can recognize it in the future. When your child has to make up manipulation as you go along, he or she will definitely learn to recognize it. In this practice, you will be simultaneously modeling for your child how to use Broken Record. Then reverse roles, with you as the manipulator and the child as the assertor, using the dialogues given here that are appropriate for your child.

The prefatory response in these practice dialogues may depend on the age of your child. Older children can use the same humanizing preface that I suggest adults use: "I understand [what you say, how you feel], but I . . ." This humanizing preface to Broken Record quickly becomes habit requiring little or no thought. But children younger than ten often become anxious and tongue-tied in emotional disputes with their peers and others. It helps if they have a simple, routine task that makes them think, thereby reducing anxiety.

Therefore you might do as STAR suggests teachers have their pupils do, and ask your child to preface his or her Broken Record responses with a mirroring statement. A mirror only reflects what is presented to it, and a mirroring statement only repeats what has just been said. Your younger child will find it calming, and thus find it easier to pay attention to what another says, if the child is using his or her thinking brain to reflect back verbally what the other person has said before repeating the Broken Record response. For example: "You want to borrow my bike [MIRRORING], but I want to ride it to the park myself [BROKEN RECORD]." Both "I understand" and mirror-prefacing responses are important, since they tell peers (as well as others) that your child is not discounting or ignoring what they say but still wants to do what he or she thinks best.

However, some children under ten years of age have a problem with short term memory. These kids get confused and distracted in trying to use the mirroring preface because they have difficulty remembering the specific words another person has used. If this is the case with your younger child, have the child skip the prefatory response and just use simple, unadorned Broken Record. Start teaching your child Broken Record with the following dialogue.

DIALOGUE 17

Daughter Gets the Food She Ordered at Big Max's When the Server Makes a Mistake
Age level: Seven through seventeen
Setting: Your daughter (or son) is at a fast-food shop and has ordered a plain hot dog. At an outdoor table she unwraps the hot dog and finds it smothered with mustard, relish, and catsup. If your child is in the middle or older age range, she (or he) decides to get a fresh hot dog from the girl behind the counter. If your child is younger, you are there with her (or him). Your younger child complains to you that the hot dog is not right. You ask your child to go up to the counter and get a fresh one.

DAUGHTER: I ordered a plain hot dog, and this is covered with stuff. I would like a plain hot dog, please.

GIRL: I distinctly remember you ordering one with everything on it.

DAUGHTER: I understand that [or, You remember me ordering one with everything on it: MIRRORING], but I ordered a plain hot dog and I want a fresh one. [BROKEN RECORD]

GIRL: Everybody thinks they can change their order once they get it.

DAUGHTER: I understand, but I ordered a plain one and I want a fresh hot dog. [BROKEN RECORD]

GIRL: Are you calling me a liar?

DAUGHTER: (Not responding to baiting) I understand, but I ordered a plain one and I want a fresh hot dog. [BROKEN RECORD]

GIRL: I should charge you for this.

DAUGHTER: I understand, but I ordered a plain one and I want a fresh hot dog. [BROKEN RECORD]

GIRL: Harry, give me a plain hot dog—and make sure you get it right this time!

As a parent of a pesky kid who keeps bugging you, you may find it strange to have me say your child needs to learn how to be more persistent, but this is exactly what your child requires in order to cope successfully with manipulative peers. Your child needs to learn not how to be pesky, or a pain, but how to be *persistent* in communicating straightforwardly and assertively with friends and classmates, as the following assertive replay of an earlier manipulative dialogue indicates.

DIALOGUE 18

Son Copes with a Manipulative Friend Who Wants Him to Fool Around Instead of Doing the Chores You Asked Him to Do
Age level: Seven through seventeen
Setting: A friend drops over and finds your son cleaning out the garage, a chore you asked him to finish.

FRIEND: What are you doing?

SON: Cleaning out the garage.

FRIEND: You can do that later. Let's bike down to the park.

SON: I want to get this done first.

FRIEND: Why?

SON: I promised my mom I'd get it done.

FRIEND: Tell her you're done, and let's go.

SON: You want me to go to the park [MIRROR], but I want to finish this first. [BROKEN RECORD]

FRIEND: Are you afraid your mom will chew you out?

SON: You want me to go to the park [MIRROR], but I want to finish this first. [BROKEN RECORD]

FRIEND: So she finds out! Big deal! She gives you a bad time. So what? Hasn't she chewed you out before?

SON: You want me to go to the park [MIRROR], but I want to finish this first. [BROKEN RECORD]

FRIEND: What are you, a momma's boy?

SON: You want me to go to the park [MIRROR], but I want to finish this first. [BROKEN RECORD]

FRIEND: Don't be a jerk. The rest of the guys are down at the park. You want me to tell them that you can't come because your mother said you can't?

SON: You want me to go to the park [MIRROR], but I want to finish this first. [BROKEN RECORD]

FRIEND: Aww, come on. Let's go.

SON: (Using some creative problem solving) Tell you what. You want me to go to the park. So do I. You help me clean up and we'll get there faster. [WORKABLE COMPROMISE]

FRIEND: Oh . . . okay. Where do these old tires go?

Teaching Your Child the Use of Workable Compromise and Self-Disclosure

In the last dialogue, your son resolved the conflict between himself and his friend with some creative problem solving. Whereas the adversary model of conflict resolution—i.e., I am right, therefore you must be wrong—sets things up so only one party in a disagreement or conflict can win, assertiveness training takes the viewpoint that both parties can win, or at least that neither has to lose.

Workable Compromise: Does a Compromise Have to Be Fair to Work?

Trying to get both people to gain at least part of what they want is the basis for another assertive verbal skill, Workable Compromise. Teach your child that he or she does not have to "win" every dispute with other people. In fact, your child doesn't really have to try to win anything. Encourage your child to make a deal, to offer a compromise, as in the previous dialogue, if that is possible. In doing this, both your child and the other child get something out of their interaction. Make sure that your child understands that compromises do not have to be "fair" to work, or meet all the needs and wants of both parties in a dispute. The only practical limitation on working out a compromise is that it must leave your child's (or your own) self-respect intact. For example, it will do no good at all for your daughter, just to get out of a temporary hassle, to make a compromise with her brother that he can tease her unmercifully only on Mondays, Wednesdays, and Fridays.

Let me emphasize that all the training dialogues in this book are only samples of the most common situations that children have reported to the STAR research staff. They certainly do not cover every possible situation in which your children may have to assert themselves, and it would be impossible for me to list all the situations in which assertive practice dialogues would help. Therefore, if for any reason the practice situation or topic of a sample dialogue does not fit your child, use a conflict situation or topic that you know your child would have a problem coping with, or ask your child about situations and topics that trouble him or her and use those for practice.

Self-Disclosure: An Aid in Being Persistent with People You Know and See Regularly

Now that you have seen how being assertive, even on a basic and unsophisticated level, works to get us out of impossible situations caused by manipulating our feelings of guilt, foolishness, or ignorance, you may want to try using Broken Record as a response in other manipulative dialogues already illustrated. However, I suggest that you add on one of the assertive skills we have already discussed, Self-Disclosure, in situations that call for it, thus forming a combined assertive-skill response.

For example, in the manipulative dialogue where a friend wanted to borrow your car and you made up all sorts of reasons why you couldn't lend it to him, you ended up lending your friend your car. Before replaying that dialogue more assertively, stop and think for a moment about why you really prefer not to lend your friend (or anyone else) the car. Most novice learners of assertiveness come up with all sorts of external reasons that are identical to those in the dialogue: insurance, poor brakes, my spouse will need it. Underlying these reasons is one *real* reason: People worry and feel uncomfortable whenever they lend their car. But they believe their worry is unjustified or irrational because nothing has ever happened when they lent it before, so they never come right out and assertively disclose their real feelings. If you are like most of the rest of us, you believe that your negative feelings are not a "proper" justification for your behavior. In fact, those negative feelings are the *only* realistic basis on which you have to operate.

In this particular case, you must make a decision. Be your own judge. Which is more important—your friend having what he wants, or your not feeling worried and uncomfortable? If you decide that your friend's convenience is more important than your worry, there is no problem. You simply lend him your car whenever requested and pay the price. If you decide that your feelings are more important, then you can use Self-Disclosure along with Broken Record very effectively, not only in not lending your car, but also in not destroying your friendship. Let's look at a replay of that manipulative dialogue with you being more assertive, using Broken Record in conjunction with Self-Disclosure.

DIALOGUE 19

Saying No to a Manipulative Friend Who Wants to Borrow Your Car and Pooh-Poohs Your Uncomfortable Feelings
Setting: I am your friend and co-worker and I jog up to your house on Saturday morning and begin to talk.

ME: Hi, busy?

YOU: Sort of.

ME: Good. Then you wouldn't mind if I borrowed your car this morning, would you?

YOU: Gee, Pete, whenever I lend anyone my car, I get really worried and uncomfortable. So I'd like not to lend it. [SELF-DISCLOSURE]

ME: You have nothing to worry about. I've never had an accident in my life.

YOU: But I do get worried and uncomfortable. So I don't want to lend my car. [SELF-DISCLOSURE and BROKEN RECORD]

ME: What are you worried about?

YOU: I just get worried and uncomfortable. So I don't want to lend my car. [SELF-DISCLOSURE and BROKEN RECORD]

ME: You never told me this before.

YOU: I feel silly that I never did before, but I still get worried and uncomfortable, so I don't want to lend my car. [SELF-DISCLO-SURE and BROKEN RECORD]

ME: I thought we were friends.

YOU: (Not getting baited into a discussion of "What are friends for?") I just get worried and uncomfortable, so I don't want to lend my car. [SELF-DISCLOSURE and BROKEN RECORD]

ME: You shouldn't worry like that. It's irrational. Maybe you should see a shrink.

YOU: I get worried and uncomfortable, and I don't want to lend my car. [SELF-DISCLOSURE and BROKEN RECORD]

ME: Well, this is a big disappointment. I thought I could count on you.

YOU: I feel bad that you're disappointed, but I just get worried and uncomfortable, so I don't want to lend my car. [SELF-DISCLO-SURE and BROKEN RECORD]

ME: (Sarcastically) Yes. I heard that already. Don't worry about me. I'll find a car somewhere.

YOU: How about Jim? He lives just down the street. [WORKABLE COMPROMISE]

ME: Is he in?

YOU: I don't know. Why don't you check?

ME: (Trotting off) I will. Thanks.

YOU: Anytime.

Teaching Children to Say How They Feel and What They Think

I recommend you also teach your child that disclosing personal worries is permissible. This admission does not make him or her a spineless wimp but is just part of being human. STAR stresses the importance of teaching your children to be comfortable in making assertive "I feel . . ." or "I think . . ." statements. If your son is like most boys, he very likely believes that it is wrong or weak for him to express emotions, especially to his peers. If you or someone else doesn't help him modify that belief, unless he is bright, it won't be until he is in his late teens or early twenties (if at all) that he has the insight expressed by some young men: "I finally decided that being a macho jock [the ideal male] wasn't really important, and got on with things that were."

To help your children feel comfortable about expressing feelings, routinely set aside some time to talk with them about how they feel about different subjects. Start with topics like chores and schoolwork. Then ask specifically about small things that upset them, such as a friend who promises something and doesn't do it, or how they feel when a friend keeps interrupting them when they are talking. If your child is like most youngsters, he or she will talk not about feelings but about the bothersome person—"Billy's always saying he'll help and then doesn't." To get your child to become comfortable in expressing his or her feelings, ask your child not to talk about Billy but about how he or she feels about Billy or Billy's behavior—e.g., "I don't like it when Billy . . ." or "I don't like Billy when he does that." Make sure your child understands a very important point about his or her emotions: In being his or her own judge, your child has the right to decide whether feeling upset about someone else's behavior is okay or not.

Also ask your children to express their opinions. Children rarely start sentences with "I think." That's adult behavior. So encourage "I think" statements by specifically asking your kids what they think about certain things and events: "Why do you think Billy does that a lot?" You don't have to reward them for expressing their opinions. Your asking what they think is reward enough, because it means that what they think is important. However, to make this work, you have to understand that what your kids think is not always going to be rational, clever, insightful, or correct. Our own thinking as adults cannot always be characterized as having these attributes either. This kind of thinking comes with experience and is self-correcting. So don't try to correct them, and especially don't put them down because what they think doesn't measure up to adult standards. All you want to do at this time is give them reinforcement for thinking and then expressing how they feel and what their personal opinions are.

After your children have become fairly open with you in expressing how they feel and think, they will find it much easier to use assertive Self-Disclosure (explained on pages 73–82), as shown in the following replay of a previous manipulative dialogue between a child trying to study and a friend.

DIALOGUE 20

Son Deals with a Manipulative Friend Who Doesn't Respect His Need to Study
Age level: Eleven through seventeen
Setting: Your son is studying for a test tomorrow, and his friend wants your son to come to the beach with him.

FRIEND: Let's go to the beach.
SON: I'd like to go to the beach today [SELF-DISCLOSURE], but I can't.
FRIEND: Why can't you?
SON: I have a math test tomorrow morning and I have to study for it.
FRIEND: You're good in math. You don't need to study!
SON: I wish I was, but I have to study. [SELF-DISCLOSURE]
FRIEND: What do you care about math for?
SON: I'd like to get a good grade in math. [SELF-DISCLOSURE]
FRIEND: What for? Only nerds worry about math. You want to be like them?
SON: (Ignoring manipulative baiting) I understand you want me to go to the beach with you, but I'm afraid I won't get a good grade if I don't study. [MIRRORING and SELF-DISCLOSURE]
FRIEND: We could be playing volleyball with the rest of the guys.

SON: If I don't study, I'm afraid I might not get a good grade tomorrow. [SELF-DISCLOSURE and BROKEN RECORD]
FRIEND: You've got nothing to worry about! I told everybody we'd be there at two. We have to go to the beach.
SON: Why?
FRIEND: If we don't show up, the rest of the guys can't play as a regular team.
SON: If I don't study, I'm afraid I might not get a good grade tomorrow. [SELF-DISCLOSURE and BROKEN RECORD]
FRIEND: If you don't come, what am I going to tell them?
SON: I don't know. But if I don't study, I'm afraid I might not get a good grade tomorrow. [SELF-DISCLOSURE and BROKEN RECORD]
FRIEND: The other guys won't like you for this.
SON: I hope not, but if I don't study, I'm afraid I might not get a good grade tomorrow. [SELF-DISCLOSURE and BROKEN RECORD]

Here is a dialogue for an older child who has practiced expressing feelings openly and comfortably. This dialogue, too, uses Self-Disclosure and is an assertive replay of a previous manipulative dialogue between a child and a friend.

DIALOGUE 21

Daughter Deals with a Manipulative Friend Who Wants Her to Steal a Bottle of Vodka for a Party
Age level: Eleven through seventeen
Setting: Your daughter's friend is planning a party this weekend and wants to serve liquor illegally.

FRIEND: You've got to help me out with my party this weekend.
DAUGHTER: How?
FRIEND: Bimbo said she was going to bring the booze for the punch, but her mother caught her taking it, and now she's grounded.
DAUGHTER: So?

FRIEND: So you've got to get a bottle of vodka from your father's cabinet.

DAUGHTER: I would really feel uncomfortable doing that. [SELF-DIS-CLOSURE]

FRIEND: Why?

DAUGHTER: If my dad caught me, I'd be mortified. [SELF-DISCLO-SURE]

FRIEND: Don't talk like a child. You're a lot smarter than Bimbo. You won't get caught. Besides, you and your dad are real close. If he caught you, you could sweet-talk him out of anything.

DAUGHTER: I would really feel uncomfortable doing that to my dad. [SELF-DISCLOSURE]

FRIEND: Why?

DAUGHTER: I think it just wouldn't be right to do that. [SELF-DIS-CLOSURE]

FRIEND: I thought we were good friends, and you don't care enough to help me out!

DAUGHTER: I would really feel uncomfortable stealing a bottle of vodka for you. [SELF-DISCLOSURE and BROKEN RECORD]

FRIEND: At least Bimbo tried! She's a real friend who cares.

DAUGHTER: I would really feel uncomfortable stealing a bottle of vodka for you. [SELF-DISCLOSURE and BROKEN RECORD]

FRIEND: When I really need a friend, what happens? You fink out on me!

DAUGHTER: I would really feel uncomfortable stealing a bottle of vodka for you. [SELF-DISCLOSURE and BROKEN RECORD]

FRIEND: If you cared for me more than getting caught taking some stupid vodka, you'd do it!

DAUGHTER: I would really feel uncomfortable stealing a bottle of vodka for you. [SELF-DISCLOSURE and BROKEN RECORD]

FRIEND: Don't ever ask me to steal something for you!

DAUGHTER: I won't. What are you going to wear at the party?

FRIEND: My sexy new purple outfit. I'll look terrific.

In practicing Self-Disclosure and Broken Record with your child to deal with manipulative peer pressure, explain that other kids will never be as persistent as your child can be after this practice. But it's the practice that gives your child confidence in being assertive by knowing beforehand what the outcome will be.

As was said earlier, the three main characteristics of the nonassertive person are lack of persistence, oversensitivity to criticism, and fear of being caught in a mistake. Having seen how you can teach your child the foundation of assertiveness, being persistent, let's go on to the next chapter and the second major characteristic of nonassertiveness, so that you can learn how to teach your child to be more effective and less emotional in coping with the great manipulator, criticism.

CHAPTER FOUR

Teaching Your Child to Be Human: Coping with Errors, Faults, and Criticism

A few years ago a colleague told me a story about how being assertive saved the day for one of his adult students. The student was a new vice-president at a bank in San Diego, and had just finished taking my colleague's systematic assertiveness course.

Coming into his office one morning, Jim, the vice-president, was told by his secretary that Bill, the president of the bank, wanted to see him in his suite "immediately!" Jim said that a good definition of *eternity* is the thirty seconds it takes to walk from your office to your boss's after you get a message like that, especially when your secretary's tone of voice makes you feel like a little kid who has done something to be ashamed of.

Upon entering the presidential suite, Jim noticed two things at once. The four other vice-presidents of the bank were squeezed in next to each other on a three-man couch, where Bill had silently waved each to sit as they had come in. Bill was marching up and down in front of them, holding a rolled-up set of papers in his hand. The veins on his forehead stood out, and his face was literally purple with rage. Jim didn't have to be told where to sit—he sat on the arm of the couch, lined up with the other objects of Bill's anger.

As soon as Jim sat, Bill turned to the five vice-presidents and said, "Which one of you is in charge of the idiot who prematurely released the higher interest-rate schedules for our new long-term jumbo savings certificates? We can write off the rest of this month in terms of new accounts because everyone will wait till the higher interest goes into effect on the first! That's going to cost us at least twenty-five thousand dollars!"

The immediate reaction of the other four VPs was to turn and look at each other as if saying, "Not me! It must be you." Jim's immediate reaction was to raise his hand and say, "Look no further, Bill. Publicity is in my department, so it must have been one of my people. I don't know how it happened or who did it, but I will find out. I feel really bad about this. I should have foreseen it might happen and prevented it."

While Jim was saying this, his boss visibly started to relax. As Jim described it, "Bill immediately changed. His face faded back to its normal color and his body started to sag as if he had lost his steam." When Jim finished his statement of responsibility, Bill responded to him with "Calm down, calm down. Don't worry about it. It's only twenty-five thousand."

While losing twenty-five big ones would certainly upset you or me, for a banker like Bill, who handles millions of dollars weekly, that was surely not reason enough to turn apoplectic. But if it wasn't the loss of $25,000 that upset Bill, what was it?

Bill was upset for the same reason you are when someone you work or live with makes a mistake that affects you. Because of past experience, Bill assumed that getting someone to take responsibility for a mistake would be like pulling teeth. He was angry because he thought he was in for a long, knock-down, drag-out fight with his VPs before he could convince the one responsible for the error to make sure it wouldn't happen again.

Bill was therefore visibly surprised, pleased, and sympathetic when Jim immediately took responsibility for following up on the costly mistake and relieved him of the fight he anticipated. And what was the reaction of the other VPs? When Jim assertively admitted his responsibility, each reacted in the same way as Bill. As a new VP, how long would it otherwise have taken Jim to build up his colleagues' trust in him as much as it rose in that minute or so it took him to acknowledge his section's error? Six months? A year?

For Jim, learning to confront his negative points, faults, and errors not only paid off handsomely at work but also gave him great personal relief. It is wonderful not to have to pretend you are perfect. Being able to cope verbally with a person who is angry with you for making an error is one payoff of understanding and practicing assertiveness. But the most important result of assertiveness is an internal one: that sense of personal competence Jim acquired by being able to acknowledge publicly that he was not perfect, had personal faults (by whatever standard such faults are defined), and would make errors. In short, he learned to assertively accept himself as human.

Being Your Own Judge of Your Errors and Faults

If assertiveness involves having faith in your own judgment about yourself and your positive qualities, a faith that gives you the ability to perform, then assertiveness must also involve your own judgment about your negative qualities, which may or may not foul things up for you. Jim learned to accept and feel comfortable with himself in spite of his faults, defects, and errors, by using the verbal skill of Negative Assertion. This particular verbal skill is important to your child because it teaches him or her that a good child does not have to be perfect. Negative Assertion teaches your child through practice and successful experience that it is quite all right and entirely human to make mistakes, that one should not be intimidated by them or give up trying, and that in whatever one does in life, mistakes are in fact guaranteed to happen. The use of Negative Assertion allows *you*, not someone else, to be the judge of your negative qualities and errors. You decide whether you should feel guilty, foolish, or ignorant about them.

You can see the simple but powerful effect of Negative Assertion in allowing you to take charge of your own emotions and behavior if we replay the manipulative dialogue from chapter 2 about your forgetting your promise to pick me up at noon for a dental appointment.

DIALOGUE 22

Learning to Cope Assertively with a Manipulative Friend When You Make a Mistake
Setting: *It's now one o'clock and you finally show up in your car at the entrance to my office building, where I'm still waiting for you.*

ME: Where the hell were you?

YOU: What do you mean, where was I?

ME: You were supposed to pick me up at noon, and now it's one o'clock!

YOU: I was? What for?

ME: My tooth is killing me. I could have made my own arrangements to get my tooth fixed, but you said you would make an emergency appointment with your brother, the dentist—who also needs the business.

YOU: Oh! . . . Gosh! That was really dumb of me! I forgot all about it. [NEGATIVE ASSERTION]

ME: You forgot! That does me a lot of good!

YOU: What can I say except that it was really dumb of me to forget something so important to you. [NEGATIVE ASSERTION]

ME: You could at least offer to help me out!

YOU: Sure. What can I do? (Asking what is wanted instead of volunteering a possible solution)

ME: Can you make another appointment at five-thirty?

YOU: No problem. I'm sure my brother will do that for me. Is that all?

ME: Can you drive me there at five? I still need a ride there and then home.

YOU: Sure. That's the least I can do.

ME: Well, that makes up for some of the problem you caused with your forgetfulness.

YOU: What can I say except that I blew it? [NEGATIVE ASSERTION]

ME: You could say that you are sorry.

YOU: Of course. I feel very bad about screwing things up for you. [SELF-DISCLOSURE and NEGATIVE ASSERTION]

ME: Okay. Do you have any aspirin?
YOU: Top drawer of my desk.

Once again, much or most of the other person's bad and angry feelings about the mistake are caused by anticipation of having to get into a fight about (1) whether the mistake is really a mistake, (2) whose fault it is, or (3) how important the mistake is. The mistake itself is not the major factor. The use of Negative Assertion saves the other person from going through this uncomfortable process, and he or she typically feels much better when you use Negative Assertion than when you do not.

Negative Assertion: Teaching Your Child How to Cope with His or Her Errors and Faults, and the Criticism These Generate

STAR teaches children to assert their negative points and human errors (instead of trying to hide them, as children usually do) in the same way you could have done in the previous dialogue. In teaching your own child how to use Negative Assertion to cope with human faults, get him or her out of the habit of saying "I'm sorry." As we have noted, this phrase has been made meaningless by overuse and doesn't soothe other people. Instead, have your child practice using assertive negative statements such as "That was inconsiderate of me ["I don't know why I do such dumb things," "It was really stupid of me to say that," "Boy, I really am klutzy today"] and I really feel bad about it." It is important to point out to your child, as STAR does, the difference between a person and a person's behavior. For instance, saying "Sometimes I [am inconsiderate, do dumb things, say something really stupid, am a real klutz]" does not mean that your child is an inconsiderate, dumb, stupid, or klutzy person. It means only that your child is like everyone else and behaves less than perfectly.

You may note that the verbal behavior you will be teaching your child to assert his or her negative points sounds a bit strange for a child, especially as young as seven to ten years old. Keep in mind that in teaching the child to be assertive, you are teaching him or her how to act in a more mature and competent way, so the speech patterns used will begin to sound like those of an adult—perhaps not those of a sophisticate, but definitely the language of someone capable of handling mistakes and criticism without distress. You should not worry about this, even if it sounds incongruous to you, because your children will have to start talking more and more like adults as they mature anyway, and this early practice makes the transition easier for them. STAR teaches children one of the phrases I use when I do something foolish, and then negatively assert myself out of it: "When I do something like that, I think I must be getting mentally incompetent." While that sounds more humorous coming from a young child than it does from me, it does work, and one can't fight success.

The next two dialogues point out the difference in behavior between a child taught to cope assertively with errors and personal faults, and a child who was not. The first dialogue demonstrates the typical reaction of an unassertive child caught in an error by an angry parent.

DIALOGUE 23

How a Child Not Trained to Cope Assertively with His Errors Deals Badly with Mom or Dad and Makes Things Worse Setting: You go out to the garage to inspect it late Friday night and find that your son hasn't cleaned it out for the garage sale tomorrow as he promised.

You: What did you do today? You promised that you would clean out the garage for the sale tomorrow!

Son: I thought you said the sale was Sunday.

You: Don't give me that! I distinctly remember telling you it was Saturday! What did you do after school instead of cleaning it up as you promised?

Son: I worked on my homework.

You: You did that after dinner. What did you do this afternoon?

Son: I worked on it for a while. . . .

You: For how long?

Son: About a half-hour.

You: And then what did you do?

Son: It got dark.

You: What did you do when you came home from school?

Son: It wasn't my fault! I forgot.

You: Where did you go?

Son: Nowhere.

You: I'm fed up with you saying you will do something and then you don't! You are not going anywhere until you clean up that garage! Do you hear me?

Son: Yes.

You: You're going to clean up that garage at the crack of dawn. You're not going to get out of doing what you are supposed to this time!

Son: Okay.

In the next dialogue, you can see how a child taught to assert himself, even about negative points, will cope better with your feelings of anger, and make a bad situation better instead of worse. Although it may seem strange to teach your own son how to deal with your anger and disappointment over his goofs, if *you* don't do it, he may never learn how. When you are calm and collected, use this dialogue as practice to teach your son (or daughter) how to cope with errors that affect you.

DIALOGUE 24

How an Assertive Child Takes Responsibility for Mistakes and Makes a Bad Situation Better
Age level: Seven through seventeen
Setting: The same as before.

You: What did you do today? You promised that you would clean out the garage for the sale tomorrow!

Son: Gosh! I completely forgot it! How dumb can I get? [NEGATIVE ASSERTION]

You: You forgot! You're always forgetting things! You'd forget your head if it wasn't screwed on tight!

Son: I do forget a lot of things. [NEGATIVE ASSERTION]

You: I distinctly remember telling you it was Saturday! How could you forget something important like this?

SON: It was really stupid of me. [NEGATIVE ASSERTION]

YOU: I'll say. What did you do after school instead of cleaning it up as you promised?

SON: It was dumb. I just forgot it. I feel really bad about screwing up your sale. [NEGATIVE ASSERTION and SELF-DISCLOSURE]

YOU: It will be okay if we get up at the crack of dawn and clean up then. You're going to help me clean up, and then stick around for the sale.

SON: Sure. I feel bad about this. When I screw things up like this, I think I must be mentally incompetent. [SELF-DISCLOSURE and NEGATIVE ASSERTION]

To teach your child Negative Assertion, practice on situations that are common—e.g., when other children criticise your child's mistakes: "Did you scratch the paint on my new bike?" "Can't you be more careful? You spilled that Coke all over my new shirt!" "If you'd kept your big mouth shut, we wouldn't have to rake these leaves!" "You forgot to bring my book back on the day of the test? What an idiot!" "You ate all our candy yourself and didn't save any for me? What a selfish person you are!" (See the training list of sample criticisms in the Appendix.) The situations for practice are limitless, because kids always make mistakes and are oversensitive about their negative points. Have your child practice Negative Assertion, with you as the critic, until it feels quite natural for him or her to readily admit an error or a fault, and then go on to the next verbal skill designed to cope with criticism: Fogging.

Fogging: Teaching Your Child How to Cope with Manipulative Criticism

Fogging is similar to Negative Assertion in that you always agree with your critic, but it is used for situations quite different from those in which you have clearly made an error. When someone criticizes you for making such an error, there is agreement between you and your critic that an error was made, based on some belief or system that assigns positive and negative values to things—even if you hate to admit it! Negative Assertion is used only when you and your critic completely agree that you are at fault.

Fogging, on the other hand, is used when matters are not so clear-cut —when there is not absolute agreement between you and your critic about your thoughts, feelings, or behavior. Fogging works best when there are two different beliefs (or interpretations of a belief) to choose between—yours and your critic's. In that situation, who really knows which viewpoint is best, yours or your critic's? You really have no objective way of proving your belief superior to your critic's, or vice versa. Therefore, this situation always pushes you to make your own judgment of the correctness of that for which you are being criticized. In such situations the critic is usually manipulative, and that's where you can use Fogging to your advantage.

Fogging is a clinical slang term I used for explaining this assertive skill to patients at the Sepulveda Veterans Hospital when I developed systematic assertiveness training there in 1969. I would ask them to think of how a fogbank behaves. "A fogbank does not respond to you. If you attack a fogbank, it does not fight back. If you punch a fogbank, it allows your fist to penetrate with no resistance, and then closes up afterward. If you throw a brick at a fogbank, it does not stiffen to bounce the brick off so you can pick it up and throw it at the fogbank again. After getting nowhere in trying to force a fogbank to do something, you give up and leave it alone." The name Fogging has stuck, even though it is more accurate to describe this skill as Agreeing with Truth, Agreeing with Principle, or Agreeing with Probability (the odds).

Fogging works well because it does three important things for you. First, with practice, Fogging reduces your automatic (and irrational!) sense of guilt or anxiety when you are criticized. All of us get that momentary flash of stomach-knotting panic when someone else criticizes us. Unfortunately, for some of us this sensation is more than momentary and we become quite defensive when criticized, as if we have to protect ourselves. Fogging diminishes this emotional reaction and thus allows our thinking brain to work. We are then able to evaluate the criticism and decide whether or not it is important to us.

Second, Fogging reduces the amount of criticism you will receive. A manipulator (just like the rest of us) operates under the primary psychological law of behavior—i.e., win-stay, lose-change. A manipulator uses manipulation only because it works and gives the manipulator a payoff —what he or she wants. If manipulative criticism does not work in controlling your behavior or emotions, your critic will begin to use it less and less and, we hope, change to a more mutually productive way of communicating. This is what happened to eight-year-old Mary when Chris, the STAR psychologist, taught her how to respond to merciless teasing.

Third, Fogging reduces conflict between you and your critic because it does not follow the adversary model of determining right and wrong —i.e., you do not have to prove your critic wrong for you to elect to do what you want, or for you not to feel guilty. Fogging does not take away your critic's dignity or self-respect and thereby worsen the dispute, as the adversary model often does.

How People Will Criticize You or Your Child: With Truth, with General Principles or Logic, and with the Odds

To see what the verbal assertive skill of Fogging is, and how to use it, let's look at how people typically criticize you, and how you can use Fogging to cope with such criticism.

People will criticize you in any or all of three ways. You will be criticized with the *truth*, you will be criticized using *general principles*, and you will be criticized using the *odds*. For instance, let's say you are reading this book and I decide to criticize you manipulatively using truth. I come up and say, "You're reading again, aren't you?" If I did that to you in real life, in a negative tone of voice, you would very likely feel a quick sense of panic in your gut. If you are like most of us, you would also have an involuntary reaction that prompts you to defend yourself, without first thinking through *why* you should have to defend yourself. You would automatically reply to my criticism in either of two ways: with denial or with countercriticism. Most likely, without thinking, you would stop reading, perhaps even put the book down, and say, "Oh, no, I wasn't reading anything! I was just looking at the pictures." Even if you didn't say something like that, my criticism of you, using the truth, would make you feel like saying it.

This impulse to deny is so reliable—in spite of its absurdity—that I always use it in assertiveness-training seminars to demonstrate our automatic response to criticism. The learner I select to demonstrate it feels defensive and foolish, as if I am Big Daddy and he or she is a six-year-old child caught with a hand in the cookie jar. We involuntarily feel like guilty-six-year-olds because we are not in the habit of being our own personal judges. We automatically accept what others say, without eval-uating it. The student learns, by practicing Fogging, that all manipula-tive criticism we receive has two parts: (1) at least *some* observed truth about ourselves or our behavior (in this case, 100 percent truth), and (2) the manipulator's subjective judgment of this correctly observed behav-ior (in this case rendered by my disapproving tone of voice).

Fogging is designed to teach you to make your acceptance or rejection of criticism a voluntary, thinking response instead of an automatic one. It allows you to distinguish between the observations of the critic and the critic's judgment of those observations. In Fogging, you always respond to the critic's *observations* of your behavior, and not to his or her *judgment* of it. Fogging teaches you to listen carefully to criticism rather than ignore it. Therefore, the assertive response I would want you to give to my criticism using truth is "You're right, Pete, I am reading" (to agree with truth), and then go back to reading.

If your critic is someone close and you have not been trained to be more assertive, you may begin automatically to countercriticize in order to reduce the anxiety caused by your critic. One of my colleagues loves to tell how Fogging helped improve things between her husband and herself. As she tells the story, she was resting after a hard day's work at the clinic before cleaning up the house and getting dinner ready. Her husband walked in at 5:30 and said, "This house is a mess!" Her auto-matic response was "Who are you to say anything? I've been killing myself all day. I had to run around for two hours picking up the kids and shopping for groceries. What gall! I've seen what you do at work. Half the time you have your feet up on the desk reading the paper, or you're chitchatting with the cute secretaries down by the water cooler! You should talk." The fight lasted all night.

After learning Fogging, my colleague tells how she was sitting on the kitchen floor reading *Ms.* magazine when her husband came in and said, "Dinner's not ready!" Her response to this manipulative criticism, using truth, was a simple, nondefensive "You're right," along with a smile. That response, in contrast to her previous one, triggered a laughing fit by her husband, in which she joined.

People will also criticize you using general principles, or with logic, in order to induce feelings of guilt, foolishness, or ignorance to get you to do what they want. For instance, in an assertiveness-training seminar when I pick on someone to demonstrate our common reaction to criticism, I might say, "You're taking notes again!" and then, after that person drops his or her pen in denial, I follow up with criticism using general principle, or logic. The criticism is nonsensical and irrelevant, but that makes no difference to the criticized person's gut reaction. I might say, "If you keep writing detailed notes instead of paying attention to the total point I am trying to make, you will miss a lot of the richness of my presentation. Then when you go back to your company and your boss says, in the next staff meeting, 'Sally, tell us what you learned in Dr. Smith's seminar,' you will give a detailed report that lacks an overall viewpoint."

The assertive response that I want the student to learn is "Pete, you could be right" (to agree in principle), and then to resume taking notes. This Fogging response essentially says that while my criticism may be valid in principle or according to logic, it may not apply to her specific situation, and that Sally still thinks taking notes is a good idea. By using Fogging as a response to my critique, Sally does not get into an adversary conflict in which she feels she has to prove to me that her note-taking is appropriate.

People will also criticize you using the odds, pointing out how the behavior that they do not want you to continue will probably end in disaster. In the assertiveness seminar, I follow up criticism using general principle with criticism using the odds. I then tell Sally, "If you still take notes and you go back to the company and make a disastrous presentation, I can see you five years from now. Your boss realizes, for the first time after that disaster, that you really are a lightweight ding-a-ling who can't recognize good advice. After that it's all downhill. You keep getting assigned less-important jobs, and finally get fired from the mail room at the end of the line. Having an industry-wide reputation as a loser, you can't find a job, so you take to the streets. But even as a hooker, you're a failure because you don't follow good advice. Finally, five years from now, you wind up as the youngest bag lady in Marina del Rey— all because you insisted on taking notes in this seminar!"

The assertive response I want the learner to give to my criticism using the odds is "You may be right, Pete. That may happen" (to agree with the odds), and to again go back to taking notes. This Fogging response recognizes that the scenario I presented is at least possible, *and* nothing to get anxiously defensive about. It may have a probability of only 50 billion to one, but it cannot be denied altogether. Therefore Fogging allows you to see truth in terms of probability. You feel the odds favoring a negative outcome of your behavior are low, while the manipulator claims they are high. Neither you nor your critic can prove or disprove the forecast of these odds, so the Fogging response "You may be right" lets you avoid conflict, does not take away your critic's dignity and make things worse, and allows you to get on with what you want to do.

Fogging is learned most quickly by practicing it as a response to criticism, even though in real life one rarely uses Fogging by itself, without the other verbal assertive skills. The following dialogue is one I use to demonstrate Fogging to a class of students.

DIALOGUE 25

Coping with Personal Criticism by Fogging
Setting: I am teaching assertiveness and ask the class to criticize me.

ME: Now I want you to criticize me. How I teach the course, my organization, my speech, my manners, my looks, how I dress—anything you can think of. (Smiling smugly) If you can't find anything to criticize, make it up.
STUDENT 1: (After a delay long enough for the class to realize that I have been baiting them with my egotistical statement in order to generate some criticism) You're awfully cocky!
ME: You're right. I am too cocky. [FOGGING]
STUDENT 2: And a real egotist!
ME: That's true. I certainly am too egotistical. [FOGGING]
STUDENT 3: You could shape up this seminar and make it better.
ME: You may be right. I certainly could make it better. [FOGGING]
STUDENT 4: You're too fat.
ME: I certainly could be slimmer. [FOGGING]
STUDENT 5: You are definitely an unattractive person.
ME: I could be better-looking. [FOGGING]
STUDENT 5: No, I meant that you have an unlikable personal style and personality. You must have very few friends.

ME: I could be more likable and there is no doubt I could have more friends than I do have. [FOGGING]

STUDENT 6: I doubt that anyone really, truly likes you.

ME: That's an interesting observation. Sometimes I feel that way myself. [FOGGING]

STUDENT 7: You don't respect any of the students here.

ME: I certainly could have more respect for you than I do. [FOGGING]

STUDENT 8: You dress like a slob.

ME: There's no doubt that I could dress better. [FOGGING]

STUDENT 9: That tie is stupid!

ME: It could be smarter. [FOGGING]

STUDENT 10: You are stupid.

ME: I could be smarter too. [FOGGING]

STUDENT 11: Everybody here is going to be put off by your attitude and not learn as much as they could.

ME: You may be right, and I'm sure that all of you could learn more than you have so far. [FOGGING]

STUDENT 12: You're impossible!

ME: You're right. I could be a lot easier on you than I am. [FOGGING]

In teaching your child to cope well with criticism by learning Fogging, do you have to make sure the child understands the fine points and tactics, such as agreeing with truth, principle, and probability? Not really. That information is primarily for you, to enable you to understand that you are not teaching your child some mysterious, experimental set of clinical techniques, but a well-thought-out and tested, behavior-oriented verbal skill. If your child is old enough and interested, by all means teach him or her the fine points. But to teach the child better coping, all that is really necessary is rote practice of the skill, in much the same way as we learn a new language by rote and then use it effectively without needing to be an expert on its grammar.

To start teaching your child to respond to criticism with Fogging, make a game out of it, as STAR does, with critique cards. On one side of each card, write a short criticism, such as: You're too lazy; You could wash the dishes better; Your hair is cut too long; You could have raked the leaves better; You're a sloppy person. On the other side write a

Fogging response, such as: I could be more energetic; You're right—the dishes could be cleaner; My hair could be shorter; The yard could look better; I could be neater. You can refer again to the Appendix for a list of possible criticisms and assertive responses to them, which you can use to make these critique cards. Make enough cards so that both you and your child have at least a dozen or so, and start trading criticisms and Fogging responses. After both of you have gone through the cards, reshuffle them and start over. When you feel confident that your child can reliably give you a Fogging response to criticism, then role-play a critic whom your child will fog, as in the following dialogue.

DIALOGUE 26

Teaching Your Child to Cope with Criticism Nondefensively and Thoughtfully, Using Fogging
Age level: Seven through seventeen
Setting: You criticize your child's clothes, habits, attitudes, schoolwork, etc., and your child does nothing but fog your criticism. If your child forgets, and gets defensive, your next criticism is "Ha! You got defensive and forgot to fog!"

You: That outfit looks terrible!
Child: You may be right. It could look better. [FOGGING—AGREEING WITH THE ODDS]
You: That shirt looks as if you slept in it!
Child: It could use an iron, couldn't it? [FOGGING—AGREEING IN PRINCIPLE]
You: And those pants! Doesn't your mother wash your clothes?
Child: They look that way, don't they? [FOGGING—AGREEING IN PRINCIPLE]
You: You have no taste at all. The colors in that shirt are disgusting.
Child: I could have picked a less colorful shirt to wear. [FOGGING —AGREEING IN PRINCIPLE]
You: Anybody who dresses like this doesn't care about himself [herself].
Child: You may be right. I probably could care more. [FOGGING—AGREEING WITH THE ODDS]

You: If you don't care about yourself, you won't try hard enough at school.

Child: You're right. I could try harder. [FOGGING—AGREEING IN PRINCIPLE]

You: I'll bet your grades are not as good as they could be.

Child: You're right. They could be better. [FOGGING—AGREEING IN PRINCIPLE]

You: That's because you don't study hard enough.

Child: You may be right. Maybe I could study harder. [FOGGING—AGREEING WITH THE ODDS]

You: You didn't really study tonight, did you?

Child: (Getting defensive and forgetting to fog) Yes I did! You saw me.

You: You didn't really study!

Child: But I did!

You: You're arguing with me now.

Child: No I'm not! I did study!

You: You're arguing!

Child: (Silent, realizing he or she has been fooled into not fogging you)

You: What a dummy! You got sucked into an argument when you're supposed to fog me.

Child: (Still silent)

You: And now you're just sitting there when you're still supposed to fog anything I say.

Child: (Either catching on or prompted by "What are you supposed to say when I criticize you?") You're right. I did get sucked in. [FOGGING—AGREEING WITH TRUTH]

You: And you got defensive.

Child: You're right. I did get defensive. [FOGGING—AGREEING WITH TRUTH]

You: You got so flustered and nervous you didn't know what to say.

Child: That's true, I didn't know what to say. [FOGGING—AGREEING WITH TRUTH]

You: You're still nervous.

Child: (Forgetting) No, I feel fine.

You: If you're not nervous, then how come you forgot to fog me again?

Child: (Catching on) You're right. I did forget again. [FOGGING—AGREEING WITH TRUTH]

You: And you're still a bit nervous.

CHILD: I probably am. [FOGGING—AGREEING WITH THE ODDS]

You: You're twiddling your thumbs!

CHILD: (Immediately stops twiddling thumbs)

You: And now you stopped!

CHILD: (Looks down and unhitches his or her fingers and places hand behind back)

You: Now you've put your hands behind your back so I can't see them! And you forgot to fog whatever I say. I sucked you in again!

CHILD: (Catching on) You're right. I was twiddling my thumbs, and I forgot to fog you. [FOGGING—AGREEING WITH TRUTH]

You: You'll never learn this!

CHILD: I probably won't. [FOGGING—AGREEING WITH THE ODDS]

You: Gosh, you're really dumb! Your sister does this better and she's two years younger than you.

CHILD: You may be right. [FOGGING—AGREEING WITH THE ODDS]

You: You have been really slow in learning how to fog.

CHILD: You may be right. I could have learned faster. [FOGGING—AGREEING WITH THE ODDS]

You: You're a phony, too. You can fog if it's easy. But when I make you nervous, you act like a jerk and forget everything.

CHILD: You're right. When I get nervous, I probably do act like a jerk. [FOGGING—AGREEING WITH THE ODDS]

You: And a phony! But you won't admit it!

CHILD: You may be right. I probably won't. [FOGGING—AGREEING WITH THE ODDS]

You: I give up on you!

CHILD: You probably should. [FOGGING—AGREEING IN PRINCIPLE]

You: Now you're getting smart with me.

CHILD: I probably am! [FOGGING—AGREEING WITH THE ODDS]

This dialogue points out two phases that all learners go through in learning to fog criticism. The first is just learning the Fogging response:

You may be right; That's possible; I'm sure you feel that way; etc. The second phase is learning to fog when someone makes you automatically feel guilty, ignorant, or foolish. Both are important, but the second phase is where your child receives the real payoff from learning Fogging. When learners finally realize that they are getting nervous, *and* recognize they have no reason to hide or deny this, they have reached an insight as big as one can get from ten years of expensive couch time in a shrink's office.

To give your child this beneficial experience, start by criticizing things that he or she expects will be criticized, like shirt colors and wrinkled clothes. Then switch to "real," unexpected criticism, like insisting that studying (or enough studying) wasn't done, or giving negative interpretations of innocuous behaviors such as scratching an ear, twiddling thumbs, or tapping feet. When you act as if these things were major sins, the child is very likely to become defensive and not know why. But if you continue your role-playing and criticism of your child's automatic reaction of genuine confusion and feeling of foolishness—repeatedly, and with prompting, if necessary—he or she will soon realize that there is nothing to be anxious or feel foolish about. When that point is reached, the child will be able to fog unexpected "real" criticism as well as the expected practice criticism.

Once this realization occurs, your child has intuitively learned the whole basis for Fogging. Then your child simply needs to (a) practice responding to the different things for which he or she may be criticized in order to eliminate the automatic defensive reaction, and (b) practice fogging in conjunction with the other verbal assertive skills (detailed in later chapters) to solve social conflict problems with peers, with teachers and other adults, and with you, the parent.

If at first Fogging feels unnatural to you, you are in very good company. Several years ago a friend pointed out that Ben Franklin, the first great American scientist and statesman, discovered for himself the benefits of Fogging, but found it initially difficult. The following excerpt from *The Autobiography of Benjamin Franklin* is lengthy but well worth reading.

My List of Virtues contain'd at first but twelve: But a Quaker Friend having kindly inform'd me that I was generally thought proud; that my Pride show'd itself frequently in Conversation; that I was not content with being in the right when discussing any Point, but was overbearing and rather insolent; of which he convinc'd me by mentioning several Instances; I determined endeavouring to cure myself if I could of this Vice or Folly among the rest, and I added *Humility* to my list, giving an extensive Meaning to the Word. I cannot boast of much Success in acquiring the *Reality* of this Virtue; but I had a good deal with regard to the *Appearance* of it. I made it a Rule to forbear all direct Contradiction to the Sentiments of others, and all positive Assertion of my own. I even forbid myself agreeable to the old Laws of our Junto, the Use of every Word or Expression in the Language that imported a fix'd Opinion; such as *certainly, undoubtedly,* &c., and I adopted instead of them, *I conceive, I apprehend,* or *I imagine* a thing to be so or so, or it so appears to me at present. When another asserted something, that I thought an Error, I deny'd my self the Pleasure of contradicting him abruptly, and of showing immediately some Absurdity in his Proposition; and in answering I began by observing that in certain Cases or Circumstances his Opinion would be right, but that in the present case there *appear'd* or *seem'd* to me some difference, &c. I soon found the Advantage of this Change in my Manners. The Conversations I engag'd in went on more pleasantly. The modest way in which I propos'd my Opinions, procur'd them a readier Reception and less Contradiction; I had less Mortification when I was found to be in the wrong, and I more easily prevail'd with others to give up their Mistakes and join with me when I happen'd to be in the right. And this Mode, which I at first put on, with some violence to natural Inclination, became at length so easy and so habitual to me, that perhaps for these Fifty Years past no one has ever heard a dogmatical Expression escape me. And to this Habit (after my Character of Integrity) I think it principally owing, that I had early so much Weight with my Fellow Citizens, when I proposed new Institutions, or Alterations in the old; and so much Influence in public Councils when I became a Member. For I was but a bad Speaker, never eloquent, subject to much Hesitation in my choice of Words, hardly correct in Language, and yet I generally carried my Points.

In concluding his account of how he was changed by mastering this nondefensive, nonadversary psychological skill, Franklin says: "In reality there is perhaps no one of our natural Passions so hard to subdue as *Pride*. Disguise it, struggle with it, beat it down, stifle it, mortify it as much as one pleases, it is still alive, and will every now and then peep out and show itself. You will see it perhaps often in this History. For even if I could conceive that I had compleatly overcome it, I should probably [be] proud of my Humility."

Benjamin Franklin was so self-assured and had such confidence in himself that he reportedly took as a compliment a humorous but cutting remark made about his age and his libido during the first Constitutional Convention: "He is old enough to be the father of half the convention, and is the father of the other half." One does not have to read history to know his likely response to that remark: "You're probably right!"

In using any of the verbal assertive skills, particularly Fogging or Negative Assertion, remember that these skills are for use in situations of *social* conflict, not legal or physical conflict. If, as you back out of your driveway, someone comes limping up to you and says, "You just ran over my foot," the appropriate response is not "You may be right," or "How dumb of me to do that," but "Here is the name of my lawyer [or insurance agent]." If a mugger says to you, "Your money or your life," you don't, as Jack Benny did when the mugger repeated himself, say, "I'm thinking! I'm thinking!" Nor do you say, "I understand that things in the urban ghetto are rough, Mr. Mugger, but you can't have my money." When a policeman tells you to move along at the scene of a disturbance, you do not reply, "You may be right that it's dangerous here, officer, but I have my civil rights." All that will get you is a whack over the head and a ride downtown in a police van. Learning to be assertive does not mean that you forget to use your common sense!

Assertive Inquiry: Teaching Your Child How to Cope with Compliments and Criticism from Those Who Are Important or Close to the Child
Positive Inquiry (for Coping with Compliments) and Negative Inquiry (for Coping with Criticism)

Like Fogging, the verbal coping skill of Assertive Inquiry (positive or negative) is designed to help you and your child deal with other people's judgments of you, either positive (compliments) or negative (criticism). While compliments may be difficult for your child to handle, or may even be manipulative in intent—"That's a great outfit—you look terrific today! Can you lend me your lunch money?"—it is criticisms rather than compliments that are more common. Like the rest of us, therefore, your child needs to concentrate on practicing the negative half of Assertive Inquiry (Negative Inquiry) to cope with criticism from people he or she will interact with over and over again: classmates, friends, teachers, family.

It is important that you point out to your child, as STAR does, that criticism from other people is only an opinion—their personal judgment of his or her behavior—not a rule set down in heaven or Congress or the Supreme Court, which one must automatically accept. Unfortunately, in trying to cope with this criticism, your *un*trained child will either passively accept the opinion as fact or will get into a verbal fight with the critic to protect himself or herself. Both these options make the situation worse for your child, not better.

Negative Inquiry teaches your child to explore the other person's opinion instead of simply accepting it or fighting it. Since Negative Inquiry is not adversary and does not challenge or threaten the critic, this prompts him or her to abandon the manipulation and to examine the hidden agenda or want that underlies the criticism and is the real cause of the conflict.

For example, your son may get a lot of criticism from his best friend. That criticism will be manipulative in nature, focusing on his behavior or his lack of baseball skills or his difficulties with his classmates. What it won't address is the real reason for the criticism: that the friend is angry and upset because your son (following your firm instructions) won't let him—or anyone else—ride his bike. By using Negative Inquiry to deal with this criticism, instead of getting angry, your son will prompt his friend to finally acknowledge that what he is really upset about is the bike. When this hidden agenda is revealed, your son can make a thinking, voluntary choice about whether or not to accept his friend's judgments.

Negative Inquiry is, in fact, the verbal assertive skill that Chris, my colleague from STAR, taught eight-year-old Mary (see chapter 1) to enable her to cope with peer criticism and teasing. It is not usually necessary to use Negative Inquiry in conflict situations involving people you are not likely to see again, such as clerks, waitresses, flight attendants, or porters. If there is no ongoing relationship, the other person's concealed wants or agendas are totally irrelevant; all you want to accomplish is to stop him or her from manipulating you. Fogging and Broken Record are the simplest ways to deal with that manipulation.

To teach your child the simple verbal mechanics of Negative Inquiry, do what I do with adults in my assertiveness seminars. I get up in front of the class and say, "When you were in the third grade and the teacher came in and said 'Good morning, class,' what did you all say?" The seminar students then all reply in unison, "Good morning, teacher!" I then say, "Now you've got it! That's the way you are all going to learn Negative Inquiry. I am going to wander around the room and make judgment statements about objects and people. You will all respond to each of my judgments with Negative Inquiry by asking, 'What is it about [the object or person I have judged] that is bad [tacky, poor, cruddy]?' For example, if I say, 'This coffee cup is poorly designed,' what would you say?" The class responds in unison, "What is it about the coffee cup that is [or means it is] poorly designed?" The class and I then have the following dialogue.

DIALOGUE 27

A Classroom Demonstration of Coping with Personal Criticism by Using Negative Inquiry
Setting: I am standing in front of a class of thirty students who are learning how to assertively respond to criticism based on some private belief of the critic.

ME: This blackboard is quite poor.
CLASS: What is it about the blackboard that means it is poor? [NEGATIVE INQUIRY]
ME: These seats are quite uncomfortable.
CLASS: What is it about the seats that is uncomfortable? [NEGATIVE INQUIRY]
ME: The lunch we had was terrible.
CLASS: What is it about the lunch that was terrible? [NEGATIVE INQUIRY]
ME: (Wandering among the students) Bill's moustache is inadequate.

CLASS: What is it about Bill's moustache that is inadequate? [NEGA-
TIVE INQUIRY]

ME: Nancy's hair is too fussy.

CLASS: What is it about Nancy's hair that means it's too fussy? [NEGA-
TIVE INQUIRY]

ME: Nancy's hair is too brown.

CLASS: What is it about Nancy's hair that means it's too brown? [NEG-
ATIVE INQUIRY]

ME: (Pointing out that another person's judgment is arbitrary) Nancy's
hair is exactly the right color.

CLASS: What is it about Nancy's hair that means it's exactly the right
color? [POSITIVE INQUIRY]

ME: Joe's eyes are too green.

CLASS: What is it about Joe's eyes that means they're too green? [NEG-
ATIVE INQUIRY]

ME: Joe's eyes are too close together.

CLASS: What is it about Joe's eyes that means they are too close together? [NEGATIVE INQUIRY]

ME: Joe's eyes are too far apart.

CLASS: What is it about Joe's eyes that means they are too far apart?
[NEGATIVE INQUIRY]

ME: Debbie's dress is not stylish.

CLASS: What is it about Debbie's dress that means it isn't stylish?
[NEGATIVE INQUIRY]

ME: (Picking up a copy of *When I Say No, I Feel Guilty* to point out
that assertive inquiry into a judgment-opinion can be either positive
or negative) This book is fantastic!

CLASS: What is it about that book that means it's fantastic? [POSI-
TIVE INQUIRY]

ME: Bunny is so sexy.

CLASS: What is it about Bunny that means she's so sexy? [POSITIVE
or NEGATIVE INQUIRY]

ME: This class is really unsophisticated.

CLASS: What is it about us that means we are unsophisticated? [NEGA-
TIVE INQUIRY]

ME: This Negative Inquiry routine you are using is a real pain.

CLASS: What is it about our using Negative Inquiry that is a real pain?
[NEGATIVE INQUIRY]

ME: You just won't buy anything I say without questioning it.

CLASS: What is it about our not buying anything you say without questioning it that makes it a real pain? [NEGATIVE INQUIRY]

ME: I have to think about what I'm saying.

CLASS: What is it about having to think about what you are saying that is a real pain?

ME: Okay, class. Terrific job!

CLASS: What is it about the job we did that is terrific? [POSITIVE INQUIRY]

When your child responds to criticism based upon someone's judgment-opinion with an inquiry like "What is it about the way I catch the softball that is bad?" your child is really asking, in a nondefensive and nonantagonistic way, "What is your belief about softball that makes my playing bad?" In teaching Assertive Inquiry to your child, tell him or her, as I do students in my assertiveness seminars, "When you negatively or positively inquire about someone's opinion, don't automatically accept what the other person tells you just because it seems to make sense, and then stop your inquiry. When you inquire about an opinion, reserve your own judgment about it until your critic gives you no more information, or finally stops being manipulative and gives you an assertive response such as 'Well, dammit, that's just the way I see it!' Also, don't respond with 'What makes you think . . . is bad?' That will be taken as a sarcastic disagreement. Just pretend you are a neutral visitor from Mars who hasn't visited here since people were walking around wrapped in what looked like colorful bedspreads, and you are taking a survey to update your files. You want to find out what people believe and what they base their opinions on."

Assertive Inquiry, either negative or positive, into another person's judgment does three things for your child. First, it gives the child something meaningful and productive to say in response to criticism, consequently lowering any anxiety the criticism may have caused. Second, it prompts the person who offers the critical judgment to examine the basis for making that judgment. Third, Assertive Inquiry allows your child to think about the criticism and make his or her own informed judgment about it based upon the inquiry—i.e., to reject it, if manipulative, or to accept it, if constructive and helpful.

Practice Negative Inquiry with your child as the following dialogue illustrates. The subject of the criticism can be anything—clothes, haircuts, attitudes, athletic coordination, etc. In this practice, you can play the role of yourself or one of your child's peers. If you play yourself, you will want to view this exercise as one designed to help your child cope with criticism and not be intimidated by it. It should not be a means for you to use real criticism intended to change your child's choices or behavior. That will defeat the purpose of the exercise. If you want your child to listen to your real criticism of him or her, wait a bit until the child has had enough practice with Fogging, Negative Assertion, and Negative Inquiry to be able to cope effectively with it and not be intimidated by it, or by you. If you can intimidate your child, so can others, including your child's peers, and that is what you are trying to eliminate.

Remember, the primary purpose of teaching your child assertiveness is to help him or her gain the ability to think and judge for himself or herself, even if that judgment and thinking do not always agree with your own. This is a small price to pay for the benefits STAR has shown children get from learning to be more assertive. Keep this in mind, and in early practice sessions, make your criticism as humorous as possible, as the following dialogue tries to do.

DIALOGUE 28

Teaching Your Child to Cope with Criticism Productively Using Negative Inquiry
Age level: Seven through seventeen
Setting: You criticize your child about his or her clothes to give the child practice in using Negative Inquiry.

You: You are not going to wear that to school, are you? It's awful!
CHILD: What is it about my outfit that's awful? [NEGATIVE INQUIRY]
You: It really looks tacky.
CHILD: What is it about my outfit that makes it look tacky? [NEGATIVE INQUIRY]

You: A T-shirt with tiny letters that say "If you can read this, you're too close!" is a bit gross.

CHILD: What is it about my T-shirt saying that that's gross? [NEGATIVE INQUIRY]

You: It's the colors, too, that make it gross.

CHILD: What is it about its colors that makes it gross? [NEGATIVE INQUIRY]

You: Who ever heard of an olive-drab T-shirt with orange and purple roses as a trim?

CHILD: What is it about an olive-drab T-shirt with roses that's gross? [NEGATIVE INQUIRY]

You: It makes you look like a marine who has no sense of color coordination.

CHILD: What is it about looking like a marine that's gross? [NEGATIVE INQUIRY]

You: It's not looking like *any* marine, but one without any taste or color sense. Let's understand what's important here.

CHILD: What is it about my T-shirt looking as if I have no taste or color sense that is bad? [NEGATIVE INQUIRY]

You: Well, it's not the T-shirt so much as the checked skirt [or shorts].

CHILD: What is it about my skirt that makes me look bad? [NEGATIVE INQUIRY]

You: It's the red-and-white checks. They make you look like you're wearing a tablecloth from a cheap café.

CHILD: What is it about my skirt looking like a tablecloth that is wrong? [NEGATIVE INQUIRY]

You: It means you have no taste.

CHILD: What is it about my looking as if I have no taste that is wrong? [NEGATIVE INQUIRY]

You: People will think your elevator doesn't go all the way up.

CHILD: What is it about people thinking my elevator doesn't go all the way up that's wrong? [NEGATIVE INQUIRY]

You: Well, if you don't care how you look, neither do I.

CHILD: What is it about my not caring how I look that's wrong? [NEGATIVE INQUIRY]

You: I can't think of anything else to tell you.

CHILD: There must be other things wrong with my outfit. [NEGA-
TIVE INQUIRY prompt]
YOU: There are, but I give up.
CHILD: Okay. If you think of anything else, I'm counting on you to tell
me.

After your child has learned to handle the mechanics of forming a
simple, nondefensive inquiry response to criticism, go on to situations
like the one in the next dialogue.

DIALOGUE 29

*Teaching a Younger Child How to Use Negative Inquiry to Cope
Comfortably with an Older Child's Manipulative Criticism*
Age level: Seven through seventeen
*Setting: You are role-playing an older brother who is
manipulatively criticizing his younger brother about the way he
plays basketball. The intent of the criticism is to get younger
brother to give up playing so older brother can practice,
one-on-one, with a friend.*

SON 1: You are a really lousy basketball player.
SON 2: What is it about the way I play basketball that is lousy? [NEGA-
TIVE INQUIRY]
SON 1: You don't dribble well.
SON 2: What is it about the way I dribble that is bad? [NEGATIVE
INQUIRY]
SON 1: You slap it too hard.
SON 2: What is it about slapping it too hard that is wrong? [NEGA-
TIVE INQUIRY]
SON 1: It bounces too high.
SON 2: What is it about bouncing it too high that is wrong? [NEGA-
TIVE INQUIRY]
SON 1: The guy guarding you will take it away from you. Only a jerk
lets that happen.
SON 2: What is it about playing like a jerk that is bad? [NEGATIVE
INQUIRY]

Son 1: No one wants to play with a jerk like you.

Son 2: What is it about no one wanting to play with me that is bad? [NEGATIVE INQUIRY]

Son 1: You're a little punk who can't play basketball.

Son 2: What is it about being a punk who can't play basketball that is bad? [NEGATIVE INQUIRY]

Son 1: Are you going to stand out here and shoot baskets forever?

Son 2: What is it about my shooting baskets forever that is bad? [NEGATIVE INQUIRY]

Son 1: Wally is coming over soon and we are going to play one-on-one.

Son 2: The three of us can play.

Son 1: You would hold the game up.

Son 2: What is it about my holding the game up that is bad? [NEGATIVE INQUIRY]

Son 1: Wally would get bored and leave.

Son 2: You and I could play if he does that.

Son 1: You're no fun to play with.

Son 2: Okay. (Clearly realizing that the criticisms are manipulative instead of constructive and going back to shooting baskets)

Because these illustrative dialogues are training dialogues to give your child a lot of practice, they are much longer than any real-life situation would require. In real life, a typical Assertive Inquiry interaction usually lasts only a minute or two before the critic realizes that manipulative criticism is a waste of time.

To sum up, there are three very important skills for coping with all the confusing verbal manipulation that I guarantee will be heaped upon you or your child whenever you make a mistake, want to do something the other person doesn't, or say no to someone else. First is Negative Assertion, a skill to be used when you know you have made a mistake and the person affected by the mistake confronts you with it. Negative Assertion effectively deals with the angry or manipulative reaction you will get from that person, who typically is more concerned about getting you to take responsibility for the mistake than about the effects of the mistake itself. Negative assertion is also used to cope with personal faults, defects, or some mental or physical attributes you may have that are commonly viewed as negative; it enables you to judge them realistically and in proportion to their importance in your life.

Next is Fogging, a coping skill that enables you or your child to separate a critic's valid observations about you or your behavior from the invalid judgments the critic has made about you or your behavior. Fogging allows you to make your own evaluation of the importance and relevance of the criticism without having to argue or prove your critic wrong in order to justify that judgment.

Finally, there is Assertive Inquiry (positive or negative) which allows you or your child to deal with the possible hidden agendas of a critic with whom you have a long-term relationship. Negative Inquiry does not give manipulative criticism any payoff, but prompts the critic to examine his or her hidden agenda and assert his or her real wants to see if a workable compromise can be reached.

Up to now, we have looked at each of the assertive verbal skills separately, and I have pointed out their use in very stylized ways. Practicing these skills using simple responses is the best way to learn them initially, even though they sound elementary and repetitive. The reason I stress the practice of a stylized response is that it becomes overlearned and somewhat automatic. This automatism is valuable when assertiveness skills are first used in actual situations, because your child is likely to be nervous and not thinking too clearly. A response learned to the point of being automatic is much more likely to be remembered under stress.

Let's turn now to the next chapter, the first in a series of three that show you how to teach your child to use the verbal skills in combination with one another to resolve conflicts with other children, with teachers and staff at school, and with other family members.

CHAPTER FIVE

Teaching Your Child to Assertively Cope with Other Children: Saying No, and Asking for What Is Wanted

What can you tell your child about how to behave assertively toward someone else? How should your child assert himself or herself to a friend, or to a teacher, to you, or to a boss at a part-time job after school, or to a waitress at the fast-food shop? While the skills used to assert oneself with all these people are the same, the specific goals that these skills are directed toward are often set by the built-in (a priori) social rules, or social structure, particular to each situation. These rules tell us how to behave in the situation without our having to do much thinking or planning beforehand. Since manipulation can present itself suddenly, this can be very helpful in coping with it. While it may sound like an impossible task to teach your children how to behave assertively in the many different situations they can find themselves in, it is not, because social conflicts fall within three specific categories.

The Three Types of Social Conflict Your Child Will Experience: Commercial, Authority, and Equal Relationship Situations

Any social situation we find ourselves in will fall into one of three categories: commercial situations, where money is involved; authority situations, where one person can tell another what to do; and equal situations, where two people have to work out answers to their problems and neither has any authority over the other.

Unless we think about it, we assume that all social situations are similarly structured and have the same generally accepted social rules that direct the ways we should behave toward one another. Upon close examination, however, we can see that these three classes of situations —commercial, authority, and equal—have different degrees of structure. Commercial situations have the greatest a priori structure, and equal situations the least, with authority situations somewhere in between. In a commercial interchange, you expect to buy or sell something, with the seller offering merchandise or a service, and the buyer offering money in exchange for it. Even before they meet, both parties in a commercial situation know the a priori rules on how they are expected to behave. In some commercial situations there is a legal contract written up that spells out the smallest details of how each party should behave toward the other, perhaps for years to come. Real-estate transactions are a good example of the amount of a priori structure a commercial situation can have.

Authority situations, on the other hand, have only a moderate amount of built-in structure that indicates how each party in the interaction is to behave. At work, a boss tells an employee what to do (usually within reason), and the employee knows that he or she will receive a paycheck for doing what the boss wants. Interactions between teachers and students also fall into the authority classification. When I teach, I know beforehand that I will present material that the students will learn, and that they will ask me questions about that material and I will answer them. But the rules of the authority situation are limited. I do not have to tell the students what to do outside the classroom or lecture hall— thank God!

A parent-child relationship starts out as an authority situation and evolves (we hope!) into an equal-relationship situation. Initially, you are everything to your child: provider, boss, teacher, judge. Eventually, as your child matures and is able to think and decide for him or herself, you become a treasured and valuable friend and are no longer the boss, teacher, or judge of your now adult, or almost adult, offspring.

Contrary to what we commonly believe, there are no generally accepted a priori social rules or structure in equal relationships between men and women today, as there were some twenty to thirty years ago. Thirty years ago, relationships between men and women almost always fell into the authority classification, since everyone behaved as if men were superior to or more expert than women, no matter what common sense told us. Today's absence of structure in an equal-relationship situation between a man and a woman makes it extremely difficult for us to decide how to behave.

We try to get around this difficulty by making assumptions, usually one-sided (and therefore manipulative), about how wives should always behave toward husbands; husbands toward wives; friends toward each other; girlfriends toward boyfriends; co-workers and classmates toward each other, etc. If both parties automatically accept these assumptions —if, for instance, a wife assumes she should always do what her husband asks—there is no obvious conflict. More often than not, however, the parties do not automatically accept each other's assumption of what the a priori rules should be. Therefore, the guidelines on how to behave toward one another need to be worked out by both parties —spouses, friends, co-workers, or classmates—and renegotiated as often as needed.

Since our social rules in any situation make it easier for us to know how to behave and what to expect, most adults find it less anxiety-provoking to first practice learning to be assertive in a commercial situation, where there is lots of social structure; then in an authority situation, where there is less structure; and finally in an equal situation, where there is the least structure. This is like learning to swim at the shallow end of the pool, where you always have the bottom to stand on until you become proficient and confident, instead of starting at the deep end, where you are on your own. Assertiveness in a commercial situation is the simplest to teach adults, because most of the rules for commercial situations are spelled out in detail, and because the more rules there are that indicate clearly how everyone should behave, the less alone and anxious we feel. Novice learners are less fearful of asserting themselves when they feel that they have God, the federal government, the Supreme Court, and righteousness behind them and everyone knows the proper thing to do.

For practical reasons, however, teaching children to be assertive, especially younger ones, follows a step-by-step path that is almost the reverse of the one used for adults. It works better to view children's commercial interactions as authority situations since children usually find themselves interacting with adults there. But authority situations are more difficult for children to handle than for adults. Children see themselves as powerless in authority situations, whereas most adults have learned through experience that in authority situations we are not completely at the mercy of our boss, physician, lawyer, or teacher. Your child has yet to learn this.

Your child has to learn also to discriminate between those situations in which the person who has authority is acting as an authority, giving orders, and those in which the person has assumed a different role, such as friend or counselor, and is making a request. Most children do not know how to make this discrimination. You need to point out that teachers and other school staff, like parents, do not *always* interact as authority figures with children; and that at such times teachers' requests do not have to be automatically obeyed. When your daughter is studying for a test to be given in the afternoon, and the morning study hall teacher asks her to help sort papers, it is not in her best interest to assume that she has to agree to that request. If she does agree, it is because she assumes that in an authority situation or relationship, the rules of teacher-student always apply. You have to correct this misconception. If she can discriminate between orders and requests with respect to what you want from her as a parent, she can certainly do it with respect to her teachers if she is taught that the rules of compliance in authority situations are limited.

Because of this complexity, and the similarity of commercial and authority situations in childhood—except for the simplest commercial interactions with adults, such as at cafeterias and fast-food shops— commercial situations can be handled best after children gain some experience and confidence in asserting themselves first to peers. Examples and dialogues involving commercial situations your child may encounter are found in chapter 6.

The equal-relationship situation is one where we have the most freedom to do what we want, because it has the least fixed social structure. It is also the least complicated one in which to teach a younger child to be assertive, because (a) your child does not have to unlearn a lot of arbitrary social guidelines, taken as holy writ, on how friends and classmates should always behave toward each other, and (b) as a rule, children have less anxiety in asserting themselves with peers, because peers are not seen as authority figures who must at least be deferred to, if not obeyed.

Except for matters like common courtesy and other constraints we place upon our behavior in the interests of civility, you can tell your child that in equal-relationship situations, there are no absolute rules that one *has* to obey lest all sorts of bad things happen. If there are no universally accepted rules on how spouses, lovers, and co-workers should always behave, your child can be certain there are also none for friends, classmates, and playmates. Friends do not always have to agree for their relationship to survive or prosper, and you can assure your child that disagreements between friends and classmates are not only normal but to be expected. Since equal-relationship situations offer the younger child the most freedom to learn to be assertive, it will be best to start off by letting your child practice putting all of his or her assertive skills together to cope with peer conflict and disagreement.

Practice in Putting All the Assertive Skills Together

Eight-year-old Mary (in the first chapter) learned how to cope with criticism when Chris taught her how to assertively inquire about the teasing she received from her classmates. That skill turned things around for her, but Mary still had a lot to learn after that positive experience. Learning how to cope with problems other people give us in equal relationships involves more than not getting upset when we are criticized. Used together, the assertive verbal skills are designed to give us the psychological "room" to think, and then to work out our solution to the conflict situation in which we find ourselves. There is no hard-and-fast rule that any one skill is the best for any particular situation, even though we may use some skills much more than others. Each of them contributes to our ability to make our own judgments on what is best for us in handling social pressure from other people. Depending on the situation we find ourselves in, we may use only one, or some, or all of them.

There is an old joke about a famous out-of-town violinist who gets lost in New York traffic on his way to perform at Carnegie Hall. The musician asks a cabdriver, "How do I get to Carnegie Hall?" and the cabby replies, "Practice, man! Practice!" The cabby's advice also applies to your child's learning to be more assertive. These skills are designed to mesh effortlessly with each other, and after some practice in using them in realistic situations, you and your child will find their use simple and effective in resolving problems.

To see how your child can use all or any of the assertive skills, this chapter gives you a set of realistic dialogues in which assertive skills are combined to deal with peer conflict—as when another child is trying to get your son or daughter to do something unacceptable, or your child is making a request of a classmate. First read through these dialogues, then role-play the pushy or manipulative partner with whom your child needs to be more assertive. While coaching your son or daughter in how to respond to your manipulations, you can use a simple or more complicated assertive response. Begin with simple ones. As your child becomes more skilled, the assertive response can become more complex and sophisticated. Simple conflict situations are also the best initial settings for practice—for example, which movie to go to on a Saturday afternoon with a friend, or what to eat at the snack bar. While we adults see such situations as trivial, to a very "good" child or a shy one without much experience in being assertive, such situations are formidable, and an important first step in learning to say what one wants in the face of social opposition.

The practice dialogues in this and the remaining chapters are based on real-life situations commonly reported as troublesome by children in the STAR research project. If your child is like most children, practicing with these social-conflict situations will be worthwhile. The sequence of dialogues in this chapter goes from the simplest, for younger children, to the more complex, for older children. I recommend, however, that even your older child begin with the simple dialogues and work up to the more complex ones appropriate for his or her age level.

DIALOGUE 30

Daughter Learns to Compromise with a Friend on What Movie to See
Age level: Seven through ten
Setting: Your daughter's friend is talking to her on Saturday morning about what the two of them are going to do together that afternoon.

DAUGHTER: So what do you want to do?

FRIEND: I want to go to the movies.

DAUGHTER: Okay. What do you want to see?

FRIEND: The double bill at the Bijou. *Halloween VIII* and *Rocky VI.*

DAUGHTER: I'm not sure my stomach can take a double bill like that. [SELF-DISCLOSURE]

FRIEND: It will be fun!

DAUGHTER: It may be, but I'd rather see something else. [FOGGING and BROKEN RECORD]

FRIEND: Don't be such a wimp!

DAUGHTER: You're right. I am a wimp sometimes, but I don't want to see another *Halloween* or *Rocky.* [NEGATIVE ASSERTION and BROKEN RECORD]

FRIEND: Everybody is going to be there!

DAUGHTER: I'm sure they will be, but I still don't want to see those movies. [FOGGING and BROKEN RECORD]

FRIEND: Well, what do you want to see?

DAUGHTER: How about a comedy? There's a Bill Murray flick at the Bayshore. [WORKABLE COMPROMISE]

FRIEND: Yuck! He's so gross!

DAUGHTER: Yes. But I like him. [FOGGING and SELF-DISCLO-SURE] How about a rock movie? *The Leper Colony* is at the Port-hole. [WORKABLE COMPROMISE]

FRIEND: But we'd have to get a ride there and back.

DAUGHTER: That's true. [FOGGING] Come on, let's see that one. We could take the bus. Or maybe my mom or dad would drop us off and pick us up later. [WORKABLE COMPROMISE]

FRIEND: Let's ask your mom. I hate buses.
DAUGHTER: Okay.

After each of these practice dialogues, as is done with STAR, talk over the situation with your child. Be sure that he or she understands that the practicing has two purposes: to make the child less nervous about the situation, and to understand how to be assertive in it. If your child complains that this practice is boring, say, "That's great!" As we have pointed out, the skills are supposed to be overlearned until the practice does get boring. Then ask your child, "Which do you prefer, to be bored learning how to deal with a pushy friend, or to feel nervous, foolish, and dumb?" To keep your child's interest, ask if he or she has any ideas on how to deal with the friend or classmate that would be better than the way used in practice. If the child's idea is a poor one, explain why you think so, but it may still be worth trying the idea out in another practice so your child can see what happens. If the idea seems appropriate, rerun the practice dialogue using that idea. It is important to prompt, and get, this type of feedback from your child during this learning process.

The next dialogue is another simple one to use in the early stages of practice. In this situation your daughter or son has to deal with a friend who always knows what's right for everyone else. Children, like adults, often have to deal with dogmatic peers. Such children learn their rigid attitudes from their own families, which tend to see things in black and white, rather than with the flexibility that acknowledges shades of gray. They learn from their parents that their viewpoints are not only absolutely correct but crucial in coping with life's variability. An adult can usually recognize that the advice from such a rigidly oriented friend is dogmatic, but a young child is likely to be intimidated by it. Moreover, although this advice is usually benign, it can be harmful if the dogmatically reared child, when older, starts using drugs or alcohol. Then that child's dogmatic insistence on the "rightness" of good foods or healthy practices may switch to the "rightness" of drugs and alcohol.

The basic problem for your child is not determining what is claimed to be "good" for him or her, but recognizing dogma for what it is: a rigid set of rules designed to influence or control his or her behavior. The following dialogue is set up to give your child practice in coping with dogma, good or bad.

DIALOGUE 31

Daughter Learns How to Deal with a Health or Drug Zealot
Age level: Seven through thirteen
Setting: Your daughter and a friend are at a snack bar making selections.

FRIEND: What are you having?
DAUGHTER: A cheese Danish.
FRIEND: Don't you know that stuff is no good for you?
DAUGHTER: I'm sure it's not as healthy as some other stuff, but I like it. [FOGGING and SELF-DISCLOSURE]
FRIEND: It will rot your teeth!
DAUGHTER: It may, but I still like cheese Danish. [FOGGING and BROKEN RECORD]
FRIEND: You shouldn't eat it! Have an apple instead.
DAUGHTER: You're right. I probably should eat an apple instead. But I still like Danish. [FOGGING and BROKEN RECORD]
FRIEND: It's bad for you.
DAUGHTER: I'm sure it is. [FOGGING]
FRIEND: It will make you fat!
DAUGHTER: Probably. [FOGGING]
FRIEND: You have no willpower.
DAUGHTER: You're right. I don't [NEGATIVE ASSERTION] So I'm going to eat it. [BROKEN RECORD]
FRIEND: That's terrible. Does your mother know you eat that stuff?
DAUGHTER: I understand what you're getting at, but I'm still going to eat it. [BROKEN RECORD]
FRIEND: Why you are so stubborn?
DAUGHTER: I don't know. Why do you think I am? [NEGATIVE INQUIRY]

In the next, very short dialogue, your son has to deal with a child who cuts in front of him in line.

DIALOGUE 32

Son Learns to Cope when a Classmate Cuts into Line
Age level: Seven through seventeen
Setting: Your son is patiently waiting in the lunch line at school when another boy cuts in front of him as he reaches the serving area.

SON: I beg your pardon.
LINE JUMPER: Yes?
SON: (Smiling) You're behind me.
LINE JUMPER: Oh. Right here?
SON: Yes.
LINE JUMPER: Okay. Thanks.

The reason this dialogue is so short is that it is so effective. Its whole point is that your child does not have to act as an agent of society, keeping everyone in line, and put the other child down by saying, "What do you think you're doing, cutting in line in front of everybody? The line forms at the rear!" While most of us feel like saying this when someone cuts in front of us, it is usually ineffective. When you say this, any of three things can happen. If the person who cuts in is larger than you, he may turn and say, "So what?"—challenging you to either fight or keep quiet. If the line jumper is more civilized, he will say something like "Gosh! I'm on the way to the hospital. My wife is in the back seat of our car going into labor. I just thought I'd pop in and get a dozen doughnuts for her!"—making you feel guilty for questioning his behavior. Or the line jumper can simply ignore what you say.

With the verbal assertion shown in the dialogue, your son (or daughter) does not try to protect everyone in the line. The rest of the children have the option of saying to the line jumper, each in turn as he appears in front of them, "You're behind me," passing him along to the end of the line. If the line jumper ignores your child's polite request to take a place in back of him or her, then the dialogue becomes one of assertively responding to manipulation with a persistent Broken Record, etc., as in any other assertive sequence. The line jumper is much more likely to accede to your child's request if it is couched in personal terms and is not a punitive, supposedly authoritative statement based upon society's rules and regulations.

Seeing Assertiveness as the Freedom to Decide in the Face of Peer Pressure, Not Just a New Set of "Shoulds" to Replace the Old Ones

Peer pressure to conform to the opinions, tastes, fads, and behaviors of the group with which your child socializes can be overwhelming at times. The next two dialogues, about dressing identically and having the same haircut, are good starting points for dealing with peer pressure. Talk with your son or daughter about the social pressures to conform that teens and preteens put upon one another. Most children want to blend in and belong at a certain age. You can point out that there is nothing wrong with wanting to belong, even to the point of wearing the same clothes and getting the same haircuts. But also point out that *unquestioning* conformity to a subgroup's rules, wants, or even whims may, in the not too distant future, be a luxury with too big a price tag. If conforming to dress and hair styles is automatic, conforming to the subgroup's mores on academic achievement, substance use, and premature sexual behavior may become automatic, too.

Point out that whatever haircut or style of clothes your children wear is relatively unimportant and not the issue. Being able to make voluntary choices about conforming and not conforming is. Say that you want them to learn how not to be pressured into automatically conforming, but if they decide themselves that they want to be like the rest of the kids, that's okay. Practice resisting social pressure to conform, using dialogues like the following ones. When your child shows that he or she can deal with peer pressure effectively in your practice sessions, make the strong point that it's now up to the child to decide whether to go along with the group and take responsibility for the consequences of that decision.

In the first of the two dialogues on social conformity, your daughter has to cope with a group of friends who want her to buy an expensive outfit so they all can go to the school game dressed in the same colors.

DIALOGUE 33

Daughter Copes with Peer Pressure to Conform
Age level: Ten through thirteen
Setting: Your daughter approaches and sits down with a group of friends having lunch at school.

DAUGHTER: Hi.

FRIEND 1: Hi. We've decided that all of us are going to the game Friday dressed the same.

DAUGHTER: I don't understand. What do you mean "dressed the same"?

FRIEND 2: We decided that we should all wear the same outfit in the same colors to show school spirit.

DAUGHTER: What outfit? Blue jeans and yellow shirts?

FRIEND 3: No. Blue pleated skirts, yellow sweaters, yellow socks, and blue tennies.

DAUGHTER: I haven't got an outfit like that.

FRIEND 1: We're all going shopping tomorrow to buy one.

DAUGHTER: I don't like the idea that we should all dress the same. [SELF-DISCLOSURE]

FRIEND 2: Oh, get with it. We'll all look fantastic!

DAUGHTER: I'm sure you will. But I still don't like the idea. [FOGGING and BROKEN RECORD]

FRIEND 3: Why not?

DAUGHTER: I don't know why. But I don't like it. [SELF-DISCLOSURE and BROKEN RECORD]

FRIEND 1: Maybe you can't afford a new outfit.

DAUGHTER: Maybe you're right. But I would like us to go to the game together the way we always do. [FOGGING and SELF-DISCLOSURE]

FRIEND 2: That will be a drag.

DAUGHTER: Maybe it will, but I still would like us to go as we usually do. [FOGGING and BROKEN RECORD]

FRIEND 3: If we all dress the same, the guys will notice us.

DAUGHTER: I'm sure they will! But I would like us to go together the way we usually do. [FOGGING and BROKEN RECORD]

FRIEND 1: You're turning into a real drag!

DAUGHTER: Maybe I am. But I still want us to go as we usually do. [FOGGING and BROKEN RECORD]

FRIEND 2: (Threateningly) Well, you don't have to sit with us if you don't want to wear the same outfit.

DAUGHTER: What is it about my not wanting to wear the same outfit that means I shouldn't want to sit with you? [NEGATIVE INQUIRY]

FRIEND 2: We wouldn't want you to feel odd!

DAUGHTER: What is it about your all wearing the same outfit and my sitting with you that means I should feel odd? [NEGATIVE INQUIRY]

FRIEND 3: Well, nothing. We just thought that wearing the same outfit is a great idea.

DAUGHTER: Maybe it is. You all wear the same outfit and I'll dress the way I usually do. How's that? [FOGGING and WORKABLE COMPROMISE]

FRIEND 2: It won't be as good with only three of us wearing the same thing.

DAUGHTER: Probably not. But don't let me spoil your fun. You wear what you want, and I'll wear what I want. That sound okay to you? [FOGGING and WORKABLE COMPROMISE]

FRIEND 1: I guess. . . .

In the next dialogue, your son faces the same group pressure from his friends to conform.

DIALOGUE 34

Son Copes with Peer Pressure to Conform
Age level: Ten through thirteen
Setting: Your son approaches a group of his friends to join them at lunch and sees that all of them have Mohawk haircuts.

SON: Hi!

FRIEND 1: Boy, do you look bad!

SON: I do?

FRIEND 1: Really bad!

SON: What is it about the way I look that's bad? [NEGATIVE IN-QUIRY]

FRIEND 2: That squirrely haircut.

SON: What is it about my haircut that's squirrely? [NEGATIVE IN-QUIRY]

FRIEND 3: It's not cool like ours!

SON: What is it about your haircuts that's cool? [POSITIVE IN-QUIRY]

FRIEND 2: Mohawks are really neat. You should get one too!

SON: They do look cool. But I like my hair long. [FOGGING and SELF-DISCLOSURE]

FRIEND 1: Get with it! You look like a nerd!

SON: I probably do, but I still like my hair long. [FOGGING and BROKEN RECORD]

FRIEND 2: We're going to form a Mr. T. club. I you don't wear a Mohawk, you can't join.

SON: No, thanks. I like my hair the way it is. [BROKEN RECORD]

FRIEND 3: Why don't you want to wear a Mohawk?

SON: I don't know. I just like my hair long. [SELF-DISCLOSURE and BROKEN RECORD]

FRIEND 3: Do you think your haircut looks better than ours?

SON: (Remembering that questions do not have to be answered) I just like my hair long. [BROKEN RECORD]

FRIEND 2: Everybody looks at us wherever we go.

SON: I'm sure they do. [FOGGING]

FRIEND 1: You would look good with one too.

SON: You're right. I would. But I think I'll stick with the one I've got. [FOGGING and BROKEN RECORD]

FRIEND 3: Don't say we didn't try to get you to look good.

SON: I won't.

With the experience of practice dialogues for coping with obvious peer pressure, your child will be able to place in perspective more subtly manipulative peer pressure, such as pressure to conform to the social group by cheating, not studying; by taking drugs or alcohol; or by engaging in sexual activity prematurely.

In high school, peer pressure to conform is even greater than at middle- and elementary-school levels. High-school kids want to be liked and to prove themselves socially as mature, admirable almost-adults. The problem with teenagers trying to be adult is that very few of them know what adult behavior and attitudes are. Consequently, teenagers will imitate each other—rather like the blind leading the blind. The behaviors that commonly result from this group conformity are sometimes humorous, sometimes sad.

Teenagers want to be like each other because at this tumultuous time in their lives there is social safety in numbers. It is very important, therefore, that the teenager (preferably the preteen) learn to discriminate between harmless group pressures to conform and be liked and manipulative group pressure to join in risky behaviors.

Situations in which peers push sex, alcohol, and drugs are played out in a later sequence of dialogues. For now, let's look at a classmate trying to get your daughter to cut class and go to the movies in the afternoon. Under pressure from her friend, your daughter has to decide for herself what is okay for her. Whatever she decides to do in this practice is okay, since the object of being assertive here is simply to give her the verbal ability to fend off peer pressure while thinking on her feet, deciding what she wants to do, and taking the responsibility for it.

DIALOGUE 35

Daughter Decides Yes or No for Herself under Peer Pressure
Age level: Eleven through seventeen
Setting: There is one class period left in the afternoon and your daughter and a classmate are walking toward the classroom.

FRIEND: Let's not go to class.
DAUGHTER: Why not?
FRIEND: Let's cut out and go to a movie instead. That would be a lot more fun than this math class.
DAUGHTER: You're right, it would, but I would feel really uncomfortable cutting class. [FOGGING and SELF-DISCLOSURE]
FRIEND: Why?

DAUGHTER: I guess I'm afraid we'll get caught. [SELF-DISCLOSURE]

FRIEND: We won't if we're smart.

DAUGHTER: Maybe, but I'm not sure I really want to cut class. [FOGGING and SELF-DISCLOSURE]

FRIEND: You and I don't need to go to this class. We're both A students, and today's only a review!

DAUGHTER: You're right, but I don't know. . . . I've never cut class before. [FOGGING and SELF-DISCLOSURE]

FRIEND: Neither have I. It's about time we did!

DAUGHTER: Maybe you're right. But you're not supposed to cut class. [FOGGING]

FRIEND: Oh, don't be such a Goody Two-Shoes.

DAUGHTER: You're right. I *am* too much of a Goody Two-Shoes. I really would like to cut class. Let's go before the buzzer sounds! [NEGATIVE ASSERTION and SELF-DISCLOSURE]

FRIEND: Right on!

As you can see, learning to be assertive is not the adoption of a "good" set of shoulds to replace a "bad" set of shoulds. I always make it a point to tell learners in my assertiveness seminars that at times I really don't want to be assertive. "Today," I tell them, "I'd rather be a flake!" That comment, which seems to undermine everything I have given them up to that point, invariably starts the following dialogue between myself and the students.

LEARNER 1: But if assertiveness has such good results in straightening out conflict and making things better between people, you should always try to be assertive.

ME: You may be right, but today I don't care. I don't want to be assertive. [FOGGING, SELF-DISCLOSURE, and BROKEN RECORD]

LEARNER 2: That's totally inconsistent with what you have said up to now.

ME: It may very well be inconsistent, but today, I'd rather be a flake. [FOGGING and BROKEN RECORD]

LEARNER 3: That's dumb!

ME: What is it about my wanting to be a flake that's dumb? [NEGATIVE INQUIRY]

LEARNER 2: You are confusing the hell out of me.

ME: I probably am. But I still don't want to be assertive. [FOGGING and BROKEN RECORD]

LEARNER 3: How can you assertively say that you don't want to be assertive?

ME: Easy! Listen to this! Today I don't want to be assertive. I'd rather be a flake! [SELF-DISCLOSURE and BROKEN RECORD]

LEARNER 1: But it's a logical contradiction and doesn't make sense!

ME: It may very well be illogical, but today I'd rather be a flake. [FOGGING and BROKEN RECORD]

LEARNER 3: Each time we try to get you to be assertive, you say you don't want to be assertive, and back up not being assertive by being assertive!

ME: Right! What is it about assertively wanting to be nonassertive that is wrong? [NEGATIVE INQUIRY]

LEARNER 2: I don't know.

ME: Now you're catching on. What is it about my wanting a goal that you may or may not not approve of, or even understand, and then dealing with you assertively to attain that goal, that is wrong? [NEGATIVE INQUIRY]

LEARNER 1: Nothing.

ME: You mean I can now decide to go along with you, to change my mind and be assertive, and I still don't need your approval to do so?

LEARNER 3: You can do anything you want to.

I finish the dialogue with my students by placing what we talked about in perspective. "Right! Keep in mind that the assertive skills are just skills. They are a very efficient means to an end, and not the end itself. The skills are just tools, and nonmoral the way a hammer or chisel is nonmoral. With that hammer and chisel, you can carve a great work of art or a pornographic print block. You can be a nasty s.o.b. and express that nastiness assertively. You can even pick your nose assertively if that's what you want. Or you can be a real prince, and be an efficient, assertive prince. It's up to you. You are your own judge and you are responsible for all your behavior, including your assertive behavior. The goals you assertively seek have nothing to do with being assertive. If you want, you can refuse to be assertive, even though it does good things for you!"

As I try to point out to learners with this dialogue, teaching people to be assertive means teaching them to think, to make judgments about what is appropriate, and to carry out that judgment, usually in the face of social opposition. If your daughter assertively decides that her friend's idea is a good one—to have some fun and excitement by cutting a boring and useless class where they were just going to kill some time—I would applaud her decision. Clinically speaking, I am more concerned about youngsters who show no spark of youth and daring than about those who take chances occasionally to test things out. These more daring youngsters want to find out what life is really about, and it's stupid of us to punish them for that.

Once your child feels comfortable in simple situations like those given so far, and handles your attempted manipulation well, go on to situations that will cause him or her to feel a bit more anxious about being assertive, as in the following dialogues.

DIALOGUE 36

Daughter Learns to Say No When a Friend Wants to Borrow Something Personal
Age level: Seven through seventeen
Setting: A friend is trying to talk your daughter into lending her record collection for use at the friend's party. Your daughter has learned the hard way that her friend is manipulative. She uses the full range of assertive skills, as needed, to cope with this new manipulation.

FRIEND: Hi!
DAUGHTER: Hi! What's up?
FRIEND: I am in the most terrible jam.
DAUGHTER: (Restraining herself from asking "What jam?") Really?
FRIEND: Yes.
DAUGHTER: Oh.
FRIEND: Aren't you going to ask me about it?
DAUGHTER: (Refusing to bite) Do you want me to?
FRIEND: Of course. Why do you think I said I was in a jam?
DAUGHTER: (Straightforwardly) I don't know.

FRIEND: I don't have a single record that I can play at my party Friday night!

DAUGHTER: (Showing empathy) Gee, that's too bad.

FRIEND: You have to lend me your set of the Funky Punks.

DAUGHTER: I understand you're in a jam, but I don't want to lend out my set to anybody.

FRIEND: Why not?

DAUGHTER: I'm worried that they might get scratched, so I don't want to lend them out to anyone. [SELF-DISCLOSURE and BROKEN RECORD]

FRIEND: But they won't get scratched at my party. I promise.

DAUGHTER: You may be right, but I don't want to take the chance. [FOGGING and BROKEN RECORD]

FRIEND: That's being selfish. I lend you things.

DAUGHTER: You may be right. You have lent me things before. [FOGGING]

FRIEND: I thought we were good friends.

DAUGHTER: We are. If you want to borrow something else, that's okay. But not my Funky Punks. [FOGGING and BROKEN RECORD]

FRIEND: It's not fair.

DAUGHTER: I feel the same way when someone tells me that. I know how you feel. It probably isn't fair. [SELF-DISCLOSURE and FOGGING]

FRIEND: I promise I won't scratch your records.

DAUGHTER: I'm sure you feel you won't, but I still don't want to lend them out. [FOGGING and BROKEN RECORD]

FRIEND: You lent me your records before. You didn't tell me "I'm worried" then!

DAUGHTER: You're right. I did lend you my records before, and I didn't tell you I was worried. I feel bad about that. I should have told you. It was dumb of me not to. [FOGGING, SELF-DISCLOSURE, and NEGATIVE ASSERTION]

FRIEND: What am I supposed to play at my party?

DAUGHTER: I don't know.

FRIEND: You're a lot of help.

DAUGHTER: You're right. I'm not much help. Is there anything I can do besides lend you my Funky Punks? [FOGGING and WORKABLE COMPROMISE]

FRIEND: Who can I borrow some records from?
DAUGHTER: Donna?
FRIEND: Maybe . . . Who else?
DAUGHTER: Bill?
FRIEND: Great! He's a real pushover. What kind of records does he have? Do you have his phone number?

One of the big fears that children have—a totally irrational one, I might add—is that if they say no to a friend, that friend will not like them (Assertive Right VII: goodwill) and the refusal will end their friendship. Be frank with your child and point out that some friendships will never survive the slightest conflict, because there is not enough in common between the two friends. But also assure him or her that in the long run being assertive with friends strengthens friendships, rather than weakens them. In the next dialogue, your son (or daughter) has to cope with a friend who simply wants company at an inappropriate time.

DIALOGUE 37

Son Learns to Say No When a Friend Wants to Visit at an Inconvenient Time
Age level: Seven through seventeen
Setting: Your son is working on a project important to him when a friend calls him on the phone.

FRIEND: Hi. I thought I'd come over and we could watch TV.
SON: Gee, I'm pretty busy now.
FRIEND: What are you doing?
SON: Just something I want to work on. (Remembering the difference between "I want" and "I have to," and that he doesn't have to automatically answer any questions he is asked)
FRIEND: Can't you do it later?
SON: That's possible, but I would like to get as much done as I can now. [FOGGING and SELF-DISCLOSURE]
FRIEND: What's so important that you have to do it now?
SON: As I said, just something I want to work on. [BROKEN RECORD]

FRIEND: Man, this is incredible! I thought we were friends!

SON: We *are* friends, but this is just something I want to try to get finished. [FOGGING and BROKEN RECORD]

FRIEND: Well, excuse me!

SON: I feel bad not saying "Come on over," but this project is important to me. [SELF-DISCLOSURE and BROKEN RECORD]

FRIEND: Well, what is it?

SON: When I'm done with it, I'll let you know, okay? [WORKABLE COMPROMISE]

FRIEND: It had better be good.

SON: I hope so too. [SELF-DISCLOSURE]

In the next dialogue your daughter has to deal with a friend who borrowed her homework and has forgotten to return it on the morning it is due.

DIALOGUE 38

Daughter Learns What to Do When a Friend Makes a Big Mistake
Age level: Seven through seventeen
Setting: Your daughter meets her friend at the entrance to school.

FRIEND: Hi.

DAUGHTER: Hi. Got everything done?

FRIEND: Yes.

DAUGHTER: Okay. Give me mine and I'll hand it in.

FRIEND: I've got it right here somewhere. . . . Oh, gosh! I left it on the table at home.

DAUGHTER: You haven't got it?

FRIEND: No. I'm really sorry.

DAUGHTER: That really makes me sick. (SELF-DISCLOSURE) The assignment is due this morning and Ms. Grinch said she would mark us down if we handed it in late.

FRIEND: What can you do?

DAUGHTER: You'll have to tell her that you borrowed my paper to look at and forgot it.

FRIEND: How could you ask me to do that? It will make me look like a fool.

DAUGHTER: It may. [FOGGING] But I don't know how else to keep from getting marked down.

FRIEND: You could say you're sick and go home. That would be the easiest way.

DAUGHTER: I could, but I want you to take responsibility for your goof. [FOGGING and BROKEN RECORD]

FRIEND: Me? Why is it my responsibility?

DAUGHTER: Do you want to go home and get my paper? [WORKABLE COMPROMISE]

FRIEND: It will take me an hour to do that. Class will be over by then and we'll both be marked down.

DAUGHTER: So I want you to tell Ms. Grinch that you had my paper at home and you forgot it. [BROKEN RECORD]

FRIEND: She will think I copied your paper.

DAUGHTER: You didn't copy it, did you?

FRIEND: No. I just wanted to see how you wrote it.

DAUGHTER: Then that's what you tell her. [BROKEN RECORD]

FRIEND: But she might mark my paper down because I looked at yours.

DAUGHTER: She may, but I doubt it. Teachers like students to work on projects together. [FOGGING]

FRIEND: But it still sounds suspicious.

DAUGHTER: Why did you want to read my finished paper?

FRIEND: So I could compare our writing styles and see if I could improve mine.

DAUGHTER: What is it about wanting to improve your writing style by looking at my paper that's suspicious? [NEGATIVE INQUIRY]

FRIEND: When you put it that way, nothing, I guess. But I'll still feel like a fool!

DAUGHTER: I'm sure you will. I would feel the same way if I borrowed your paper and forgot it the morning it had to be handed in. [FOGGING and SELF-DISCLOSURE]

FRIEND: But what do I say to her?

DAUGHTER: Simple. You go up to her with me and say, "Ms. Grinch, I did a really dumb thing and I feel very bad about it. I borrowed . . . [NEGATIVE ASSERTION and SELF-DISCLOSURE]

As you can see from this dialogue, it doesn't much matter how a social conflict starts. When a friend wants something from your child, or your child wants something from a friend, unless the other child has had some assertiveness training, I can almost guarantee that your child will face emotional manipulation by the friend. This does not mean that your child's friend is a bad friend, but only that he or she doesn't know how to cope with conflict except by manipulation. In the next dialogue your son has to deal with angry friends who blame him for their disappointment.

DIALOGUE 39

Son Learns to Deal with Intimidation
Age level: Seven through seventeen.
Setting: Your son is in the locker room getting dressed when two of his fellow members of the Soccer Club approach him.

SON: What's up, guys?
PLAYER 1: You know what's up. You blew the game!
SON: You're right. I missed the kick on the last goal attempt. That was really clumsy. [NEGATIVE ASSERTION]
PLAYER 2: If we'd had somebody else playing your position, we would have won the game.
SON: You may be right. [FOGGING]
PLAYER 2: I know we're right. This isn't the first time you've screwed up.
SON: No, it isn't. [NEGATIVE ASSERTION]
PLAYER 1: We think you ought to quit the team.
SON: I'm sure you feel that way. What does the coach say? [FOGGING]
PLAYER 1: This has nothing to do with the coach. He's too soft on guys like you.
SON: I'm sure he is. But I'm staying. [FOGGING]
PLAYER 2: We're not going to play with you anymore.
SON: Oh? Are you going to quit? I wish you wouldn't. [SELF-DISCLOSURE] We wouldn't have any team without you guys.

PLAYER 1: That's right. We want *you* to quit!

SON: I'm sure you do. But I'm staying. [FOGGING and BROKEN RECORD]

PLAYER 2: If you stay, we won't win any games.

SON: Maybe we won't, but I'm still staying. [FOGGING and BROKEN RECORD]

PLAYER 1: That's not fair. We kill ourselves to win, and someone like you comes along and fouls things up.

SON: You're right. It's not fair. [FOGGING]

PLAYER 2: We don't want to play with you.

SON: I'm sure you don't. But I wish you wouldn't quit the team because I'm not. [FOGGING and SELF-DISCLOSURE]

PLAYER 1: You're not hearing anything we tell you.

SON: I'm sure it seems that way, but I'm still not quitting. [FOGGING and BROKEN RECORD]

PLAYER 2: I think we ought to complain to the coach.

SON: If you feel that bad about it, I think you should too. If I were in your shoes, I certainly would. [SELF-DISCLOSURE]

PLAYER 1: Let's go. He doesn't have any school spirit!

SON: I probably don't have as much as I should, but I'm staying. [FOGGING, SELF-DISCLOSURE and BROKEN RECORD]

In setting up the foregoing dialogue for your son or daughter, be very frank about how he or she can be criticized by other people in *anything*, even playing a fun game for a school athletic club. A good rule to follow in placing criticism in perspective: The more important what it is you do, the more criticism you will receive.

In the next dialogue, your daughter has to deal with two friends who don't like each other and are angry at *her*, too.

DIALOGUE 40

Daughter Learns to Cope with Fighting Friends and Angry Criticism
Age level: Seven through seventeen
Setting: Your daughter has invited two friends over to spend the night.

FRIEND 1: (In front of Friend 2) Why did you invite *her* over?

DAUGHTER: What's the problem?

FRIEND 2: I thought you only invited *me* over to spend the night.

DAUGHTER: Hold it. Are you two guys mad at each other?

FRIEND 1: She's a real creep. I don't know why you think she's your friend.

FRIEND 2: And *she's* a creep too!

DAUGHTER: What's going on here?

FRIEND 2: Your friend over there tried to get Debbie to stop being friends with me!

FRIEND 1: Only because you told Debbie I was dumb!

DAUGHTER: This makes me really feel bad. I wanted us to have a good time because I like you both. And now you decide to have a fight. I don't like this. [SELF-DISCLOSURE]

FRIEND 1: Well, you shouldn't have invited her. I thought *I* was your friend.

FRIEND 2: And I thought *I* was your friend.

DAUGHTER: I can understand that you're both mad at each other, but both of you are my friends. Can we stop fighting and enjoy this evening? [WORKABLE COMPROMISE]

FRIEND 2: You shouldn't have invited both of us here at once.

DAUGHTER: You're right. Now I can see that was a dumb thing to do. [NEGATIVE ASSERTION]

FRIEND 1: If you want to be friends with *her,* you don't need me.

FRIEND 2: Good! Then leave.

DAUGHTER: I understand you are mad at each other. And I'm sure both of you are mad at me now. What else can we do to straighten this out except fight? [WORKABLE COMPROMISE]

FRIEND 2: I'm willing to try, but she isn't. She started it!

DAUGHTER: Maybe she did. But that's not what I'm talking about. What else can we do besides fighting each other? [FOGGING and WORKABLE COMPROMISE]

FRIEND 1: If she'd apologize, I'd forget it.

FRIEND 2: If *I'd* apologize? How about her?

DAUGHTER: I'm sure both of you would like to get an apology. Can you both give one? [FOGGING and WORKABLE COMPROMISE]

FRIEND 1: Only if she goes first.

FRIEND 2: Only if she goes first.

DAUGHTER: I'm sure you both feel wronged. How about at the same time? [FOGGING and WORKABLE COMPROMISE]
FRIEND 1: Okay.
FRIEND 2: Okay.
DAUGHTER: Super! Okay, on three. Ready? One . . . two . . .

As you can see, persistent use of assertive skills enables your child to handle just about anything, even a fight.

In the next dialogue we turn again to dealing with manipulative close friends. In this case your son has to cope with a friend who wants him to do something dishonest and risky.

DIALOGUE 41

Son Learns to Say No to a Friend Who Wants Him to Cheat on a Test
Age level: Eleven through seventeen
Setting: Your son and a friend are eating lunch at school together.

FRIEND: Did you study for the test last night?
SON: Sure. Didn't you?
FRIEND: I didn't get a chance to.
SON: How come?
FRIEND: There was a great kung fu movie on channel two.
SON: Yeah. I wanted to watch that too.
FRIEND: Do you think you will get a good grade on the test?
SON: I hope so. I studied until I fell asleep.
FRIEND: I think I'm going to flunk it.
SON: Didn't you study at all?
FRIEND: I had a lot of things to do this week. You could help me out.
SON: How?
FRIEND: Whenever I poke you in the back, hold up your test and pretend to read it, so I can see your answers.
SON: That's cheating. I don't want to do that. [SELF-DISCLOSURE]
FRIEND: Why not? Afraid you might get caught?
SON: You're right. I don't want to get caught cheating. [FOGGING and BROKEN RECORD]

FRIEND: You're chicken!

SON: You're right. I am. [NEGATIVE ASSERTION]

FRIEND: But if you don't help me, I'll flunk!

SON: You may flunk, and I'd feel bad about that. [FOGGING and SELF-DISCLOSURE]

FRIEND: If you feel so bad about my flunking, you should help!

SON: Maybe you're right, but I'm not going to hold my test up. [FOGGING and BROKEN RECORD]

FRIEND: I could look over your shoulder.

SON: You could, but I think you'd get caught. [FOGGING and SELF-DISCLOSURE]

FRIEND: If I got caught, I'd tell the teacher that you were helping me.

SON: That really makes me mad. I'm your friend, and just because I don't want to cheat, you say you're going to lie and get me in trouble! [SELF-DISCLOSURE]

FRIEND: Okay, okay! I'm sorry! But how about me? What am I going to do?

SON: Tell the teacher that you couldn't study this week and ask to take a makeup test. [WORKABLE COMPROMISE]

FRIEND: She may not go for it.

SON: She may not. You can ask her now—she's right over there. If she doesn't buy it, I could go over my notes with you now, and we could ask the study-hall monitor if we could study for the test outside, where we can talk. That would help me, too. [FOGGING and WORKABLE COMPROMISE]

FRIEND: Okay. That's a really good idea.

Whenever you role-play a friend who threatens to do something if your child doesn't comply with your wishes, coach your child not to respond with a counterthreat, such as "Okay, if you are going to lie, I am going to the teacher right now and tell her you wanted me to cheat!" Threats are next to useless in resolving conflicts; they only get both parties angry, with neither of them using his/her thinking brain to work out compromise solutions that would benefit both.

The whole point of being assertive is to see if we can get past manipulation of our emotions and solve the problems that other people foist on us. Even if we cannot solve a problem for both parties in a social conflict, at least we can use our thinking brains to make sure the conflict causes the fewest problems for us. For example, if no matter how your son tried to help his manipulative friend, the friend still threatened to lie if he was caught cheating and involve your son, the worst course of action would be for your son to express his anger by threatening to tell the teacher what his friend said. A self-protective course, if needed, would be for him to remain quiet and later tell the teacher discreetly what had happened, and let the teacher take it from there. If the friend was only bluffing and didn't cheat, the teacher would observe that. But if the friend tried to cheat and was caught, he would face the consequences alone.

Unfortunately, despite our good intentions, some people seem to do their best to destroy the relationships we have with them. Also, some people are bad friends who deliberately use us. It usually takes something genuinely shocking for us to realize we have been used and that there never was a real friendship. If something like this happens to your child, he or she will pay a hefty emotional price, but will also learn the valuable lesson that true friends, who like us for ourselves and care about us, rather than about what they can get from us, are quite rare.

Gaining the Freedom to Say No to Drugs and Alcohol

Teenagers, and even preteens, can and do get into trouble because of drugs and alcohol. A few years ago data collected in the state of California reported that approximately 14 percent of the pupils in public schools abuse alcohol to the extent that they are involved in incidents with the law, such as drinking while driving, rowdiness, or public intoxication. While the chance that your child will abuse chemical substances is statistically not great, since the number of kids who abuse drugs and alcohol is a small percentage of all teenagers, fourteen percent is still an awful lot of kids who do get into trouble because of drugs and booze. In any case, an ounce of prevention is worth a pound of cure. You can set things up in such a way that the probability of your child's abusing such substances will be very low.

Since many parents worry about the possibility of childhood drug and alcohol abuse, we'll start off with a brief discussion of the problem.

We know a great deal in the clinical sense about why people, including young people, abuse substances. Two psychological characteristics of substance abusers stand out. First, the typical chronic substance abuser has a poor self-image and uses chemical substances to compensate for a mildly stressful environment with which he or she cannot cope. (Drugs and alcohol are also used by the person with a normal self-image to compensate for overly tense or unpredictable situations. Most such people stop using drugs once the negative or intolerable situation is removed.) The second characteristic of the typical substance abuser is that he or she is nonassertive and has great difficulty handling peer pressure.

A combination of these two characteristics is present in many middle-school and high-school students, prepubertal and pubertal. Such youngsters are talked into trying or continuing to use chemical substances and become psychologically dependent upon them to cope with their poor self-images. This dependence is different from physiological addiction, which, contrary to popular belief, involves only a small percentage of substance abusers. Large-scale research indicates that only 10 percent of drug abusers are physiologically addicted to the substance they misuse. For the other 90 percent, the resolution of substance abuse is to change the psychological or social environment that prompts them to take drugs as an alternative to failure, or to give them the skills necessary to cope with that environment.

Resolving a substance-abuse problem requires understanding both what substance abuse does for the abuser (helping him or her cope with poor self-image) and the reasons why the abuser began and continues his or her psychological dependency on substances (usually peer pressure). Detoxification of the substance abuser (eliminating the physiological effects of the abused substances) is quite simple, though it may be physically uncomfortable, but it is not a cure for substance abuse. The substance abuser needs to solve the two main psychological problems that prompt chronic substance abuse.

Assertiveness training targets both these problems by increasing self-image and providing the individual with the skills to resist peer pressure. Assertiveness training, in fact, is currently used nationwide as part of the standard treatment of choice for adult alcohol and drug abuse. Assertiveness is taught to substance abusers not just to make it easier for them to say no to drugs or alcohol but to allow them to say no to a lot of other things that cause a lowering of self-image, such as pressure from manipulative friends, associates, co-workers, bosses, spouses, and other family members.

As we have seen, a child who is taught to always be good has a low self-image. If you place yourself in your child's shoes, you can see why this is so. Imagine how you would feel about yourself if you always had to be "nice" and do what other people told you to do. A good child is susceptible to being talked into using drugs because he or she is accustomed to obeying others and because drugs make it easier to cope with this low self-image.

"If this analysis is correct," you might ask, "then why didn't we have good-child drug abusers twenty or thirty years ago?" The answer is simple. Drugs weren't as widely available then as they are now. Alcohol was. Some used it recreationally, and others abused it. Many adults today use drugs in a recreational sense much as older generations used alcohol, and many alcoholics of those earlier generations started abusing alcohol in their early teens when alcohol became available to them. In fact, clinically speaking, the typical alcohol abuser cannot be distinguished from the typical drug abuser. The only difference is the substance taken, and most such people will take whatever is available, alcohol or drugs.

To give your child the best chance of not becoming dependent upon drugs or alcohol during his or her entire life span, teach your child to be assertive in all respects. Being able to think for yourself and be your own judge is a very effective means of boosting and maintaining self-respect and self-image, and self-image is the key to preventing substance abuse. The way to achieve this is to first practice being assertive in a variety of situations, including those in which one has to say no to drugs and alcohol. If your child has the ability to decide and the skill to say no, then he or she has freedom of choice when pressure is applied to use drugs and alcohol.

The next dialogue is a replay of the dialogue in which your child had to deal with a health-food zealot. This time, however, the zealot is pushing alcohol and drugs.

DIALOGUE 43

Daughter Says No to Drugs and Alcohol Offered by a Friend
Age level: Eleven through seventeen
Setting: Your daughter and a friend are at a party where,
unknown to her, drugs and alcohol are available.

FRIEND: What are you having?
DAUGHTER: A Pepsi.
FRIEND: Don't you know that stuff is no good for you?
DAUGHTER: I'm sure it's not as good as some other stuff, but I like it.
[FOGGING and SELF-DISCLOSURE]
FRIEND: It will rot your teeth!
DAUGHTER: It may, but I still like it. [FOGGING and BROKEN
RECORD]
FRIEND: You should drink something natural that gives you a high!
There's beer and wine or hard stuff.
DAUGHTER: You're right. I probably should drink something else. But
I still like Pepsi. [FOGGING and BROKEN RECORD]
FRIEND: Grow up! That stuff is for kids.
DAUGHTER: I'm sure it is. [FOGGING]
FRIEND: Not only will it make you fat, but if I get high and you are
sober, this party will be a real downer.
DAUGHTER: Probably. [FOGGING]
FRIEND: Have you ever smoked grass?
DAUGHTER: No.
FRIEND: That's terrible. I always use it at parties.
DAUGHTER: I'm sure you do. [FOGGING]
FRIEND: Do you want to try some?
DAUGHTER: Thanks for offering, but I don't feel like taking any. [SELF-
DISCLOSURE]
FRIEND: That's pretty cold. I want to help you feel good, and you act
like a dead fish!
DAUGHTER: I'm sure I seem like a dead fish, but I don't want to smoke
any grass. [FOGGING and BROKEN RECORD]
FRIEND: You're only scared you'll like it!

DAUGHTER: Maybe, but I still don't want any. [FOGGING and BRO-
KEN RECORD]

FRIEND: It isn't addictive, you know. You should try it at least once. It
doesn't turn you into a doper!

DAUGHTER: I'm sure you're right. I probably should try it once. But I
still don't want any. [FOGGING and BROKEN RECORD]

FRIEND: It's not bad for you.

DAUGHTER: I'm sure it isn't. [FOGGING]

FRIEND: You really will like it if you give it a try.

DAUGHTER: I'm sure I will, but no thanks. [FOGGING and BROKEN
RECORD]

FRIEND: You don't want to grow up, do you?

DAUGHTER: Maybe you're right. So I'm going to stay sober. [FOG-
GING and BROKEN RECORD]

FRIEND: I can find someone else to get high with me.

DAUGHTER: I'm sure you can. Bye! [FOGGING]

It is a poor strategy—as well as impractical—to try to restrict your
child to environments that are drug-free in order to lower his or her
chances of drug abuse. You have no way of knowing that a particular
situation will be free of drugs, nor does your child. The best technique
is to teach your child how to say no to drugs confidently and easily, as
illustrated in the foregoing dialogue. Children have no need for drugs,
and initially try them as an experiment, usually under peer pressure. If
children have been taught to be assertive with friends who press them
to try drugs or alcohol, they will usually decline the offer.

In the next dialogue your son has to deal with a friend who brings beer
into your own home and wants your son to drink it. The substance could
just as well be grass or hard liquor or drugs; if you want control over any
of these in your home, you can substitute it for the beer in the dialogue.

DIALOGUE 44

Son Says No to Drinking at Home with a Friend
Age level: Eleven through seventeen
Setting: Your son is home alone, and a friend who comes over to
study with him brings along two cans of beer in a paper bag.

SON: Hi! Whatcha got there?

FRIEND: Two beers! One for you and one for me.

SON: I don't know how to tell you this without sounding like a wimp, but I promised my dad that I wouldn't drink any booze unless he was with me. [SELF-DISCLOSURE]

FRIEND: You don't want one?

SON: I would like one, but I promised my dad, so . . . no. [SELF-DISCLOSURE and BROKEN RECORD]

FRIEND: Well, I'll drink both then.

SON: Fine with me. But not here. I promised my dad. [SELF-DISCLOSURE and BROKEN RECORD]

FRIEND: You mean you don't want me to drink beer here?

SON: I feel bad about it, but that's right. [SELF-DISCLOSURE]

FRIEND: That's stupid. We're not trying to do anything sneaky! Your dad drinks beer himself. He has a six-pack in the fridge. I already checked!

SON: It does seem stupid, but I promised no drinking unless he's here. [FOGGING and BROKEN RECORD]

FRIEND: How will he know? We're not trying to drink his stuff!

SON: He probably won't find out. But no drinking if he's not here. [FOGGING and BROKEN RECORD]

FRIEND: This is crazy! I can't even drink my own beer!

SON: I know it seems crazy, but no drinking when he's not here. [FOGGING and BROKEN RECORD]

FRIEND: I paid for this beer with my own money! My brother got it for me last night.

SON: I'm sure you did. Why don't you wait until my dad gets home in an hour? [FOGGING and WORKABLE COMPROMISE]

FRIEND: God! The kooks I have for friends!

SON: You're right. I am a bit kooky, but humor me. [NEGATIVE ASSERTION and WORKABLE COMPROMISE]

FRIEND: You'd better know how to do this homework.

SON: I was hoping *you* knew how to do it. [SELF-DISCLOSURE]

To control the use of alcohol or drugs in your home, two things are required: a commitment from your child not to use them or allow their use in your home, and a child who has had practice in assertiveness and experience in saying no to friends.

Coping with Peer Pressure at Social Events and on Dates

In the next set of dialogues, we turn to a problem commonly reported by youngsters in the STAR research project: how to set up the rules of partying and dating. The youngsters surveyed by STAR researchers complained that they didn't know how to communicate well enough beforehand so that both people on a date would know in advance what to expect, and so parents would know what their teenagers were doing and where they were.

In the first dialogue your daughter has to deal with a friend who insists they stay at a party beyond the time you and she agreed on. Although here it is a girlfriend who is pressuring your daughter to stay out late, the assertive skills used to say no are just as useful and appropriate in dealing with a boyfriend who pressures her on a date.

DIALOGUE 42

Daughter Tells a Friend About Getting Home on Time, and Means It
Age level: Thirteen through seventeen
Setting: It is eleven o'clock on Saturday night and your daughter reminds her friend of the time.

DAUGHTER: It's getting late.
FRIEND: It's early yet.
DAUGHTER: Remember, I agreed to get home by now, and I'm going with you in your sister's car.
FRIEND: Don't pay any attention to that. Your mom and dad don't care if you're a little bit late. They expect it.
DAUGHTER: I'm sure they do, but I don't want to be real late. [FOGGING and SELF-DISCLOSURE]
FRIEND: This party is too much fun to leave now.
DAUGHTER: It is. I'm sorry I have to leave. [FOGGING and SELF-DISCLOSURE]
FRIEND: You don't have to leave. There's plenty of time.

DAUGHTER: I'm sure there's plenty of time for you, but I want to leave now. [FOGGING and BROKEN RECORD]

FRIEND: But why? I told you, your parents don't really care.

DAUGHTER: I would feel really uncomfortable coming home late after promising I wouldn't. [SELF-DISCLOSURE]

FRIEND: Do you think they would ground you?

DAUGHTER: No, but I would still feel uncomfortable not keeping my word. [BROKEN RECORD]

FRIEND: You haven't met Bobby yet. Let me get him over here.

DAUGHTER: I feel good about your trying to fix me up, but I think it's best I leave. [SELF-DISCLOSURE and BROKEN RECORD]

FRIEND: You're just being difficult and a stick-in-the-mud.

DAUGHTER: I'm sure I seem like that, but I want to leave. [FOGGING and BROKEN RECORD]

FRIEND: Oh, all right! Let me say good-bye and get my stuff.

DAUGHTER: Okay. But don't take too long. [WORKABLE COMPROMISE]

FRIEND: Five minutes.

DAUGHTER: If you're not back in five, I'm coming to look for you. [WORKABLE COMPROMISE]

In the next dialogue of this set, your daughter deals with a boyfriend who likes to do things without planning ahead of time.

DIALOGUE 45

Daughter Gets Things Straight Before Going Out on a Date
Age level: Thirteen through seventeen
Setting: Your daughter is speaking to a boyfriend on the phone and he tells her he would like to go out on a date Friday night.

BOYFRIEND: How about going out Friday night?

DAUGHTER: That sounds like fun. I would like that. [SELF-DISCLOSURE]

BOYFRIEND: Okay, I'll pick you up at seven on Friday.

DAUGHTER: What would you like to do?

BOYFRIEND: What do you mean?

DAUGHTER: On the date. What would you like to do?

BOYFRIEND: You mean where will we go?

DAUGHTER: Exactly.

BOYFRIEND: Don't worry about that. I'll think of something.

DAUGHTER: I'm sure you will. But I'd like to know what you want to do before we go out. [FOGGING and BROKEN RECORD]

BOYFRIEND: Don't worry about it. We'll go someplace great.

DAUGHTER: I'm sure we will, but I'd still like to know where you want to go. [FOGGING and BROKEN RECORD]

BOYFRIEND: Well . . . there's lots of places we could go.

DAUGHTER: Sure there are. Do you have any idea what you would like to do, like go dancing or something? [FOGGING and WORKABLE COMPROMISE]

BOYFRIEND: Well, I haven't had a chance to look at the paper yet.

DAUGHTER: Do you want to go to a movie? [WORKABLE COMPROMISE]

BOYFRIEND: I don't know.

DAUGHTER: Is there something else you would rather do?

BOYFRIEND: I haven't thought about it yet.

DAUGHTER: Okay, how does this sound? You think about it and call me back before Friday and let me know what you want to do. [WORKABLE COMPROMISE]

BOYFRIEND: That's getting pretty rigid, you know! It doesn't allow much room for doing things naturally as they occur to you.

DAUGHTER: I'm sure it seems rigid, but I'd like to know where we're going before I go out on a date. [FOGGING and BROKEN RECORD]

BOYFRIEND: You make me feel like I'm a real flake and you don't trust me!

DAUGHTER: I'm sure you feel that way. And I'm doing this badly. But I do want to know where we're going before Friday. [FOGGING, NEGATIVE ASSERTION, and BROKEN RECORD]

BOYFRIEND: Don't you trust me to take you somewhere nice?

DAUGHTER: I'm sure it must sound that way, and I feel real awkward about this, but I do want to know where we are going before Friday. [FOGGING, SELF-DISCLOSURE and BROKEN RECORD]

BOYFRIEND: There are lots of other girls I could ask out who are not as picky as you.

DAUGHTER: I'm sure there are. [FOGGING]

BOYFRIEND: You are tough!

DAUGHTER: You are right! [POSITIVE ASSERTION]

BOYFRIEND: Okay. It's just not my style to do things in such a rigid way, but I'll decide what I want to do by Thursday and call you then to see if you would like it too. Okay?

DAUGHTER: Okay. That makes me feel really good. Thanks for inviting me out. [SELF-DISCLOSURE] Bye.

In the next dialogue your daughter has to assert herself to the same boyfriend on Friday when he calls up and wants to change where they are going.

DIALOGUE 46

Daughter Deals with Last-Minute Changes Before Going Out on a Date
Age level: Thirteen through seventeen
Setting: Your daughter picks up the phone and it's her date calling.

BOYFRIEND: Great news! A friend just gave me two box-seat tickets to the hockey game tonight! You'll really enjoy it.

DAUGHTER: You want to go to a hockey game? I thought we were going to the play?

BOYFRIEND: Yes, but I just got the tickets ten minutes ago.

DAUGHTER: I'm sure you did, but I'm not a hockey person. [FOGGING and SELF-DISCLOSURE]

BOYFRIEND: You'll love it.

DAUGHTER: I get upset with quick changes. That's why I wanted to know where we were going beforehand. [SELF-DISCLOSURE]

BOYFRIEND: Yes, but this is the Winnemucka Wharf Rats playing the San Diego Surfers! It's a regional play-off!

DAUGHTER: I'm sure it's going to be a great game, but hockey is not my cup of tea. [FOGGING and BROKEN RECORD]

BOYFRIEND: Just give it a chance. You'll like it.

DAUGHTER: When you called yesterday and said you got us tickets for that play, I was so excited. Sort of like you are now about this hockey game. [SELF-DISCLOSURE] Let's go to the play tonight, as we planned, and the next time you get free tickets for a play-off game, we'll go. How does that sound? [WORKABLE COMPROMISE]

BOYFRIEND: I may not get more tickets like these for quite a while.

DAUGHTER: That's okay. I can wait.

BOYFRIEND: You're sure you would rather go to the play?

DAUGHTER: Positively.

BOYFRIEND: Okay. But you will miss a great matchup. It doesn't matter to me. I can watch it on cable later.

DAUGHTER: Swell. That makes me feel much better. [SELF-DISCLO-SURE]

Now, let's replay an earlier dialogue about dating, this time with a daughter assertively responding to her manipulative girlfriend about different personal perspectives on sexual behavior.

DIALOGUE 47

Daughter Says No to Sexual Peer Pressure
Age level: Thirteen through seventeen
Setting: A fourteen-year-old daughter is talking to her friend
Bimbo about dating.

DAUGHTER: I've changed my mind about going out on another double date this weekend.

FRIEND: Why?

DAUGHTER: I just feel uncomfortable about it. [SELF-DISCLOSURE]

FRIEND: We talked about this before! Bobby and Fred are cool guys. You just were a real drag on Friday.

DAUGHTER: You are right, I was, but I don't want to go on another double date. [FOGGING and BROKEN RECORD]

FRIEND: Get with it. You acted like a nun! It's no fun having an audience that doesn't do anything but sit there and watch.

DAUGHTER: You're right. It's no fun for you if I just sit there and watch. [FOGGING]

FRIEND: Is there something wrong with you? Do you have a hang-up or something?

DAUGHTER: Perhaps. I just feel uncomfortable on that kind of date. [FOGGING and SELF-DISCLOSURE]

FRIEND: You shouldn't feel that way. It's unnatural.

DAUGHTER: I probably shouldn't, but I do, so I'm not going on another double date. [FOGGING, SELF-DISCLOSURE, and BROKEN RECORD]

FRIEND: What are you uncomfortable about?

DAUGHTER: I'm uncomfortable about how old we are, and getting involved sexually. [SELF-DISCLOSURE]

FRIEND: You are a real dimwit. If you're big enough, you're old enough. You're not as developed as I am, but you're big enough.

DAUGHTER: I guess I am, but I'm still not comfortable on that kind of date. [FOGGING and BROKEN RECORD]

FRIEND: You probably have an immature hang-up about it. It's really nothing. Anybody can do it.

DAUGHTER: I probably do have a hang-up. [FOGGING]

FRIEND: All you have to do is try. Fake it.

DAUGHTER: I probably could fake it, but I'd rather not go out on that kind of date again. Maybe later, but not now. [FOGGING, BROKEN RECORD, and WORKABLE COMPROMISE]

FRIEND: I can always find someone else to double-date with me.

DAUGHTER: I'm sure you can. [FOGGING]

FRIEND: Okay. But you will miss a great time.

DAUGHTER: I'm sure I will. [FOGGING]

As the dialogues in this chapter point out, it is the feelings of guilt, foolishness, or ignorance that other people try to generate within us that cause us problems in being effective in a social conflict. These problems arise, if we are vulnerable to manipulation, regardless of the subject of the conflict—whether it is a choice of movie, or lending phonograph records, or cheating, or sex, or drug and alcohol use. Children who do not know how to act assertively, and children who lack self-esteem, are especially vulnerable to these feelings because they want so much to belong, to be part of the gang and do what everyone else is doing. I can guarantee that this universal sense of wanting to belong will be exploited by your children's friends, especially their close friends. However, in spite of these very normal feelings, and with practice, children can learn to assert themselves effectively and easily in dealing with the many thorny subjects of disagreement with friends or classmates. One major plus of this practice is the ultimate realization that wanting to belong and maintaining a friendship do not mean there must be perfect harmony between two friends or that your child always has to go along with whatever a friend wants.

Let's turn now to the next chapter, which will show you how to teach your child to be appropriately assertive in a situation that causes anxiety in most children: coping with authority figures, such as teachers and other staff at school.

CHAPTER SIX

Teaching Your Child How to Get Help from, Say No to, and Assertively Resolve Problems with School Staff and Other Adults in Authority

I n asserting himself or herself to friends and classmates, your child can do an excellent job just by rote-learning the appropriate verbal skills without necessarily understanding why they work. He or she will still be able to resolve social conflicts because coping with the manipulation of young peers is quite easy with practice. Preteen classmates are manipulative, but unless your child's peers are quite precocious, they will not be expert manipulators, as we adults are.

However, when your child has to deal with teachers and school administrators, or enters high school and has to cope with other teenagers, it is helpful to him or her to know *how* an expert manipulator goes about the process of talking someone into doing what the manipulator wants. As always, you and your child should remember that a manipulator is not a bad person, just someone who has been taught that emotional manipulation is the way to get what is wanted.

The Key Words for Your Child to Remember in Organizing an Assertive Response: Understand, Agree, and Behave

Understand, agree, and *behave:* These key words tell us how a person tries to manipulate us, and also remind us how to formulate a response to manipulation. The manipulator assumes that the three words are linked—i.e., "If you understand, you must agree with me; and if you agree with me, you must behave in the way I want." When we let ourselves be manipulated, it is because we, too, believe the three key words are linked.

The unspoken argument or ploy that the manipulator uses, and expects us to accept automatically without thinking, is "You must understand what I'm telling you [Assertive Right IX: understanding]. If you don't understand, there's something wrong with you, and I'll say again why you have to do what I want. If you do understand what I'm telling you, and if you have any brains at all, then you must logically agree with what I say [Assertive Right VIII: logic]. If you don't agree, you must be really stupid, so I will start over again until you do understand, and then you will have to agree. Finally, when you do agree with what I'm telling you, and if you have any redeeming qualities at all—which I doubt—then you must care enough to shape yourself up by going along with what I say and behaving accordingly, as any decent, self-respecting, civilized, cultured person should [Assertive Right X: caring]."

In observing manipulators, you will see that they always use this argument, since manipulation is based on the adversary model of conflict resolution—i.e., "If I am right, you must be wrong. Therefore I will prove that I am right!" Hence the assertive response "You may be right, but I'm still going to do it my way" eliminates the manipulator's argument that "he who is right wins" and minimizes any psychological control he or she has over you or your child.

If we scrutinize this manipulative argument about how we should automatically respond, common sense tells us that though we may understand what someone says, this understanding has no connection whatsoever to our behavior. It also tells us that understanding what someone tells us does not mean we have to agree or even disagree with it. There is no intellectual, logical, moral, philosophical, or practical rule that says understanding something means having to either agree or disagree with it. Finally, even if we do understand someone's argument for why we should do something and *do* agree with it, that does not mean we have to behave the way that person wants us to behave. There is no rule that says agreeing with something means having to behave accordingly.

The belief that understanding, agreement, and action must be linked together is so ingrained in Western society and culture that many of my intelligent, highly educated friends and colleagues are upset when I point out this method of placing manipulation in perspective. One of my colleagues said to me, "What you are teaching people just doesn't make sense to me. I can't go along with agreeing with something and then not carrying through with it. If after I had pointed out all the reasons why we should do our research in a particular way, one of my graduate students said, 'You may be right, and I'll go along with it, but I would rather try to do it another way,' I'd kick him out of the graduate program!" My friend thought this situation posed an intellectual dilemma, but in reality it was an emotional one, as so often is the case when one of our cherished beliefs is challenged.

To illustrate this point, I gave him a personal example. I reminded him that his wife was one of the most beautiful, sexy, and intelligent women I knew. I told him that being only human, during the years I had worked with her as a professional colleague, I was tempted many, many times to put the make on her. I pointed out that I did not because of ethical, moral, and practical reasons. I also added that in spite of understanding and agreeing with all these ethical, moral, and practical reasons not to complicate my relationship with her and him, every time we meet I still feel the same way. My colleague roared with laughter, and said, "Now that makes sense! I see what you're driving at. I guess you can understand and agree with something and still not go along with it one hundred percent. Okay, I won't kick the graduate student out!"

In teaching your child how to be assertive with authorities, such as teachers, make sure he or she understands that the three key words are a reminder of how to use verbal skills in putting an assertive response together when someone in authority tries to make him or her feel guilty, foolish, or ignorant. Your child's use of the three key words is a direct assertive response to the manipulator's effort to make him or her kow-tow. The first key word, *understand,* refers to the preface of the Broken Record response (I understand what you're saying, but . . .). It also refers to the most common Self-Disclosure (I don't understand), also used as a preface to Assertive Inquiry (I don't understand. What is it about my . . . that means . . .). The key word *agree* refers to Fogging and Negative Assertion (I agree, you may be right, etc.). The key word *behave* refers to the actual message repeated by Broken Record (. . . but I still want . . .)

The School Situations that Children Most Often Have Trouble With

In teaching your child to be assertive to authority figures at school, remember that he or she is very likely to have to overcome some anxiety. For example, your child may have a fear of looking foolish, a fear that the teacher may really know what's better, or a fear that the teacher or vice-principal or counselor will be unreasonable. The most reliable and effective way of reducing or eliminating our fears, whatever they may be, is to expose ourselves to the situations that cause them and cope well in those situations. The whole basis of psychological behavior therapy is to set things up in such a way that the phobic or fearful client can't help but do well in the fear-producing situation—sort of like shooting fish in a barrel.

That is why the following practice dialogues cover some worst-case situations, however unlikely, in which your child's fears are realized. In these dialogues, most of the school staff are portrayed as graduates of either the Attila the Hun School of Education or the Old Curmudgeon Normal School of Penmanship. While it is highly unlikely that your child will encounter any school staff members like these, such portrayals are useful in allaying a child's worst fears. If your child can cope with this fictional school staff, he or she can certainly deal with the staff in your own school district, most of whom are undoubtedly capable teachers and administrators. The situations used in these dialogues to give your child practice in being assertive are those identified by STAR researchers as the ones that children most commonly have trouble with at school.

Working Out Practical Problems with Teachers

Students often assume that problems in school can't be worked out with school staff, because they perceive the staff as locked into rules and unwilling to negotiate. Consequently, the students assume that their problems cannot be solved in the school setting and retreat to home. In the first of these school-oriented dialogues, your child has to work with a teacher to solve a problem. The particular problem has been selected arbitrarily and is unimportant in itself. Any problem will do, and you may choose a different one if you wish. What is important is to give your child experience in assertive problem solving with school staff.

DIALOGUE 48

Daughter Uses Assertive Problem Solving at School When
Something Goes Wrong
Age level: Seven through thirteen
Setting: Your daughter has walked to school, and when she gets
there she finds that the family dog has followed her. Mom and
dad have both gone to work, and daughter has a test to take in
her first class. She approaches her teacher before class to see what's
the best thing to do.

DAUGHTER: Ms. Priss, I have a problem that I don't know what to do about. [SELF-DISCLOSURE]

TEACHER: What's the problem?

DAUGHTER: It's embarrassing, but my dog, Clemmie, followed me to school today, and if I take her back, I'll miss the test you are giving this morning. [NEGATIVE ASSERTION]

TEACHER: Why don't you scoot down to the vice-principal's office and call your mother to pick her up?

DAUGHTER: I wish I could, but my mother's out for the day. [SELF-DISCLOSURE]

TEACHER: Well, bringing your dog into the classroom is impossible.

DAUGHTER: What is it about bringing Clemmie into class while I take the test that is impossible? [NEGATIVE INQUIRY]

TEACHER: One just does not bring dogs into the classroom.

DAUGHTER: What is it about Clemmie that means she shouldn't be in the classroom while I'm taking the test? [NEGATIVE INQUIRY]

TEACHER: You know what I'm talking about, dear. Dogs . . . well . . . they just make messes everywhere.

DAUGHTER: Oh . . . you mean she might piddle on the floor?

TEACHER: Yes.

DAUGHTER: Clemmie doesn't do that. She's very clean and neat. I think she's a prig. [SELF-DISCLOSURE]

TEACHER: Well, she might get excited and forget herself. Dogs do that, you know.

DAUGHTER: You're right. Dogs do that when they get excited. But I don't think Clemmie will. She's really inhibited. [FOGGING and SELF-DISCLOSURE]

TEACHER: Well, we really can't take the chance. It would upset the whole class, and we have a test to take.

DAUGHTER: I could have her lie right near the door, and move my chair over to be with her. If she got excited, I could take her outside. [WORKABLE COMPROMISE]

TEACHER: No, we just can't have a dog in the classroom.

DAUGHTER: Okay. How about if I sat outside the school with her when I take the test? [WORKABLE COMPROMISE]

TEACHER: It's too chilly out there. You'd catch a cold.

DAUGHTER: I may, but I don't think so. I'm dressed warm. [FOGGING and SELF-DISCLOSURE]

TEACHER: No, we can't have that either.

DAUGHTER: I could go home and take a makeup test tomorrow. [WORKABLE COMPROMISE]

TEACHER: No. If you're not sick, I can't justify a makeup test.

DAUGHTER: I could leave Clemmie outside the school, where she is now, and take my test. I would feel uncomfortable about that, but I don't think she would get into any trouble. [WORKABLE COMPROMISE and SELF-DISCLOSURE]

TEACHER: No, we have to be concerned about our responsibilities to animals. She might wander into the street and get hurt.

DAUGHTER: Do you want me to take her home now? [WORKABLE COMPROMISE]

TEACHER: No . . . After everyone is in class, you had better bring her in here and move your chair over by the door.

DAUGHTER: Okay. I don't think she will be a problem. [SELF-DIS-CLOSURE]

In the next dialogue, your daughter has to deal assertively with a teacher who wants something unreasonable from her. Although a real-life dialogue with this amount of manipulation is unlikely, an inexperienced youngster may very well fear that something like this would happen.

DIALOGUE 49

Daughter Says No to an Unreasonable Request by Her Teacher
Age level: Seven through seventeen
Setting: A friendly teacher asks your daughter to help sort papers during a study period instead of studying. The dialogue opens with the teacher approaching your daughter.

TEACHER: I need some help.
DAUGHTER: Oh? How can I help you, Ms. Nice?
TEACHER: I need some papers sorted before the next class period.
DAUGHTER: How long do you think it will take?
TEACHER: If we both work fast, we can get it done before the bell rings.
DAUGHTER: Gee, Ms. Nice, I feel really uncomfortable saying no, but I'm studying for a test this afternoon. [SELF-DISCLOSURE]
TEACHER: Oh? What test are you studying for?
DAUGHTER: Math.
TEACHER: For a second there I thought you couldn't help me. What a shock that was!
DAUGHTER: I don't understand. I have to study for a math test. [SELF-DISCLOSURE]
TEACHER: I thought for a moment it was an important test. A good-looking girl like you doesn't have to worry about math.
DAUGHTER: Maybe, but I would feel really uncomfortable if I didn't study for it. [FOGGING and SELF-DISCLOSURE]
TEACHER: You take tests too seriously. Especially unimportant things like math. Don't worry about it!

DAUGHTER: I know I shouldn't worry, but I do. And I will feel very uncomfortable if I don't study for my test. [FOGGING, SELF-DISCLOSURE, and BROKEN RECORD]

TEACHER: I know you. You will do fine without last-minute studying.

DAUGHTER: You may be right, Ms. Nice, I probably will pass, but I will feel really uncomfortable if I don't study. [FOGGING, SELF-DIS-CLOSURE, and BROKEN RECORD]

TEACHER: You are one of the good students. I thought I could count on you.

DAUGHTER: Thank you, Ms. Nice. I feel really bad about saying no. But I would be very uncomfortable if I didn't study for my math test. [FOGGING, SELF-DISCLOSURE, and BROKEN RECORD]

TEACHER: What am I going to do? I thought you and I were friends.

DAUGHTER: I do like you, Ms. Nice, and I really wish I could help you. How about some of the other girls, like Ann or Judy? [SELF-DIS-CLOSURE and WORKABLE COMPROMISE]

TEACHER: Those two really do need to study! I can't ask them to help me.

DAUGHTER: Let me go to the other study hall for a minute. Jimmy doesn't have a test this afternoon. [WORKABLE COMPROMISE]

TEACHER: Hmmm . . . That's a good idea. I'll do that myself. Thanks.

DAUGHTER: Sure.

In the next dialogue your daughter has to deal with a real problem that may place her at an academic disadvantage. Recent behavioral studies have shown that some teachers discriminate against girls. These teachers favor boys by allowing them to answer questions from the teacher spontaneously, and follow up on boys' responses to ensure they learn, but do not do the same thing for girls.

DIALOGUE 50

Daughter Assertively Asks for Equal Treatment in Class
Age level: Seven through ten
Setting: Your daughter is in class and the teacher is asking students questions about their last geography lesson.

TEACHER: Now who knows where Chicago is?

BILLY: (Shouting out) Ohio!

TEACHER: No, Billy, what's the state right alongside Ohio?

BILLY: Illinois!

TEACHER: Right, Billy! Who knows where Pascagoula is?

MIKE: (Shouting out) Florida.

TEACHER: No, Mike. Mary?

MARY: In Georgia?

TEACHER: No.

SUE: (Raises her hand.)

TEACHER: Sue?

SUE: Mississippi.

TEACHER: Right. Mike, where's Mississippi in relation to Florida?

MIKE: To the west, on the Gulf.

TEACHER: Good boy. Now where is Sacramento?

DAUGHTER: (Speaking out) In northern California.

TEACHER: We don't shout out in this class. We quietly raise our hands like ladies.

DAUGHTER: Ms. Peoria, I don't understand. What is it about speaking out and answering that's wrong? [SELF-DISCLOSURE and NEGATIVE INQUIRY]

TEACHER: One does not just shout out answers. One raises one's hand quietly until one is called upon.

DAUGHTER: But I still don't understand, Ms. Peoria. Billy and Mike shouted out their answers. What is it about my giving an answer, when I know it, that is wrong? [SELF-DISCLOSURE and NEGATIVE INQUIRY]

TEACHER: As I said before, we quietly raise our hands like ladies and wait to be called upon.

DAUGHTER: I still don't understand. Do you want Mike and Billy to quietly raise their hands too? [SELF-DISCLOSURE and WORKABLE COMPROMISE]

TEACHER: If you keep asking these silly questions, I will have to send you to the principal's office.

DAUGHTER: I still don't understand why it is okay for Billy and Mike to give their answers, but not me.

TEACHER: Do you want to go to the principal's office, young lady?

DAUGHTER: I would rather stay here, but maybe he can tell me why it's okay for Billy and Mike to shout out their answers and I can't say anything when I know the answer. [SELF-DISCLOSURE]

TEACHER: Do you want to act like a ruffian and not know how to be a lady?

DAUGHTER: (Not being baited into a manipulative argument) I still don't understand why it is okay for Billy and Mike to give their answers, but not me. [SELF-DISCLOSURE]

TEACHER: I'm going to have to have a talk with your parents.

DAUGHTER: I wish you would, because I still don't understand. What is it about my giving an answer, when I know it, that is wrong? [SELF-DISCLOSURE and NEGATIVE INQUIRY]

TEACHER: If I let you do that, you will set a bad example for all the rest of the girls.

DAUGHTER: I don't understand. What is it about my giving answers that will set a bad example for the rest of the girls? [SELF-DISCLOSURE and NEGATIVE INQUIRY]

TEACHER: If you don't know, I'm not going to bother correcting your manners in the future.

DAUGHTER: Okay. Does that mean I can give an answer when I think I know it, like Billy and Mike? [WORKABLE COMPROMISE]

TEACHER: If you must!

DAUGHTER: Okay. Was I right? Sacramento is in northern California?

TEACHER: Yes.

SUE: (Holds up her hand.)

TEACHER: Yes, Sue?

SUE: Ms. Peoria, can I give an answer when I think I know it, too?

Assertively Coping with School Officials

Few children feel comfortable asking teachers or staff for help or permission to do something different. They don't even feel they have the right to do this. The ability to act on one's wishes is important. Children who cannot do this are often turned off by the school regimen, becoming passive students who do only what's required. If you want your child to be interested in academic learning, give him or her practice in asking for learning experiences that are personally interesting, using the next dialogue. In it, your son needs permission from the vice-principal to do something he wants. Again, for the sake of practice and experience in dealing with possible manipulation, the school staff member is portrayed as very manipulative.

DIALOGUE 51

Son Gets Permission to Do Something New and Different at School
Age level: Eleven through seventeen
Setting: Your son has to get permission to take a particular course. The vice-principal, having attended Harvard Law School for a year before going into education, has a reputation for finding reasons to say no to anything. Your son knocks on his open office door and speaks:

SON: Mr. Kant, can I speak to you for a minute or two?

VICE-PRINCIPAL: Come in and sit down. What is it you wanted to see me about, young feller?

SON: I need your permission to take an art class instead of Woodshop Two.

VICE-PRINCIPAL: You should finish the whole year of woodshop. It's a fine course. You learn a lot of practical things there. Took it myself when I was your age. Use what I learned there all the time.

SON: I really like art and I want to do wood sculpture instead of woodworking.

VICE-PRINCIPAL: What do you want to do something artsy-crafty like that for? It will never be helpful to you!

SON: Maybe not, but I'd still like to take wood sculpting instead of Woodshop Two. [FOGGING and BROKEN RECORD]

VICE-PRINCIPAL: Let me tell you something, son. It's much more important to study practical things in life than to take things that are fun.

SON: I'm sure you are right, Mr. Kant, but I'd still like to take an art class to fulfill the shop requirement. [FOGGING and BROKEN RECORD]

VICE-PRINCIPAL: This is really unusual. It may cause a problem. I'm not sure this is the right thing to do.

SON: I don't understand, Mr. Kant. What is it about my wanting to substitute Art Three for Woodshop Two that will cause a problem? [NEGATIVE INQUIRY]

VICE-PRINCIPAL: Art Three is mostly a girls' class. Won't you feel strange being the only boy there?

SON: I probably will feel strange at first, Mr. Kant, but I really want to learn about wood sculpture. Is there anything else about my wanting to take wood sculpture that is a problem? [FOGGING, BROKEN RECORD, and NEGATIVE INQUIRY]

VICE-PRINCIPAL: Well, I can't okay this unless one of the art teachers says it's okay.

SON: I've asked Mr. Flowers if he would okay my doing wood sculpting in Art Three, and he said it would be all right.

VICE-PRINCIPAL: (Grumbling to himself) He would.

SON: Is there anything else about my taking Art Three that would cause a problem? [NEGATIVE INQUIRY]

VICE-PRINCIPAL: There would be a big mess in the art studio with you chipping away at wood.

SON: You're right, Mr. Kant, but Mr. Flowers said that I could take time before class ends to clean up, just like we do in shop. [FOGGING and WORKABLE COMPROMISE]

VICE-PRINCIPAL: (Silent)

SON: Is there anything else about my taking Art Three that would cause a problem? [NEGATIVE INQUIRY]

VICE-PRINCIPAL: You will need a special bench and tools. I can't okay this unless you have them.

SON: You're right, Mr. Kant. Mr. Flowers said I could use the teacher's bench at the head of the class, and I have my own set of chisels. [FOGGING and WORKABLE COMPROMISE]

VICE-PRINCIPAL: You would have to store your tools in the art studio, and someone might steal them. The school can't be responsible for them.

SON: That might happen. If it does, I'll have to get another set. Is there anything else that might cause a problem? [FOGGING, WORKABLE COMPROMISE, and NEGATIVE INQUIRY]

VICE-PRINCIPAL: If the rest of the students hear about this, everybody will want to get out of Woodshop Two.

SON: I won't tell anybody if you don't. [WORKABLE COMPROMISE]

VICE-PRINCIPAL: Do you like photography? I could get you into photography instead of Art Three.

SON: Thank you, Mr. Kant. I feel you are trying to help me. But I really would like to learn wood sculpture. [SELF-DISCLOSURE and BROKEN RECORD]

VICE-PRINCIPAL: How about Glee Club? I could make a special exception and have that fulfill the Woodshop Two requirement.

SON: Thank you, Mr. Kant, but I'm a lousy singer, and I really want to learn wood sculpture. [NEGATIVE ASSERTION and BROKEN RECORD]

VICE-PRINCIPAL: I don't usually do this.

SON: I'm sure you don't, Mr. Kant. [FOGGING]

VICE-PRINCIPAL: Are you sure this is what you want? I don't want to see you coming back next month asking to get back into Woodshop Two!

SON: I'm sure. [SELF-DISCLOSURE]

VICE-PRINCIPAL: Okay then. Get the papers from my secretary and fill them out and I'll sign them.

SON: I really appreciate this, Mr. Kant.

VICE-PRINCIPAL: Sure. Sure. Just doing my job.

SON: (Leaving) Thanks!

In the next dialogue your son has to confront a referee in a soccer game. One player on the opposing side keeps kicking your son in the shins quite blatantly, and the referee has yet to call a foul. In confronting the referee, your son is not well advised to challenge, threaten, bluster, or even complain. Instead, he should maintain a neutral, nonaccusatory stance by pointing out a problem that everyone is concerned about, the safety of the players.

DIALOGUE 52

Son Assertively Asks for Help from the Athletic Staff
Age level: Eleven through seventeen
Setting: Between plays, your son decides to bring an opposing player's repeated fouls and poor sportsmanship to the referee's attention.

Son: Ref, I'd like to speak to you for a second.

Referee: You are holding up the game.

Son: I'm sure I am, but I'd like to speak to you for a sec. [FOGGING and BROKEN RECORD]

Referee: You have five seconds to get back in position or I'm calling a delay of game on your team.

Son: You can do that if you want, Ref, but I'll feel better if you are aware of a potentially dangerous situation where someone may be injured. [FOGGING and SELF-DISCLOSURE]

Referee: This is the last time I'm warning you to get back into position.

Son: Okay, Ref, I'll go, but will you agree that I tried to bring to your attention a dangerous and unsportsmanlike situation in case someone is injured? [WORKABLE COMPROMISE]

Referee: (Hesitating for a moment) What do you mean?

Son: Number thirty-two on the opposing team has fouled me deliberately on the last six plays.

Referee: What has he done?

Son: Kicked me in the shins to make me back off or trip.

Referee: I didn't see any fouls. Are you saying I'm looking the other way?

Son: I'm sure you didn't see them. That's why I want to bring a potentially dangerous situation to your attention. [FOGGING and BROKEN RECORD]

Referee: And you want me to pay attention to you just because your opposing player is a bit aggressive? He's supposed to be!

Son: You're right, Ref, he is. I just want to bring a potentially dangerous situation to your attention in case someone is injured. [FOGGING and BROKEN RECORD]

Referee: I have two whole teams to watch.

Son: You do, Ref. But I just want to bring a potentially dangerous situation to your attention in case someone is injured. [FOGGING and BROKEN RECORD]

Referee: Do you want to file a formal complaint?

Son: No. I just want to bring a potentially dangerous situation to your attention in case someone is injured. [BROKEN RECORD]

REFEREE: Do you want me to call both coaches over here and talk to them?

SON: No, Ref. I just want to bring a potentially dangerous situation to your attention in case someone is injured. [BROKEN RECORD]

REFEREE: Okay. I'll keep my eye on him.

SON: Thanks, Ref. I appreciate it. [SELF-DISCLOSURE]

Assertively Coping with Mistakes and Poor Decisions at School

All children break rules at some point, and unfortunately they cope with their mistakes as badly as we adults do with ours. They become very defensive when called on the carpet by school administrators, and handle it poorly. Children do foolish things sometimes just for the hell of it, but doing dumb things and learning from them are part of the process of growing up.

Some of the dumb things I and my contemporaries did in school are among my favorite memories. I remember one time when my younger brother and I were in high school together in the 1950s, during the McCarthy era. It was spring assembly day, and a state senator was going to speak to all 1,000 students and their families seated in the sports stadium. My brother got bored waiting for the event to begin, so he walked up to the microphone on the temporary stage, with the dignitaries and school administration seated behind him, and said to the crowd: "Party members, friends, and fellow travelers, we are gathered here today to celebrate the founding of the Communist party and its role in the history of mankind. Let me remind you of our gallant predecessors who have gone before: Marx, Lenin, Trotsky, Dzerzhinski, heroes all!"

At first his audience reacted with a stunned silence. Then they began to laugh, all 3,000 plus, as two football players marched him off the stage. Even the state senator was laughing—political speakers always like someone to warm up their audience beforehand. I always envied my brother for that, even if he had to take a dressing down from the vice-principal the next day.

In the next dialogue your son has to speak to the vice-principal after breaking the rules, but without letting himself become defensive or argumentative.

DIALOGUE 53

Son Faces the Vice-Principal Assertively and Respectfully When a Rule Is Broken
Age level: Twelve through seventeen
Setting: Your son reports to the vice-principal's office on Monday morning, after cutting class on Friday.

SON: (Knocking on VP's door) Ms. Rules?
VICE-PRINCIPAL: Yes?
SON: I'm supposed to report to you. Your secretary isn't here.
VICE-PRINCIPAL: Let me see. . . . Yes. Sit down. You cut your last class on Friday without permission.
SON: That's right, Ms. Rules. It was a dumb thing to cut class without getting permission first. [FOGGING and NEGATIVE ASSERTION]
VICE-PRINCIPAL: Do you know why we require that you get permission first?
SON: Not exactly, but I guess to keep everyone from cutting class on Friday afternoon. [SELF-DISCLOSURE]
VICE-PRINCIPAL: Right. If we don't insist upon it, we might as well close down the school on Friday afternoon.
SON: You're right, Ms. Rules. It was dumb to cut class without permission. I feel foolish sitting here now. [FOGGING, NEGATIVE ASSERTION, and SELF-DISCLOSURE]
VICE-PRINCIPAL: Why did you cut class?
SON: I don't know. It was just a spur-of-the-moment thing, and dumb. [SELF-DISCLOSURE and NEGATIVE ASSERTION]
VICE-PRINCIPAL: You are not going to get anywhere in life if you aren't more disciplined.
SON: You're right, Ms. Rules. [FOGGING]
VICE-PRINCIPAL: Doing things on a whim makes other people think you need to improve your character.
SON: You're right. It certainly makes me look as if I don't have much character. [FOGGING]

VICE-PRINCIPAL: I didn't say that! I said that it makes you look as if you could improve your character and be more disciplined in school affairs.

SON: I guess I misinterpreted you. [NEGATIVE ASSERTION]

VICE-PRINCIPAL: You certainly did! Now what are you going to do about making up this cut?

SON: I don't know. What can I do? [SELF-DISCLOSURE]

VICE-PRINCIPAL: I want you to apologize to your teacher for not showing up for class.

SON: I would be happy to do that. Anything else? [SELF-DISCLOSURE]

VICE-PRINCIPAL: No. This is the first time you cut class. You aren't going to make a habit out of this, are you?

SON: I hope not. [SELF-DISCLOSURE]

VICE-PRINCIPAL: Well, if you do, you'll be back in this office again! Remember what I just told you about character and academic discipline being the foundation of success in life.

SON: Yes, ma'am.

In the next dialogue your daughter has to account for making a poor decision. Last night, instead of doing her homework first thing after dinner, she decided to watch a movie on TV. After the movie, she was too sleepy to do her homework.

DIALOGUE 54

Daughter Copes with a Teacher after Doing Something Dumb
Age level: Seven through seventeen
Setting: Your daughter approaches the teacher to explain why she has no homework to turn in.

DAUGHTER: Ms. Rigids?

TEACHER: Yes?

DAUGHTER: Last night I did something really dumb. [NEGATIVE ASSERTION]

TEACHER: What's that?

DAUGHTER: I feel like a jerk having to tell you this. Last night I started to watch a movie on TV instead of doing my homework right after dinner, and after the movie I fell asleep. [SELF-DISCLOSURE]

TEACHER: So you didn't do your homework?

DAUGHTER: No, and I feel bad about it. [SELF-DISCLOSURE]

TEACHER: That's not the way to get a good grade in this class—or even a passing one.

DAUGHTER: You're right, Ms. Rigids, and I feel bad about it. [FOGGING and SELF-DISCLOSURE]

TEACHER: How come you people always find some excuse not to do your homework?

DAUGHTER: I don't know. [SELF-DISCLOSURE]

TEACHER: That's not a good answer!

DAUGHTER: You're right. It isn't. [FOGGING]

TEACHER: What am I supposed to do when students don't do what they're supposed to do?

DAUGHTER: I don't know, Ms. Rigids. And I feel bad about it. [FOGGING and SELF-DISCLOSURE]

TEACHER: You aren't going to get away with this, you know!

DAUGHTER: You're right. I shouldn't get away with it. Do you want me to do it tonight along with tomorrow's assignment? [FOGGING and WORKABLE COMPROMISE]

TEACHER: No. That's too much work for one night.

DAUGHTER: Then what do you want me to do? [WORKABLE COMPROMISE]

TEACHER: Do it on the weekend and hand it in Monday.

DAUGHTER: Okay. I still feel bad about this. [SELF-DISCLOSURE]

TEACHER: Don't worry about it. All of us do dumb things once in a while.

DAUGHTER: Okay.

Improving Academic Performance by Assertively Asking for Help in Understanding and Learning

In the next dialogue your daughter's teacher is portrayed in the worst possible light—as a very defensive, manipulative person. In all likelihood your child's actual teacher is not that way at all. But to teach children how to be assertive to an authority figure, you must teach them how to cope with their most unrealistic fears of what may happen if they are assertive to an authority figure. This training teaches them not to become defensive if their worst fears are realized and they are accused of being lazy, stupid, or worse, but to persist in requesting clarification of what is to be learned. In reality, most teachers are pleased when their students take enough interest in what is being taught to ask for clarification.

DIALOGUE 55

Daughter Gets a Teacher to Explain Things Better When She Does Not Understand
Age level: Seven through seventeen
Setting: Your daughter does not understand a particular point the teacher is making on the blackboard. She decides to ask the teacher to clarify it.

DAUGHTER: (Holds up hand.)

TEACHER: Yes?

DAUGHTER: Ms. Vague, I don't understand what you just talked about. I'd appreciate it if you would go over it again. [SELF-DISCLOSURE]

TEACHER: What don't you understand?

DAUGHTER: The whole thing.

TEACHER: I've spent the last twenty minutes explaining it all to the class. Can't you be more specific?

DAUGHTER: I wish I could be more specific too, but I don't understand it right from the beginning. Would you please explain it again? [SELF-DISCLOSURE and BROKEN RECORD]

TEACHER: That will take another twenty minutes and our class time is valuable.

DAUGHTER: It is valuable, Ms. Vague, but I'd still appreciate it if you would explain it again. [FOGGING and BROKEN RECORD]

TEACHER: Are you the only one who doesn't understand? Does anyone else need this explained again? (The class is silent.) It seems that you are the only one who didn't understand this!

DAUGHTER: I'm sure that's true, but I'd appreciate it if you would explain it again. [FOGGING and BROKEN RECORD]

TEACHER: That would be a waste of class time!

DAUGHTER: It could be, but I'd appreciate it if you would explain it again. [FOGGING and BROKEN RECORD]

TEACHER: Do you want me to hold up the whole class just because you don't understand something? That's unreasonable and selfish.

DAUGHTER: It may seem unreasonable and selfish, but I'd appreciate it if you would explain it again. [FOGGING and BROKEN RECORD]

TEACHER: If you daydream during an explanation while the rest of the class pays attention, you can't expect special treatment.

DAUGHTER: (Not bothering to deny a false accusation) You're right, Ms. Vague. If I daydreamed while the rest of the class paid attention, I shouldn't get special attention, but I'd appreciate it if you would explain it again. [FOGGING and BROKEN RECORD]

TEACHER: You should pay more attention when I explain things on the blackboard.

DAUGHTER: You're right, Ms. Vague, I should, but I'd sure appreciate your explaining it another time. [FOGGING and BROKEN RECORD]

TEACHER: Okay. But this time pay attention.

DAUGHTER: Thank you, Ms. Vague, I will.

In the next dialogue your son needs a teacher's help in clarifying an assignment. This is particularly important because children often do not understand assignments and what they have to do but are reluctant to ask for help for fear they will look stupid. It is a wise rule of thumb during elementary school to check occasionally on your child's understanding of homework assignments. If your child shows poor comprehension of assignment instructions, the following dialogue will help him or her clarify what is supposed to be done *before* trying to do it. This will prevent poor academic performance caused not by a lack of ability but by a lack of assertiveness in obtaining a clear understanding of what is wanted.

DIALOGUE 56

*Son Asks for Help from a Teacher Despite Fear of Looking
Stupid*
Age level: Eleven through seventeen
*Setting: Your son approaches his teacher at the end of class to ask
for help in clarifying a class assignment.*

SON: Mr. Busy?
TEACHER: Yes?
SON: I need some help from you on the class assignment.
TEACHER: I don't have any time now to spare.
SON: I'm sure you don't. When can I get some help from you? [FOG-
GING and WORKABLE COMPROMISE]
TEACHER: I'm overloaded with work now.
SON: I guess you are, but I'd still like to get some help from you.
[FOGGING and SELF-DISCLOSURE]
TEACHER: You don't need any help from me. You're a good student.
You can do that assignment yourself.
SON: I wish you were right, but I would feel really uncomfortable doing
it without asking you about some things first. [FOGGING and SELF-
DISCLOSURE]
TEACHER: I'm just too busy. Do you know what all the teachers have
to do now besides teaching class?
SON: No, I don't. [SELF-DISCLOSURE]
TEACHER: We have to attend a staff development meeting twice a week
for the next ten weeks to become sensitized to students' needs.
SON: I didn't know that. [SELF-DISCLOSURE]
TEACHER: Of course you didn't. I just told you. That's why I don't have
any time to go over the class assignment with you now.
SON: Okay. How about after the next class on Thursday? [WORK-
ABLE COMPROMISE]
TEACHER: Thursday is one of the days for the staff development semi-
nar.
SON: Okay. How about after next Tuesday's class? [WORKABLE
COMPROMISE]
TEACHER: Tuesday is the same thing. That's why I can't help you now.

SON: Oh ... Then how about tomorrow? I can see you during my study hall at one. [WORKABLE COMPROMISE]

TEACHER: Let me look at my schedule. ... No. When's your next study hall after that?

SON: Friday at the same time. [WORKABLE COMPROMISE]

TEACHER: Okay, Friday at one.

SON: Swell. Thanks, Mr. Busy.

Many students do not understand how they learn, and thus aren't able to view their learning process in perspective. The great majority of us learn through our mistakes, and your children are probably no exception. Unfortunately, most students think performance evaluation—such as grades—is a gauge of their natural abilities. They have no idea that if they learn how to learn, their academic performance will improve. When I was a young teenager, and into athletics as most young males of my age were then, the most amazing principle I learned was that natural talent and an unconditioned body were poor indicators of athletic ability. In the same way that I naïvely confused raw physical talent with athletic performance, most children confuse natural academic ability with academic performance. They assume that tests and papers measure their natural aptitude—i.e., they are good in a subject, or they are not, so it doesn't matter much how they try. Consequently, few students take the trouble to review their mistakes and learn better ways of doing things.

In the next dialogue your daughter decides there must be a better way to learn, and asks a teacher how to do better.

DIALOGUE 57

Daughter Asks a Teacher for More Academic Feedback to Learn How to Do Better
Age level: Eleven through seventeen
Setting: Your daughter is upset with the grade she got on a term paper. She decides to talk to her teacher about it. At the end of class, she approaches him.

DAUGHTER: Mr. Reader, I'd like to talk about my paper on the FBI, if you have the time now.

TEACHER: Sure. What about it?

DAUGHTER: I felt that I had done a good job. I spent a lot of time on this paper, and was very disappointed when I got a C-minus. [SELF-DISCLOSURE]

TEACHER: Well, that's all it deserved.

DAUGHTER: I don't understand, Mr. Reader. What is it about my paper that made it deserve only a C-minus? [NEGATIVE INQUIRY]

TEACHER: Well, for one thing, it was too long. You were supposed to write a ten-page essay, and this is sixteen pages long.

DAUGHTER: I don't understand. If you had said the paper should be limited to sixteen pages, would it still have deserved only a C-minus? [NEGATIVE INQUIRY]

TEACHER: Well . . . probably. You didn't say anything in sixteen pages that you couldn't have said in ten.

DAUGHTER: I was too wordy? [NEGATIVE INQUIRY]

TEACHER: Yes. Part of the purpose of writing term papers is to learn to write, and you could write much more concisely with some thought and planning.

DAUGHTER: Is there anything else about my paper that made it deserve only a C-minus? [NEGATIVE INQUIRY prompt]

TEACHER: Yes. You made a lot of assumptions about why the FBI's powers are limited, and why it can't automatically operate in a state's jurisdiction.

DAUGHTER: What is it about saying that Congress limited FBI powers, because of traditional distrust of national police going back to colonial times, that was wrong? [NEGATIVE INQUIRY]

TEACHER: You may very well be right, but you didn't say that your assumption was a hypothesis or a theory. You wrote it as if it were fact, and you had no sources to back you up.

DAUGHTER: I felt that was an important idea. How do I say that without making my paper deserve only a C-minus? [SELF-DISCLOSURE]

TEACHER: Simple. You say, "One interesting hypothesis is . . ." and then say the same thing you did.

DAUGHTER: That's all that was needed?

TEACHER: That's it.

DAUGHTER: Wow! Is there anything else that made my paper deserve only a C-minus? [NEGATIVE INQUIRY prompt]

TEACHER: An A student checks for spelling errors. You had four that you didn't catch.

DAUGHTER: My problem is that I'm a lousy speller. I read it and it looks okay. I would have to look up every word in my paper. [NEGATIVE ASSERTION]

TEACHER: That's one way of becoming a good speller. Or you could have someone you trust proofread it for you to catch errors you miss.

DAUGHTER: Gosh, I must be dumb! I never thought of that. I always felt that was cheating. [NEGATIVE ASSERTION and SELF-DIS-CLOSURE]

TEACHER: Of course not. Use all the help you can get to learn and perform well.

DAUGHTER: Anything else? [NEGATIVE INQUIRY prompt]

TEACHER: That's about it.

DAUGHTER: I would like to rewrite my term paper and give it back to you to see how well I could do following your advice. Would you do that for me? [WORKABLE COMPROMISE]

TEACHER: I can't change your grade, you know. That wouldn't be fair to everyone else.

DAUGHTER: You're right, Mr. Reader. It's not fair. It was really dumb of me not to ask you these things before I wrote the paper, and I feel really bad about it. But I can't learn to do it better unless I can correct the things I'm doing wrong. Will you let me try? [FOGGING, SELF-DISCLOSURE, and WORKABLE COMPROMISE]

TEACHER: Okay, but don't get so upset. It's only a term paper. That's only twenty percent of your grade. You will be writing lots of papers before you get out of school.

DAUGHTER: Swell. Thanks.

Teachers are human like everyone else. They sometimes make mistakes or are imprecise. That does not mean they are not good teachers. To interact effectively with teachers, your child needs to perceive them not as supermen and -women but as special and helpful human beings who can teach him or her even if they are less than perfect.

In the next dialogue your son decides that what the teacher said in class is confusing and has to be clarified.

DIALOGUE 58

Son Learns More by Asking a Teacher to Clarify Things
Age level: Eleven through seventeen
Setting: Your son thinks his teacher has made a mistake in class.
He goes up to the teacher after class to find out diplomatically
what's wrong.

SON: Ms. Smart?

TEACHER: Yes?

SON: This may be dumb, but I'm a bit confused. You said today that Magellan was the first one to circumnavigate the globe. [NEGATIVE ASSERTION and SELF-DISCLOSURE]

TEACHER: Yes. That's true.

SON: That's what's confusing me. In last night's reading homework, the text said that Magellan died in the Philippine Islands before his ship got back to Europe. That's just a little more than two-thirds of the way. [SELF-DISCLOSURE]

TEACHER: That's true.

SON: That's what's confusing me. What you said and what the book said can't both be true. [SELF-DISCLOSURE]

TEACHER: Well, Magellan is given credit for circumnavigating the globe because it was his idea, his ship, and his expedition that accomplished it, even if he didn't make it personally.

SON: So Magellan didn't really circumnavigate the globe, but his surviving crew members did?

TEACHER: Technically that's true.

SON: What's so terrible about giving the names of the crew members who actually did circumnavigate the globe, instead of Magellan? [NEGATIVE INQUIRY]

TEACHER: Well, we probably don't know their names anymore, and people find it easier to give credit to the person in charge. History has been criticized a lot for that lately.

SON: Okay, then what's so terrible about saying, "The first people to circumnavigate the globe were Magellan's crew, even though we don't know their names anymore"? [NEGATIVE INQUIRY]

TEACHER: Nothing, except we would sound a little silly saying, "The first people to circle the earth did it in Magellan's ship, but we don't know who they all were." So we say that Magellan did it. At least we know his name. But to tell the truth, nowadays we're really not sure that Magellan's crew *were* the first ones to circumnavigate the globe. There is some indication that the early sailors from the Mediterranean area, perhaps the Egyptians or the Phoenicians, may have, and it's quite likely that the early Chinese did.

SON: Again, I don't understand. What's so bad about saying that in a history text? [SELF-DISCLOSURE and NEGATIVE INQUIRY]

TEACHER: We have only indications that the Middle Eastern sailors did, not hard evidence. As for China, Western historians usually considered Chinese history a collection of mythical stories. So even if the Chinese were first, it was a lot easier to credit Magellan because we knew that he, or at least his crew, actually did it.

SON: This is a lot more complicated than the textbook says it is.

TEACHER: It is. That's what makes it fun to learn if you're interested.

SON: I am. [SELF-DISCLOSURE]

TEACHER: If you're really interested in these kinds of historic details, I can give you the names of a couple of really good books in the public library.

SON: Thanks. I'd like that. [SELF-DISCLOSURE]

Getting Help from Experts

Many pupils hesitate to ask for help because they make the childish assumption that asking for help means there must be something wrong with them. The next dialogue deals directly with a fear that your child may have. Without an assertive attitude about requesting help from other people, he or she is likely to assume that one has to prove that one deserves to be helped. In this dialogue the intermediary person your daughter first talks to does not understand that one is entitled to help without having to justify every request. Your daughter is called upon to do so by a school nurse, and has to stick to her guns about keeping her personal life private.

DIALOGUE 59

Daughter Assertively Asks for Personal Help at School
Age level: Eleven through seventeen
Setting: Your daughter wants some counseling about problems affecting her schoolwork and decides to talk to the nurse about getting an appointment with the school psychologist.

NURSE: Come on in. What's wrong with you?

DAUGHTER: Nothing really, Ms. Butcher. I want to see the school psychologist for counseling.

NURSE: If you want to see the psychologist, there must be something wrong with you. What is it?

DAUGHTER: I don't know. I just want to talk to the psychologist. [SELF-DISCLOSURE and BROKEN RECORD]

NURSE: Well, let's have it.

DAUGHTER: I don't know. I just want to talk to the psychologist [SELF-DISCLOSURE and BROKEN RECORD]

NURSE: You can't get an appointment unless there's something wrong. Her time is valuable.

DAUGHTER: I'm sure it is. But I still want to talk to the psychologist. [FOGGING and BROKEN RECORD]

NURSE: Well, I can't send you to her unless you talk to me first.

DAUGHTER: I don't understand. What is it about my wanting to talk only to the psychologist that is wrong? [SELF-DISCLOSURE and NEGATIVE INQUIRY]

NURSE: If we let everyone speak to the psychologist whenever they felt like having a chat, she would be overloaded and nobody would get help.

DAUGHTER: I'm sure you're right, but I still want to speak to the psychologist. [FOGGING and BROKEN RECORD]

NURSE: We're getting nowhere here. Why don't you want to tell me what's going on?

DAUGHTER: I just feel uncomfortable about certain things. [SELF-DISCLOSURE]

NURSE: What things?

DAUGHTER: I want to speak to the psychologist about them. [BROKEN RECORD]

NURSE: Don't you trust me?

DAUGHTER: I'm sure it must seem that way, but I just want to speak to the psychologist. [FOGGING and BROKEN RECORD]

NURSE: That's unreasonable of you. I told you why you should speak to me first. You may be wasting the psychologist's valuable time. She has a lot of students to see.

DAUGHTER: I'm sure you're right, but I still want to speak to the psychologist. [FOGGING and BROKEN RECORD]

NURSE: Okay, but I sure hope you're more willing to talk about what's bothering you with her.

DAUGHTER: I do too. [SELF-DISCLOSURE]

NURSE: Take this slip to Ms. Ego's office and make an appointment.

DAUGHTER: Okay. Thanks.

NURSE: Humph!

Most children are intimidated by expertise and afraid to ask questions. Asking would reveal their ignorance, and this might be pointed out to them in front of their friends and peers. In the next dialogue your daughter has to assertively deal with two experts, one of whom tries to monopolize the conversation even though your daughter wants to learn something.

DIALOGUE 60

Daughter Learns Something New Even Though a So-called Expert Tries to Intimidate Her
Age level: Eleven through seventeen
Setting: Your daughter and a friend are walking through the exhibit booths set up in the school gym on Career Choice Day. Your daughter's friend stops to talk to the counselor at the business-career booth. The friend is bright and seems to know a lot about this area. She and the counselor get into a technical discussion about business machines. Your daughter is left out of the discussion, but this career area interests her, and she decides to see if she can learn something about it.

FRIEND: Hi, Mr. Ops.

COUNSELOR: Hello.

FRIEND: Is that the new Zenword processor?

COUNSELOR: Yes. It was loaned it to us for Career Choice Day.

FRIEND: Is it the same as the Leadingword processor?

COUNSELOR: No. It's much faster and sets a lot of things up for you automatically.

FRIEND: Does Zenword justify more easily than the Leadingword machine?

COUNSELOR: Yes, much more.

DAUGHTER: I don't understand, Mr. Ops. What does *justify* mean? [SELF-DISCLOSURE]

FRIEND: Oh, you don't need to know that. You're not into business applications.

DAUGHTER: You're right, I'm not. But it sounds interesting. What does *justify* mean? [FOGGING, SELF-DISCLOSURE, and BROKEN RECORD]

FRIEND: It just means to line up the margins in a special way.

DAUGHTER: I don't understand. What do you mean "line up the margins in a special way"? [SELF-DISCLOSURE]

FRIEND: Like right justification or left justification, or centering, or proportional printing. It's too complicated to explain to you.

DAUGHTER: I'm sure it is complicated, but I would like to know what you're both talking about. [FOGGING, SELF-DISCLOSURE, and BROKEN RECORD]

FRIEND: If you want to know, you should take Keyboarding One.

DAUGHTER: I'm sure I could learn it that way, but I'd like to understand what you're both talking about now. [FOGGING, SELF-DISCLOSURE, and BROKEN RECORD]

FRIEND: It would be impossible to explain it all to you now.

DAUGHTER: [Note: Whenever someone tells you something is impossible, automatically translate *impossible* to mean difficult.] I'm sure it would be difficult, but I'd appreciate it if you would explain what you are talking about. [FOGGING, SELF-DISCLOSURE, and BROKEN RECORD]

FRIEND: You wouldn't understand it.

DAUGHTER: Perhaps not, but I'd still appreciate it if you two explained it to me. [FOGGING, SELF-DISCLOSURE, and BROKEN RE-CORD]

COUNSELOR: Here, let me give you a demonstration. It's not that complicated. Let's print out a sample text with ordinary left justification, the way correspondence is usually typed. Then we can print it out with right justification, where both margins are straight and even, and then we'll print out the same thing with proportional printing, the way things look in a printed book.

DAUGHTER: Terrific. Thanks, Mr. Ops. I'd like that. [SELF-DISCLO-SURE]

Identifying and Then Solving Personal Problems with Teachers and Staff

In dialogues 61 and 62, children have the opportunity to gain perspective on how they relate to teachers they dislike or are troubled by. A very good way to gain this perspective is to teach your child how to run an internal Negative Inquiry dialogue with himself or herself. For your child to learn this sophisticated use of the Negative Inquiry skill, as in the following dialogue, prompt him or her to list the bothersome things about the disliked teacher, and then prompt him or her with negative inquiries to help the child explore why they are troubling.

The specifics—or "whys"—that your child comes up with may be matters that can be resolved if (a) your child can first identify them using Negative Inquiry, and (b) will then talk to the teacher about them. Dialogue 62 points out how this could be done.

On the other hand, if the only "whys" your child can give for unease about a teacher are related to grades, then it will be worthwhile for your child to look at his or her own academic performance and study habits to see if this unease or dislike is justified. Dislike for a teacher is often a technique for blaming poor academic performance on the teacher, instead of on poor study habits.

In the most complex case, where your child cannot come up with specifics on what the teacher does, other than "He [or she] doesn't like me," it may be that your child is unknowingly doing something that irritates the teacher, as often happens between two human beings. If that is so, the final dialogue in this chapter may be helpful.

The examples used in dialogues 61, 62, and 63 are simple ones that illustrate how assertive skills can be used to improve relations between students and teachers. Real-life situations may be just as simple or more complex. The assertive skills will enable your child to cope with student-teacher relationships of both kinds.

DIALOGUE 61

Getting Specific Details on Why Your Child Has Trouble with a Particular Teacher
Age level: Eleven through seventeen
Setting: Your child has complained to you about a teacher, and you are trying to help him or her identify what the problem is and get specifics that can be discussed with the teacher.

You: What is it about Mr. Enigma that bothers you? [NEGATIVE INQUIRY]

CHILD: He never smiles.

You: What is it about Mr. Enigma's not smiling that bothers you? [NEGATIVE INQUIRY]

CHILD: He always seems unfriendly.

You: What is it about Mr. Enigma's seeming unfriendly that bothers you? [NEGATIVE INQUIRY]

CHILD: It makes me feel he doesn't like me.

You: What is it about feeling Mr. Enigma doesn't like you that's bad? [NEGATIVE INQUIRY]

CHILD: It makes me feel I can't speak to him.

You: What is it about feeling that you can't speak to Mr. Enigma that's bad? [NEGATIVE INQUIRY]

CHILD: Suppose I don't understand, or I have a problem. Who can I ask for help if he doesn't like me?

You: Is there anything else about Mr. Enigma that bothers you? [NEGATIVE INQUIRY prompt]

CHILD: He's so brainy.

You: What is it about Mr. Enigma's being brainy that's bad? [NEGATIVE INQUIRY]

CHILD: He knows everything.

You: What is it about Mr. Enigma's seeming to know everything that bothers you? [NEGATIVE INQUIRY]

Child: It makes me feel really dumb.

You: What is it about Mr. Enigma's seeming to know everything that means you should feel dumb? [NEGATIVE INQUIRY]

Child: I don't know. I just feel dumb when he calls on me.

You: What is it about Mr. Enigma's calling on you that makes you feel dumb? [NEGATIVE INQUIRY]

Child: The way he looks at me.

You: What is it about the way Mr. Enigma looks at you that makes you feel dumb? [NEGATIVE INQUIRY]

Child: He looks as if he thinks I won't know the answer.

You: Sort of condescending?

Child: What's that mean?

You: Like he's just playing a game with you?

Child: Yeah.

You: Anything else about Mr. Enigma that bothers you? [NEGATIVE INQUIRY prompt]

Child: No. I can't think of anything else.

You: Maybe you could have a talk with Mr. Enigma and tell him about this. It seems important to you. [WORKABLE COMPROMISE]

Child: How can I do that?

You: We could practice. I'll be Mr. Enigma and you be you, and you tell him about your problem. [WORKABLE COMPROMISE]

Child: Okay.

The next dialogue gives your child practice in talking to a teacher who makes him or her uneasy.

DIALOGUE 62

Your Child Deals Assertively with a Teacher Who Makes Him or Her Nervous
Age level: Eleven through seventeen
Setting: After class, your child approaches the teacher and discusses the problem identified by using Negative Inquiry in the previous dialogue.

CHILD: Mr. Enigma?

TEACHER: Yes?

CHILD: If you have a couple of minutes, I'd like to talk to you about a problem I have.

TEACHER: Sure. That's part of my job.

CHILD: This may sound really dumb, but I feel that you don't like me. [NEGATIVE ASSERTION and SELF-DISCLOSURE]

TEACHER: What in the world gave you that idea?

CHILD: As I said, it sounds dumb, but it bothers me. I never see you smile, and you're serious all the time. It makes you seem unfriendly, and so I feel nervous about asking you anything. Like now. [NEGATIVE ASSERTION and SELF-DISCLOSURE]

TEACHER: Hmmm . . . You don't have anything to be nervous about, but I guess you're right—I don't smile much. I didn't realize it made you nervous.

CHILD: And when you ask me questions in class, you make me feel really dumb. [SELF-DISCLOSURE]

TEACHER: How do I do that?

CHILD: I don't know. Just the way you look at me, I guess. [SELF-DISCLOSURE]

TEACHER: How do I look at you?

CHILD: Again, this sounds really dumb, but the way you look at me makes me feel you expect me not to know the answer. [NEGATIVE ASSERTION and SELF-DISCLOSURE]

TEACHER: Well, I don't always expect you to know the answer, but I don't think you are dumb either.

CHILD: That's a relief, but the way you look at me still makes me feel that way. [SELF-DISCLOSURE and BROKEN RECORD]

TEACHER: Hmmm . . .

CHILD: I know this may sound silly, but maybe you could look at me differently than you usually do. [SELF-DISCLOSURE and WORKABLE COMPROMISE]

TEACHER: Okay, how would you like me to look?

CHILD: Maybe you could smile? [WORKABLE COMPROMISE]

TEACHER: That's all?

CHILD: That would make me less nervous.

TEACHER: Why?

CHILD: I think it makes you look friendlier. [SELF-DISCLOSURE]

TEACHER: Okay, but sometimes I have a lot on my mind. I might forget.

CHILD: That's okay. If you do, how about me smiling at you to remind you? [WORKABLE COMPROMISE]

TEACHER: Sure. It will be interesting to see if you get more answers right when I smile.

CHILD: I may not get more answers right, but I will feel less nervous. [NEGATIVE ASSERTION and SELF-DISCLOSURE]

TEACHER: Okay.

CHILD: Thanks, Mr. Enigma. I appreciate it. [SELF-DISCLOSURE]

If an internal Negative Inquiry dialogue does not produce some specifics on what a teacher does that's upsetting, it may very well be that your child unknowingly does some things that the teacher does not like. One way to resolve this problem is given in the next dialogue, the last of this series. Here your child uses Negative Inquiry with the teacher to improve their relationship.

DIALOGUE 63

Your Child Improves Relations with a Teacher Who Has Been Annoyed with Him or Her
Age level: Eleven through seventeen
Setting: Your child decides to find out if he or she is doing something that upsets or annoys the teacher, and approaches the teacher at the end of class.

CHILD: Ms. Sensus?

TEACHER: Yes?

CHILD: I'd like to talk to you for a few minutes if you have the time. [SELF-DISCLOSURE]

TEACHER: Sure. What do you want to talk about?

CHILD: Please correct me if I'm wrong, but I get the feeling that I do something in class that irritates or annoys you. My problem is that I don't know what it is, and I feel bad about upsetting you. [NEGATIVE ASSERTION and SELF-DISCLOSURE]

TEACHER: You don't upset me.

CHILD: I don't?

TEACHER: Well, only a little.

CHILD: What is it that I do that upsets you? [NEGATIVE INQUIRY prompt]

TEACHER: You never seem to be paying attention.

CHILD: (Not stopping here on the assumption that all he or she has to do is pay more attention, but trying to get specifics that will be useful in changing the upsetting behavior) What is it that I do that makes me look like I'm not paying attention? [NEGATIVE INQUIRY]

TEACHER: You always seem to have your head buried in your book when I'm talking or when I'm writing things on the blackboard, or you stare off into space.

CHILD: (Again, not assuming this is sufficient information but continuing to try to understand why this is important to the teacher) What is it about my looking at the book when you're talking or writing things on the blackboard that upsets you? [NEGATIVE INQUIRY]

TEACHER: It makes me feel you don't trust me—as if you have to check with the book to see if what I'm telling you is right.

CHILD: (Not denying or discounting teacher's feelings by trying to explain) I didn't know that upset you. [SELF-DISCLOSURE]

TEACHER: Well, it's no big thing.

CHILD: What is it about my looking off into space that upsets you? [NEGATIVE INQUIRY]

TEACHER: It seems as if you don't care about what I'm saying to the class.

CHILD: (Again, not letting it go at that) What is it about my seeming not to care that upsets you? [NEGATIVE INQUIRY]

TEACHER: It's as though you feel that what I teach in this class isn't important enough to pay attention to.

CHILD: I didn't know that upset you. [SELF-DISCLOSURE]

TEACHER: It's no big thing, really.

CHILD: I don't mean to upset you. When I look in the book, I'm looking for examples of what you're saying. And when I stare off into space, I'm thinking about what you say. [SELF-DISCLOSURE]

TEACHER: Okay, but you should be more disciplined. Look for examples in the textbook when you do your homework.

CHILD: How about if I ask you for examples? [WORKABLE COMPROMISE]

TEACHER: As long as we don't spend too much time on them.

CHILD: How about if I ask you a question about what I'm thinking about when you say something? [WORKABLE COMPROMISE] ·

TEACHER: As long as it doesn't get us too much off schedule. We have a lot of material to cover.

CHILD: Okay. Is there anything else I do that upsets you in class? [NEGATIVE INQUIRY prompt]

TEACHER: Yes. You screw up your face when you're writing things down. You shouldn't do that. It makes you look like an illiterate, and you're a good student.

CHILD: What is it about my looking like an illiterate that upsets you? [NEGATIVE INQUIRY]

TEACHER: This is an English composition class, remember. I don't want my students looking like dum-dums in other classes. I want all of you to look like people who can write and communicate.

CHILD: Okay, I'll try not to make faces when I write. But if I forget, will you remind me? [WORKABLE COMPROMISE]

TEACHER: How? I don't want to embarrass you in front of the class.

CHILD: If I make a face when I write, you make a face when I look up, okay? [WORKABLE COMPROMISE]

TEACHER: The whole class might laugh at you!

CHILD: And at you! But who cares? It will be our joke. Okay? [WORKABLE COMPROMISE]

TEACHER: Okay.

CHILD: Thanks. I really feel better now. [SELF-DISCLOSURE]

TEACHER: So do I.

Coping Assertively with Adults in Commercial Situations

So far this book has given you only one simple example for teaching your child how to cope assertively with social conflict in a commercial situation—the Broken Record dialogue at the fast-food shop (dialogue 17). Practice in coping assertively in commercial situations is unrealistic for younger children, who do most or all of their commercial interactions with you as the mediator between them and the people behind the counter. But as your children mature, begin using money, and become more independent of you, they must also learn that an adult in a commercial setting is not an authority figure, who can arbitrarily order them around. At that point it is a good idea to give them practice in handling manipulative or even overbearing clerks or cashiers in stores and other business establishments. Before you begin, make sure your child knows the rules of thumb for being assertive and effective in a commercial situation: (1) Do not give up on what you want, and (2) avoid, if you can, going along with any special "deal," swap, or delay in compensating you for missing money, defective or missing merchandise, or unacceptable service.

In the first of these dialogues, your daughter has to assert herself in a commercial situation at school.

DIALOGUE 64

Daughter Gets Her Correct Change Back from the School Cashier
Age level: Eleven through seventeen
Setting: Your daughter gets into a dispute with the cashier at the school cafeteria over the correct change.

CASHIER: Here's your change.
DAUGHTER: Thank you. (Looks at change for a moment.) Wait a minute. I should get forty-five cents back. This is twenty cents.
CASHIER: (Puzzled, looks at change.) Hmm . . . No. That's right. You gave me a dollar and a quarter, and your lunch costs a dollar five.
DAUGHTER: No. I gave you one dollar and a fifty-cent piece.
CASHIER: No, you didn't! It was a quarter!
DAUGHTER: I'm sure you feel that way, but I gave you one dollar and a fifty-cent piece, and I'd like the correct change. [FOGGING and BROKEN RECORD]
CASHIER: No way! I don't make mistakes like that!
DAUGHTER: I'm sure you feel you don't make mistakes like that, but I gave you one dollar and a fifty-cent piece, and I'd like the correct change. [FOGGING and BROKEN RECORD]
CASHIER: Are you telling me that my vision is bad? I know the difference between two bits and a half-dollar!
DAUGHTER: I'm sure you do. But I gave you one dollar and a fifty-cent piece and I'd like the correct change. [FOGGING and BROKEN RECORD]

CASHIER: If you want to make a complaint, go see Mr. Feeder, the manager.

DAUGHTER: I don't want to make a complaint, I just want my correct change. [BROKEN RECORD]

CASHIER: Well, you will have to go see him.

DAUGHTER: Please call Mr. Feeder over here.

CASHIER: I can't leave the cash register.

DAUGHTER: There are lots of other people behind the counter. Please get one of them to call Mr. Feeder. [BROKEN RECORD]

CASHIER: You are holding up the line. Everybody else wants to get served.

DAUGHTER: I'm sure they do, but so do I. I gave you one dollar and a fifty-cent piece and I want my correct change. [FOGGING and BROKEN RECORD]

CASHIER: (Calling one of the servers over) Sally, ask Mr. Feeder to come here. (Sally moves off, and returns in a few seconds with the manager.)

MANAGER: What's the problem?

CASHIER: Mr. Feeder, this kid is accusing me of cheating her out of some change.

MANAGER: (Turning to daughter) Are you accusing Ms. Cassrege of cheating you?

DAUGHTER: (Ignoring accusation) I gave Ms. Cassrege one dollar and a fifty-cent piece. My lunch costs a dollar five. I got twenty cents change. It should be forty-five cents. I want my correct change. [BROKEN RECORD]

MANAGER: Lots of you kids try this to get extra money besides your lunch allowance.

DAUGHTER: I'm sure they do, Mr. Feeder, but I gave the cashier a dollar and a fifty-cent piece, and I want my correct change. [FOGGING and BROKEN RECORD]

MANAGER: We'd go broke if we believed all you kids who claim they got shortchanged.

DAUGHTER: I'm sure you would. But I gave the cashier a dollar and a fifty-cent piece and I want my correct change. [FOGGING and BROKEN RECORD]

MANAGER: Why don't you have your mother call me about this tomorrow?

DAUGHTER: I'm sure you'd like me to, Mr. Feeder, but I gave the cashier one-fifty and I'd like my correct change. [FOGGING and BROKEN RECORD]

MANAGER: (Silently looks at daughter for a few moments, and then reaches into cash register drawer and hands her twenty-five cents more.)

DAUGHTER: (Smiling) Thank you, Mr. Feeder! (She moves off to eat her lunch.)

MANAGER: (Turning to cashier) Can't you tell the difference between your own mistake and when a kid's trying to con you?

You can use the next dialogue, to teach your child, as STAR and PLUS do, how to get an exchange or a refund for defective merchandise.

DIALOGUE 65

Son Learns to Exchange Defective Merchandise
Age level: Eleven through seventeen
Setting: Your son purchased a baseball at a sporting-goods store yesterday, and while practicing pitching with a friend, he noticed the seams were starting to come apart. He takes it back to the store to get an exchange or refund.

CLERK: What can I do for you, young man?

SON: I bought this baseball here yesterday. When I tried it out this afternoon, the seam came apart. Right here. See?

CLERK: What were you doing with this ball?

SON: Practicing my pitching.

CLERK: How? Did you throw it up against a brick wall?

SON: If it hits a brick wall, is it supposed to come apart?

CLERK: No, this is one of our best makes. But lots of kids throw good baseballs like this at walls and just ruin them.

SON: I'll bet they do, but I was practicing pitching and it came apart. I'd like to exchange it for another one.

CLERK: What kind of ground were you practicing on? If you were playing on asphalt or concrete, that might wear out the stitches.

SON: I'm sure it would, but I practice on the grass at the school softball field, so I'd like to exchange it for a good one. [FOGGING and BROKEN RECORD]

CLERK: Was the catcher standing in front of a wire batting cage? Sometimes the wire is broken and cuts the stitches.

SON: No, it just came apart when I was practicing, so I would like to exchange it for a good one. [BROKEN RECORD]

CLERK: Are you sure this is the ball you bought yesterday? It looks like it's had a lot of use.

SON: I'm sure it does. Practice on the field does get it dirty. I would like to exchange it for a good one. [FOGGING and BROKEN RECORD]

CLERK: (Reaching under the counter) I have another used one just like it here. It's marked up like yours. You can have this one for the one you bought.

SON: I understand you want me to exchange my new one for your old one, but I bought a new one and I want a new one in exchange. [SELF-DISCLOSURE and BROKEN RECORD]

CLERK: This is dirty and marked!

SON: Yes, it is, but I bought a new one yesterday and I want a new one in exchange. [FOGGING and BROKEN RECORD]

CLERK: How can you expect me to give you a new one for one that's marked up and used?

SON: (Remembering that questions do not have to be answered) I bought a defective new ball yesterday, and I want a new one in exchange. If you don't want to give me a new ball in exchange, you can refund my money. [BROKEN RECORD and WORKABLE COMPROMISE]

CLERK: We don't give refunds.

SON: If you don't want to refund my money, give me a new ball in exchange. [WORKABLE COMPROMISE]

CLERK: You can't expect to get a new ball for this one.

SON: If you don't want to give me a new ball in exchange, you can refund my money. [WORKABLE COMPROMISE]

CLERK: That's unreasonable!

Son: I'm sure you feel that way, but if you don't want to give me a new ball in exchange, you can refund my money. [FOGGING and WORKABLE COMPROMISE]

Clerk: Do you have your sales slip?

Son: Right in the box.

Clerk: Pick a new ball off the shelf, but this time look at it first and make sure it's not defective.

Son: Yes, sir.

Similarly, with the next dialogue, you can teach your child, as STAR and PLUS do, how to rectify a mistake made by a commercial establishment.

DIALOGUE 66

Daughter Learns to Get What She Paid For
Age level: Eleven through seventeen
Setting: Your daughter purchased three records yesterday from a record store. When she got home, one was missing. She returns to the record store today with the package of records to get her third record.

Daughter: (Walking up to the clerk at the counter) Hello. I bought three records here yesterday, and only two were put in my bag. I would like the third record I bought.

Clerk: Do you have your sales slip?

Daughter: It's in the bag with the records.

Clerk: Let's see . . . That's right, three records.

Daughter: Yes, the Placebo Dominguez album is missing.

Clerk: Did you look around at home?

Daughter: Yes, and I want the record I bought. [BROKEN RECORD]

Clerk: Did you take the bus? If you did, you should call them up. Lots of people leave things on the bus.

Daughter: No, and I want the record I bought. [BROKEN RECORD]

CLERK: It's not our policy to replace records once you leave the store with them.

DAUGHTER: I'm sure it is, but I never got my record and I want it. [FOGGING and BROKEN RECORD]

CLERK: Teenagers try this all the time—say that a record is missing and then try to get another one.

DAUGHTER: I'm sure they do, but I want the record I bought. [FOGGING and BROKEN RECORD]

CLERK: How do I know you're telling me the truth?

DAUGHTER: (Ignoring a silly question) I bought a Placebo Dominguez record here yesterday, and want the record I bought. [BROKEN RECORD]

CLERK: You don't have to get huffy about it.

DAUGHTER: You're right, I don't have to get huffy, but I want the record I bought. [FOGGING and BROKEN RECORD]

CLERK: This is very unusual.

DAUGHTER: I'm sure it is, but I want the record I bought. [FOGGING and BROKEN RECORD]

CLERK: Why don't you go home and look again for the record, and if you can't find it, come back next week.

DAUGHTER: I'm sure you would like me to, but I want the record I bought. [FOGGING and BROKEN RECORD]

CLERK: It's impossible for me to give you a record to replace the one you got.

DAUGHTER: I'm sure it is difficult, but I bought a Placebo Dominguez record here yesterday and I didn't get it. I want the record I bought. [FOGGING and BROKEN RECORD]

CLERK: Let me check with the computer . . . Hmmm . . . Our computer says we have none in stock. All sold out. Sorry. Come back next week.

DAUGHTER: I checked before talking to you. You have one copy in the rack, obviously the one I bought yesterday. I want my record. [BROKEN RECORD]

CLERK: Well, why didn't you say so in the first place? If the computer says they're all sold, that must be yours.

DAUGHTER: I should have said that first. [FOGGING]

CLERK: Why don't you get it and I'll put it in your bag and seal it.
DAUGHTER: Okay, but I want to count the records before you seal it.
[WORKABLE COMPROMISE]
CLERK: If you feel you have to.
DAUGHTER: I feel I have to. [SELF-DISCLOSURE]

As a child begins to grow up, parents sometimes get a shock, at least the first time, when a daughter or son walks in the front door looking very different from the child who left that morning, with a haircut that the hairdresser, barber, or a friend talked him or her into. If your daughter comes home with a hairstyle that you don't particularly like, you will recover eventually. However, an ill-chosen hairstyle may have more of a negative effect on your daughter than on you. Suppose the new cut is a disaster and your daughter knows it, as well as knowing that she was talked into it. She could have resisted peer pressure or even expertly wielded adult pressure, but she didn't, or she didn't know how. In those vulnerable teenage years, a haircut can be a constant negative reminder, for weeks or even months, of her inadequacy in protecting her own self-respect and social image, both very important to teenagers.

To prevent your daughter's being manipulated into changing her personal appearance—unless she wants to herself—you can use the following dialogue to teach her, as PLUS does, how to cope with a hairdresser or friend who wants to experiment with the latest hair fashion fad by trying it out on her.

DIALOGUE 67

Daughter Learns to Cope Assertively with a Pushy Hairdresser
Age level: Thirteen through seventeen
Setting: Your daughter sits down and tells the hairdresser what kind of cut she wants.

DAUGHTER: Just a trim, please.
DRESSER: You ought to cut it shorter. It would look much better.
DAUGHTER: It might, but I like it long.
DRESSER: Everybody's having it cut short for the summer.

DAUGHTER: I'm sure they are, but I'll just have a trim, thank you. [FOGGING and BROKEN RECORD]

DRESSER: It would be much cooler and more comfortable.

DAUGHTER: I'm sure it would, but no thanks. [FOGGING and BROKEN RECORD]

DRESSER: I guess your mother would get upset if you cut it.

DAUGHTER: She might. [FOGGING]

DRESSER: My mother was the same way. It wasn't until I was twenty that I could decide for myself how to cut my hair.

DAUGHTER: That must have been embarrassing when you went to get your hair cut.

DRESSER: It was. But you'd still look better in a short cut. Do you want to see some pictures of the new short cuts?

DAUGHTER: Sure. But I still want a trim.

DRESSER: Okay, it's your hair. You can do what you want with it.

DAUGHTER: Right. Just a trim and shape it. [FOGGING and BROKEN RECORD]

While you and I know from our own teenage experience that your daughter will eventually recover perfectly from a disaster at the hairdresser, keep in mind that teenagers, both boys and girls, are highly sensitive and generally cope poorly with supposed social defects or faults. The purpose of teaching children assertive social thinking and reasoning is not just to get them through their teenage years but to enable them to grow and learn from them. Practice dialogues like the previous one will help your child avoid needless embarrassment, as will earlier dialogues that teaches preteens or teens that they, and not their peers, are the judges of what is a fault or a defect and what is not.

Coping Assertively with Adults in Work Situations

I hope that as your child goes through high school or prep school, he or she has the privilege of working in a part-time job. I say "privilege" because a part-time job for a teenager is a wonderful and practical learning experience, regardless of your family's financial situation. Teenagers generally see the money they earn from a job as the important payoff of working, but ideally they will also experience something even more important—the excitement and pleasure of being able to set their own goals, and to succeed more often than fail at working out the practical problems attendant on these goals.

Is a part-time job a valid aspect of a young person's educational experience? Does working at a job early in life set up a motivational framework that gives your child a perspective on the pleasures of being productive as an adult? There are no simple answers to these questions, but to the degree that one can generalize correctly about living, I think it's fair to say that productivity is the basis for most human happiness. If this is true, then to increase your children's likelihood of being happy in life, you want to increase their chances of being productive.

All my clinical and human experience underlines a common observation: People are happier when they are doing something than when they are doing nothing. My almost automatic response when someone tells me that he or she is worrying a lot is to ask, "How busy are you? Do you have a job? Do you have a lot of free time? How do you use it?" You will recognize from your own experience that you tend to worry more when you have the time to worry! That statement is not an endorsement for the Protestant work ethic. It is a statement of fact. When I can work productively, I know how much happier I am.

So, should you consider a part-time job, in addition to going to school, a necessary part of your child's education? Frankly, yes. Although the real-life experience of working is no guaranty of later happiness and personal satisfaction, I think it stacks the odds of such an outcome in your child's favor. Over the years I have known personally and professionally a large number of families with teenagers, many of whom worked part-time and a lesser number who did not. In the families of teenagers who did not work, I observed more parental dissatisfaction with their children's motivation and achievement. The working teenagers also seemed happier, more motivated, less moody, and, to me, more interesting people.

If you agree that it can be a very positive experience for your kids to work part-time as well as go to school, you can help them get the most out of their experience by teaching them how to cope with conflict on the job. Point out that assertiveness works there as well as everywhere else there is social conflict, and use the next two training dialogues to teach your children, as PLUS does, how to cope with on-the-job errors, whether made by them or by the boss.

DIALOGUE 68

Son Learns to Work Things Out Assertively with a Boss Who Makes Mistakes
Age Level: Fourteen through seventeen
Setting: Your son works part-time after school and weekends at the local fast-food shop. Today when he goes in to work, he is met by an angry boss.

Boss: Where were you yesterday afternoon?
Son: Me? At school. Why?
Boss: You were supposed to be here at two-thirty!
Son: Gee, Mr. Burger, I'm supposed to be at school on Thursday afternoons.
Boss: Nobody told me that! How can I make up a schedule if nobody tells me when they are supposed to be in school?
Son: I don't know, Mr. Burger. I feel bad about this, but I gave you my schedule when you hired me. [SELF-DISCLOSURE]
Boss: That was for summer school!
Son: You're right. I thought you would keep the same work schedule, so I planned my school schedule around it. I should have checked with you first. [FOGGING and NEGATIVE ASSERTION]
Boss: Didn't you look at the bulletin board in my office on Monday?
Son: I didn't know that you have a bulletin board in your office. [SELF-DISCLOSURE]
Boss: Well, you're supposed to look at it every workday!
Son: I didn't know that, Mr. Burger. [SELF-DISCLOSURE]
Boss: You should have!
Son: You're right. I should have known. It was dumb of me not to know. [FOGGING and NEGATIVE ASSERTION]
Boss: If you had looked at the bulletin board, you would have known that I scheduled you for Thursday afternoons, and you could have let me know you couldn't be here.
Son: You're right, Mr. Burger. If I had known, I could have let you know. [FOGGING]
Boss: Now I have to reschedule someone else for Thursday afternoons. That's trouble I don't need.

SON: I'll bet. [FOGGING]
BOSS: You look at the bulletin every day, you hear!
SON: Yes, sir.
BOSS: And you let me know right away if there's a screw-up, you hear?
SON: Yes, sir.
BOSS: Okay. It's not your fault. That dumb Jimmy should have told you what to do when you hired on!
SON: I guess so, Mr. Burger. [FOGGING]
BOSS: Okay, get to work.
SON: Yes, sir.

Most young people have difficulty adjusting to working because their inexperience naturally causes mistakes. Their experience in handling mistakes at school, even their successful experience, does not as a rule enable them to cope well with mistakes made on the job. At school, when mistakes are made, not much happens beyond the child's being urged or made to learn from the mistake. The child usually does not get kicked out of school for making mistakes, but on the job he or she can be penalized or fired for them.

You can use the final training dialogue of this chapter to teach your child, as PLUS does, how to cope with the errors that inexperience guarantees will happen, and with the possible angry reaction of the people he or she works with.

DIALOGUE 69

Daughter Is Late to Work and Must Deal with an Angry Supervisor
Age level: Fourteen through seventeen
Setting: Your daughter is fifteen minutes late at the fabric shop where she works part-time after school. A schoolmate who gives her a ride to work didn't show up, so she had to catch the bus. As she walks into the shop, the manager begins to dress her down for not being on time.

MANAGER: It's about time!
DAUGHTER: I'm late. [NEGATIVE ASSERTION]

MANAGER: You bet you're late! This is going to come out of your paycheck!

DAUGHTER: I don't blame you for being mad, Ms. Snip. I'm upset about it myself. [SELF-DISCLOSURE]

MANAGER: You *should* be upset. I've been waiting on customers behind this counter for fifteen minutes wondering if you would show up. I could have been doing other things.

DAUGHTER: I'm sure you could have, Ms. Snip. It was dumb of me to be late. [FOGGING and NEGATIVE ASSERTION]

MANAGER: Well?

DAUGHTER: I don't understand.

MANAGER: Why were you late?

DAUGHTER: I'm not sure what happened to my ride. She didn't show up, so I had to catch the bus. [SELF-DISCLOSURE]

MANAGER: That's no excuse. It's your responsibility to be here on time.

DAUGHTER: You're right, Ms. Snip. It's my responsibility. [FOGGING]

MANAGER: What are you going to do about it?

DAUGHTER: About my ride?

MANAGER: Yes.

DAUGHTER: I don't know. I could ask my friend to let me know if she's sick or something, so I could get another ride, or leave a bit earlier. [SELF-DISCLOSURE and WORKABLE COMPROMISE]

MANAGER: I get very upset when I don't know if you're coming in or not.

DAUGHTER: I'm sure you must, Ms. Snip. How about if I phone you if I think I can't get here on time? [FOGGING and WORKABLE COMPROMISE]

MANAGER: Well, that would help, but you are supposed to be here on time every day.

DAUGHTER: You're right. I am, Ms. Snip, and I'll certainly try my best to be here on time. [FOGGING and WORKABLE COMPROMISE]

MANAGER: Well, that's okay, I guess. Put your things in your locker and get back here behind the counter.

DAUGHTER: Yes, ma'am.

This chapter has covered a wide range of problems your child may have in dealing with adults seen as authorities: practical problems, disciplinary problems, problems in understanding material to be learned or what is wanted, and problems with adults in commercial situations in or out of school. It assumes children will have difficulty articulating what they want from teachers, school staff, and other adults, and the practice dialogues are designed to prompt them to communicate straightforwardly with adults. With practice using the assertive skills, your child will more easily resolve such problems, including those that arise between teacher and student that can interfere with the prime purpose that teachers and students see each other for: teaching and learning.

Now let's turn to the next chapter, where both you and your child can learn to improve relations within the family using the same systematic assertive skills.

CHAPTER SEVEN

Teaching Your Child How to Be Assertive Within the Family

It is in your own interest to teach your children to be assertive with each other within the family. If your family is like most, your children probably rely on you to work out their disputes for them, and during the average week that can add up to much unnecessary work and a lot of tension and frustration that can drain a beleaguered parent. As we have seen, even a young child can learn to be assertive with classmates, and learn how to solve problems and social conflicts successfully in other settings. When children are successful in assertively working out compromises that give them a "piece of the action," they are more likely to try to work out disputes with brothers and sisters without relying on you, and without anger and verbal or physical fighting. Assertive children can contribute greatly to the equanimity of your family.

As you will see, the application of the assertive skills to deal with criticism, or improve communication, and solve problems in the family does not differ much from one situation to another or one dialogue to another. The assertive skills are fundamentally simple in concept and in use, and if a child has been trained to be assertive in other settings, that learning will eventually generalize to places like home. However, do not be tempted to skimp on the practice of these skills with your child. Relying on a child's learning the universality of assertive skills through his or her own real-life experience is not an efficient or effective method of teaching assertiveness—or anything else for that matter. Given the logistics—how many different situations can your child be assertive in each day?—this may take years. A better teaching method is to give your child practice in as many different situations as possible. Lots of practice is important, even though the situations used for practice may resemble each other.

There are emotional as well as intellectual reasons that practice in similar situations is important. The STAR researchers, and I myself, have learned through teaching and clinical experience that children (as well as adults) may not automatically transfer newly learned skills from one situation to a similar one if the second situation has a lot of anxiety associated with it. When we become anxious, our thinking brains tend to shut down and two plus two may not add up to four. Consequently we tend not to see that a new situation in which we have to assert ourselves may be basically similar to one in which we have already been successful.

To overcome this tendency not to transfer skills to new settings, the STAR researchers and I strongly recommend that you give your child as much practice in as many different situations as possible to reduce any anxiety your child may feel about dealing with social conflict, even what you and I would see as trivial social conflict. Some of the most common conflict situations at home, as reported by the STAR research project, are dealt with in the following dialogues.

Coping with Personal Criticism from Brothers

To start with, let's look at a very painful situation for some young girls: merciless teasing from their brothers. There are a number of psychological theories as to why this common phenomenon occurs. They range from useless statements implying nothing can be done about it because teasing is a genetic form of male dominance and aggression over females, to the very ingenious, suggesting that male sibling teasing is a psychological coping device to prevent sexual interest between brothers and sisters. No matter what we may guess is the theoretical cause, if we can believe the frequent clinical complaints of adult women who claim that chronic childhood sibling teasing was a significant element in their adult insecurity, the reduction of such teasing is a worthwhile goal.

The experience of the STAR project in teaching assertive techniques to young and older children has shown that chronic teasing can be extinguished simply and effectively. The first four dialogues in this chapter are designed to teach your daughter (or son, if necessary) how to respond to criticism or teasing from family members in an assertive and nondefensive way. In the first of these dialogues, your younger daughter (or shy son) has to cope with teasing from a brother. The first version of the dialogue illustrates a typical nonassertive response by a younger girl to her brother's criticism and teasing. Compare the first version with the second. You can use the latter to teach your child, as STAR and PLUS do, how to eliminate this teasing by responding to it assertively.

DIALOGUE 70

Daughter Learns to Deal with General Chronic Teasing by Her Brother
Age level: Seven through ten
Setting: Your daughter is watching TV in the evening with her brother, and starts up a conversation.

DAUGHTER: Do you think the show on channel five is any good?
BROTHER: You drip! What a stupid question to ask!
DAUGHTER: It's not a stupid question!
BROTHER: You are always asking stupid questions! Everything you do is stupid!
DAUGHTER: I don't think I'm stupid!
BROTHER: That's because you're too stupid to know that you're stupid!
DAUGHTER: Why do you always tease me and pick on me? It isn't fair!
BROTHER: You deserve it.
DAUGHTER: Why?
BROTHER: Look at yourself. Not only are you dumb, you're ugly, too!
DAUGHTER: I am not ugly!
BROTHER: You are the ugliest thing I ever saw!
DAUGHTER: (Crying) Mom!

By comparing this version of the dialogue with the following assertive rerun, you can see the difference between the way most young girls defensively and anxiously respond to a brother's teasing and the way an assertively trained daughter will respond unemotionally to the same type of teasing. In so doing, she will give it no payoff. Consequently, brother will not tease as much in the future.

Setting: The same as above.

DAUGHTER: Do you think the show on channel five is any good?

BROTHER: You drip! What a stupid question to ask!

DAUGHTER: I don't understand. What is it about my asking you if the show on channel five is any good that's stupid? [NEGATIVE INQUIRY]

BROTHER: You are always asking stupid questions! Everything you do is stupid!

DAUGHTER: I don't understand. What is it I do that is stupid? [NEGATIVE INQUIRY]

BROTHER: You're such a little twerp! Everything you do is stupid!

DAUGHTER: Perhaps I am. But I still don't understand. What is it I do that is stupid? [FOGGING and NEGATIVE INQUIRY]

BROTHER: You're too stupid to know that you're stupid!

DAUGHTER: Maybe. But I still don't understand. What is it I do that is stupid? [FOGGING and NEGATIVE INQUIRY]

BROTHER: You are always asking questions.

DAUGHTER: I don't understand. What is it about my always asking you questions that is stupid? [NEGATIVE INQUIRY]

BROTHER: If you were smart, you wouldn't have to always ask questions!

DAUGHTER: I don't understand. What is it about my always asking you questions that means I'm not smart? [NEGATIVE INQUIRY]

BROTHER: If you can't figure that out by yourself, why should I tell you?

DAUGHTER: You mean you don't want to tell me why you think I'm stupid anymore? [NEGATIVE INQUIRY prompt]

BROTHER: Why should I?

DAUGHTER: Is there anything else about me that you don't like? [NEGATIVE INQUIRY prompt]

BROTHER: I want to watch the movie.

DAUGHTER: Do you think the show on channel five is any good?

BROTHER: What's the name of it?

DAUGHTER: "The Frozen Slime in Concert at Wolfpark."
BROTHER: That sounds okay. Do you want to watch it?
DAUGHTER: Let's give it a try, and if it's no good, we can come back
   to this one. [WORKABLE COMPROMISE]
BROTHER: Okay.

This dialogue uses Negative Inquiry extensively to deal with brother's criticism. In the best case, the use of Negative Inquiry will reveal any hidden agenda he may have that prompts him to chronically tease his sister. For example, it may be that he himself gets teased by his young friends when he associates with his sister, so his teasing is a coping method to keep his sister at a distance when his young friends are around. In the worst case, Negative Inquiry will not bring any hidden agenda to light, but brother gets no payoff for teasing: Sis does not squirm emotionally or distance herself from him. Consequently, as long as sis responds to it assertively and unemotionally, his teasing will be heard less and less.

The next dialogue deals with a situation that occurs between older brothers and sisters, hence the teasing or criticism is a bit more sophisticated, even subtle. As in the preceding dialogue, a typical defensive, nonassertive response style is shown first, to be compared with a nondefensive, assertive rerun.

DIALOGUE 71

Daughter Learns to Deal with Brother's Chronic Criticism of Her Beliefs
Age level: Fourteen through seventeen
Setting: Your daughter is talking to her brother, and he begins to put her down by teasing her about her beliefs.

DAUGHTER: Don't you believe that people are basically good?
BROTHER: Do you believe in Santa Claus?
DAUGHTER: No, not anymore.
BROTHER: How about the Easter Bunny?

DAUGHTER: You're trying to make fun of me!

BROTHER: The tooth fairy?

DAUGHTER: I'm trying to talk seriously about something and you just have to make fun of it!

BROTHER: If you would say something realistic instead of just cutesy-pie stuff, you wouldn't get made fun of!

DAUGHTER: It's not cutesy-pie to believe that people are basically good!

BROTHER: Tell me another one starting with "Once upon a time. . . ."

DAUGHTER: You don't want to listen to anybody's opinion except your own.

BROTHER: I have a very open mind if someone says something intelligent once in a while.

DAUGHTER: Are you saying that I'm dumb?

BROTHER: If you believe in things like that, what else can you be?

DAUGHTER: I don't criticize you when you say what you believe.

BROTHER: That's because I don't believe in the Easter Bunny the way you do. Wise up and grow up.

Now let's look at how you can teach your daughter, as STAR and PLUS do, to respond to this type of situation using a nondefensive, nonemotional style.

Setting: The same as before, except that your daughter assumes something can be worked out with her brother.

DAUGHTER: Don't you believe that people are basically good?

BROTHER: Do you believe in Santa Claus?

DAUGHTER: I guess that sounds as if I do, but do you think people are good? [FOGGING and BROKEN RECORD]

BROTHER: How about the Easter Bunny? Do you believe in him, too?

DAUGHTER: I guess that means that you don't believe that people are basically good. But I'd like it better if you would give me a straightforward answer. [SELF-DISCLOSURE]

BROTHER: Do you believe in the tooth fairy?

DAUGHTER: I'd like it better if you would give me a straightforward answer, instead of being sarcastic and witty. [BROKEN RECORD and WORKABLE COMPROMISE]

BROTHER: If you would say something realistic instead of just cutesy-pie stuff, I wouldn't be sarcastic.

DAUGHTER: What is it about believing that people are basically good that means I'm unrealistic? [NEGATIVE INQUIRY]

BROTHER: Tell me another one starting with "Once upon a time. . . ."

DAUGHTER: Very witty! But what is it about believing that people are basically good that means I'm unrealistic? [NEGATIVE INQUIRY]

BROTHER: Grow up!

DAUGHTER: What is it about believing that people are basically good that means I'm immature? [NEGATIVE INQUIRY]

BROTHER: Look around you at what people do, dummy. They behave as if it's everyone for himself.

DAUGHTER: Is it impossible for you to answer a question I ask you without being sarcastic and trying to put me down? [WORKABLE COMPROMISE]

BROTHER: If you believe in things like that, what else can you expect?

DAUGHTER: I don't like it when you put me down for asking you a question. I would like it very much if you weren't sarcastic to me. [SELF-DISCLOSURE]

BROTHER: If you would stop believing in the Easter Bunny, I would stop being sarcastic.

DAUGHTER: Maybe I like believing in the Easter Bunny. I'm sure that's dumb according to you, but I'd like to talk to you about things without your getting sarcastic. [FOGGING and BROKEN RECORD]

BROTHER: Like I said. If you would stop believing in the Easter Bunny, I would stop being sarcastic.

DAUGHTER: What is it about my believing that people are basically good that's bad? [NEGATIVE INQUIRY]

BROTHER: It's dumb!

DAUGHTER: What is it about believing something dumb that's bad? [NEGATIVE INQUIRY]

BROTHER: It makes you look like a dumb, stupid ass.

DAUGHTER: What is it about my looking like a dumb, stupid ass that's bad? [NEGATIVE INQUIRY]

BROTHER: It makes all of us look dumb too!

DAUGHTER: You too?

BROTHER: Yes. I don't want other people to think I'm dumb just because my sister acts like that.

DAUGHTER: How about if I only ask you questions in private? Will that make you look dumb to other people? [WORKABLE COMPROMISE and NEGATIVE INQUIRY]

BROTHER: No, I guess that's okay.

DAUGHTER: And you won't get sarcastic? [WORKABLE COMPROMISE]

BROTHER: Only if you are not incredibly naïve.

DAUGHTER: I'll try not to be, but I can't guarantee it. And if you are sarcastic just because you think I'm naïve, I'm not going to like it. I do want to talk to you about things when I'm not sure of them. [WORKABLE COMPROMISE and SELF-DISCLOSURE]

BROTHER: Okay.

Both dialogues 70 and 71 have two goals: to desensitize a child so he or she does not respond anxiously to teasing or criticism from brothers or sisters, and to improve communication between the children in the family. As the next dialogue points out, however, there are times, particularly in sensitive situations, when just learning not to be unduly upset by teasing is reward enough. You can use the next dialogue to teach your child, as STAR and PLUS do, how to minimize malicious teasing and nonconstructive criticism by giving it no reward or payoff. This is in contrast with the previous dialogue, where it is assumed something can be worked out.

DIALOGUE 72

Daughter Learns Not to Be Bothered by Brother's Chronic Teasing and Criticism about Her Looks
Age level: Thirteen through seventeen
Setting: Your daughter is on the phone with a boyfriend, and from the tone of the conversation, it becomes clear that he is reneging on asking your daughter out to a school dance. After she hangs up, her brother begins to needle her about being rejected.

BROTHER: That's what you get for counting your chickens before they hatch!

DAUGHTER: I don't understand. [SELF-DISCLOSURE]

BROTHER: He's not going to ask you to the dance, is he?

DAUGHTER: I guess not. It's very upsetting. [SELF-DISCLOSURE]

BROTHER: That's what I meant. You counted your chickens before they were hatched.

DAUGHTER: I guess I did. Dumb of me, wasn't it? [NEGATIVE ASSERTION]

BROTHER: I'll say! You even bought a new dress for the dance, didn't you?

DAUGHTER: Yes. That's what makes me so mad! [SELF-DISCLOSURE]

BROTHER: You've got nothing to be mad about. You're lucky he even thought of asking you, even if he changed his mind.

DAUGHTER: (Abandoning the effort to communicate anything important about how she feels to her brother) You're right. I should feel lucky. [FOGGING]

BROTHER: I'll bet he feels relieved now.

DAUGHTER: He probably does. [FOGGING]

BROTHER: He almost made a big mistake and took you out.

DAUGHTER: It seems that way. [FOGGING]

BROTHER: If I were you, I'd give up. Nobody in their right mind would want to take you out.

DAUGHTER: You may be right. [FOGGING]

BROTHER: You don't seem very upset about it.

DAUGHTER: I don't seem like I'm upset, do I? [FOGGING]

BROTHER: Maybe you could date a blind man.

DAUGHTER: I could, couldn't I? [FOGGING]

BROTHER: Well, I've got better things to do besides talk to you.

DAUGHTER: I'm sure you do. [FOGGING]

BROTHER: Yep.

DAUGHTER: I'm not much fun to tease, am I? [FOGGING]

BROTHER: No.

DAUGHTER: Anytime you want to talk about dating, let me know.

BROTHER: No, thanks.

DAUGHTER: Okay.

Given the value of practicing assertion in as many situations as possible, until it is as overlearned as the ABC's, let's now look at a slightly different situation in which your child may be teased.

Coping with Criticism from Sisters as Well as Brothers

In the next dialogue your younger daughter has to deal with criticism from the rest of the children in the family for deciding to do what she likes instead of what they like. In this situation your daughter may have to pay the price of doing things alone if she decides not to conform to what other people, even her older sister and brother, think is appropriate.

DIALOGUE 73

Younger Daughter Learns to Deal with Criticism from Sister and Brother
Age level: Seven through seventeen
Setting: Your daughter decides to wear a sweater her aunt knitted. When she walks into the living room with it on, her brother and sister start picking on her for wearing it.

SISTER: You are not going to wear that tacky sweater, are you?
BROTHER: Yeah! Uncool.
DAUGHTER: Oh? What is it about this sweater that's tacky? [NEGATIVE INQUIRY]
SISTER: It looks horrible!
BROTHER: Yeah, ugly!
DAUGHTER: I don't understand. What is it that makes it look horrible? [SELF-DISCLOSURE and NEGATIVE INQUIRY]
SISTER: It's just barfo!
BROTHER: Yeah! Gag and vomit!
DAUGHTER: I still don't understand. What is it that makes it look bad? [SELF-DISCLOSURE and NEGATIVE INQUIRY]
SISTER: Nobody wears a sweater like that anymore!

BROTHER: Yeah! Nobody!

DAUGHTER: Is that it? It just looks old-fashioned? [NEGATIVE IN-QUIRY prompt]

SISTER: The color is all wrong.

BROTHER: Yeah! Puky.

DAUGHTER: Anything else besides the color? [NEGATIVE INQUIRY prompt]

SISTER: Isn't that enough?

BROTHER: Yeah! Too much.

DAUGHTER: It may be, but is there anything else that makes it look tacky besides the style and color? [FOGGING and NEGATIVE INQUIRY prompt]

SISTER: (Making a personal statement for the first time) I think that's plenty to make you look gross.

BROTHER: Yeah! El grosso extremo.

DAUGHTER: (Following up on her sister's personal dislike) What is it about my wearing a sweater that makes me look gross that upsets you? [NEGATIVE INQUIRY]

SISTER: All the guys will laugh at you behind your back.

BROTHER: Yeah! Laugh!

DAUGHTER: What is it about my being laughed at that upsets you? [NEGATIVE INQUIRY]

SISTER: When they see us together, they'll think I'm like you.

BROTHER: Yeah! Who needs you?

DAUGHTER: Well, how about if we don't stay together when I wear it? [WORKABLE COMPROMISE]

SISTER: Okay.

BROTHER: Yeah! Neat!

DAUGHTER: Okay. I kinda like the sweater myself. [SELF-DISCLO-SURE]

The preceding dialogue is a simple example of how not to be in-timidated into conforming to what a group arbitrarily wants its members to do. It may seem trivial to you, but it is actually very important. I assume you will want your child to have the ability to decide indepen-dently whether or not to go along with the current group fad, whether in dress style, slang, sex, alcohol, or drugs. If so, then it is best to start practicing in the "shallow end of the pool," so to speak—i.e., with simple, mundane examples, like wearing a favorite sweater that no one else likes.

Coping with Emotional Game Playing by Brothers or Sisters

Something that all of us experience, whether we want to or not, is emotional game playing by people we interact with. To get back at us because we upset them or won't do things their way, many people use manipulative game playing intended to punish us emotionally by making us feel bad or guilty. The husband who sulks, mutely staring off into space, and the wife who runs off into the bedroom and sobs (with the bedroom door open) following an argument are both playing emotional games intended to punish their spouses.

Your children are no exception to this common reality. One often sees children use emotional game playing on one another when they do not get their way. And unless the child who is on the receiving end of this game playing has some experience in recognizing it and coping with it, it can have a devastating emotional effect.

The next dialogue is an example of how to teach your child, as STAR and PLUS do, to deal with emotional game playing by someone close. In this dialogue your older daughter has to cope assertively with a younger sister who plays emotional games instead of dealing with situations straightforwardly. If the intent of the game playing is to make your older daughter feel bad, the best sequence in trying to minimize game playing is to (a) teach your older daughter to talk about the game playing in order to find out why it is being used; and, if that doesn't eliminate it, then (b) teach her to ignore the game playing and act as if it doesn't bother her. The game player's intent is to manipulatively punish another person for upsetting the game player, or for not doing what the game player wants. If game playing doesn't work—i.e., the person doesn't behave as if he or she is being punished —then there is no payoff for using it. Consequently, game playing will diminish in the future.

DIALOGUE 74

*Daughter Learns to Cope with Younger Sister Who Sulks and
Plays Emotional Games*
Age level: Eleven through seventeen
*Setting: Your older daughter and her younger sister occasionally
have arguments. After each argument, younger daughter gives
older daughter the silent treatment to make her feel guilty. Older
daughter decides to see if she can straighten things out with her
sister so that their arguments will not be so distasteful.*

DAUGHTER 1: I want to talk to you.

DAUGHTER 2: About what?

DAUGHTER 1: When we argue or fight, you won't speak to me for days
afterward. That upsets me. [SELF-DISCLOSURE]

DAUGHTER 2: Good!

DAUGHTER 1: Is that why you won't talk to me afterward? To make me
feel bad?

DAUGHTER 2: You deserve it!

DAUGHTER 1: I don't want to get into another fight. Can we just talk
about it without fighting? [SELF-DISCLOSURE and WORKABLE
COMPROMISE]

DAUGHTER 2: If you don't want to fight, then don't complain.

DAUGHTER 1: What is it about my complaining that's bad? [NEGA-
TIVE INQUIRY]

DAUGHTER 2: You're the one who is nasty, and then you want to
complain?

DAUGHTER 1: I don't understand. What is it I do that's nasty? [NEGA-
TIVE INQUIRY prompt]

DAUGHTER 2: You always put me down.

DAUGHTER 1: Now I really don't understand. What is it I do that puts
you down? [SELF-DISCLOSURE and NEGATIVE INQUIRY
prompt]

DAUGHTER 2: The way you talk to me when we argue.

DAUGHTER 1: Okay, what is it about the way I talk to you that's bad?
[NEGATIVE INQUIRY]

DAUGHTER 2: You look down your nose at me when I say something you don't like.

DAUGHTER 1: I don't understand. Give me a for instance of what I do that's bad. [SELF-DISCLOSURE and WORKABLE COMPROMISE]

DAUGHTER 2: Every time I say something, you say, "For sure!" or "Oh, really?" or "Gross!"

DAUGHTER 1: What is it about the way I say those things that's bad? [SELF-DISCLOSURE and NEGATIVE INQUIRY prompt]

DAUGHTER 2: You don't care, and you make fun of me when you say that. As if what I say doesn't count.

DAUGHTER 1: I don't listen to what you say? [NEGATIVE INQUIRY prompt]

DAUGHTER 2: Yes.

DAUGHTER 1: I didn't know that upset you so much. You just come right back at me. [SELF-DISCLOSURE]

DAUGHTER 2: What do you expect me to do?

DAUGHTER 1: You could tell me that I hurt your feelings badly. [WORKABLE COMPROMISE]

DAUGHTER 2: You would like that.

DAUGHTER 1: Maybe it would seem as if I did, but I don't when we can't talk for days. [FOGGING and SELF-DISCLOSURE]

DAUGHTER 2: Then why don't you stop putting me down? You could just say that you don't think I'm right.

DAUGHTER 1: I didn't know I did, and I feel bad about it. If I forget, will you remind me of it? [SELF-DISCLOSURE and WORKABLE COMPROMISE]

DAUGHTER 2: Will you stop if I do?

DAUGHTER 1: I'll try. [WORKABLE COMPROMISE]

DAUGHTER 2: Okay.

DAUGHTER 1: Great! Are we friends?

DAUGHTER 2: Yes.

The goal of the preceding dialogue is to teach the assertive child to make the communication between him or her and other children straightforward and workable. Even with the best of intentions, there is no guarantee that this happy result will occur. If a conversation such as the above dialogue does not work, make sure your child understands that the second method of coping successfully with emotional game playing is to pretend that it has no effect on him or her. The response that works when all else fails is given by Assertive Right IX (understanding). A simple "I don't understand. What's the matter? What are you upset about?" will invariably evoke the manipulative response "Nothing! Nothing at all!" If this manipulation, intended to make your child read minds, is met with "Okay. I thought you were upset, but I must have been mistaken," the emotional game playing will be short-lived.

Learning to Control Personal Possessions

It is important for a child to have some personal possessions. Personal possessions help children learn to recognize themselves as individuals, who can decide, independently of others, what to play, what to wear, what to do. Early practice in making individual judgments about inconsequential things sets the stage for taking responsibility later for judgments about more-important things, such as studying, academic achievement, drinking, sex, or substance abuse. Learning to make these early judgments is an important part of growing up. If children cannot make decisions about their personal things, then the stage is set for their becoming excessively dependent on others to tell them what they should do.

You can use the next two dialogues to teach a child, as STAR and PLUS do, how to keep brothers and sisters from infringing upon his or her personal things. At the same time, and following from that, you will be automatically teaching the child how to keep others from interfering with his or her self-respect. The best way to handle this area of childhood interaction between brothers and/or sisters is for the child to take a mutual-problem-solving stance in protecting his or her personal belongings.

Make sure your children know that what's important here is the ability to make a voluntary decision about their belongings and the ability to back that decision up. The personal articles themselves are not important, nor does it matter who uses them. In short, the purpose of this dialogue is not to teach your children to be selfish. Your children may have some difficulty with this idea. Brothers and/or sisters may be very possessive, to the point of driving you to distraction with their demands that you protect their property and make sure things are "fair." This often happens because they have not been successful in controlling their personal articles—i.e., who uses what, and when. Successful assertive experience will give them confidence in their ability to do this, and with this boost in their self-respect, the idea of not needing absolute control over personal things will seem less strange to them. Of course, if your son or daughter doesn't mind others using his or her personal things, there is no problem as long as the child can enforce rights to personal possessions and self-respect when the need arises.

DIALOGUE 75

Younger Son Learns to Work Out a Compromise with His
Brother About Personal Belongings
Age level: Seven through seventeen
Setting: After your younger son lends his brother his baseball
glove, a week passes without its being returned. Your younger son
approaches his brother to get it back.

SON 1: You haven't given me my catcher's mitt back yet.

SON 2: I have to play a couple of more games.

SON 1: I'm sure you would like to, but I'd also like my glove back. [FOGGING and BROKEN RECORD]

SON 2: It's only a couple of more games.

SON 1: Probably, but I'd like my mitt back. [FOGGING and BROKEN RECORD]

SON 2: You don't need it right now.

SON 1: Perhaps, but I'd like my mitt back. [FOGGING and BROKEN RECORD]

SON 2: But I'm playing catcher now. I need a catcher's mitt.

SON 1: I'm sure you do, but I'd like my glove back. [FOGGING and BROKEN RECORD]

Son 2: Are you going to play in a game today?

Son 1: Probably not, but I'd like my glove back. [FOGGING and BROKEN RECORD]

Son 2: You don't need it today.

Son 1: I don't understand. Are you playing a game today? [SELF-DISCLOSURE]

Son 2: No, but Jimmy and I are going to practice pitching.

Son 1: Okay, you lend me your first baseman's glove while you use my mitt. [WORKABLE COMPROMISE]

Son 2: That's not fair. My glove is almost brand-new.

Son 1: It probably isn't fair, so I want my mitt back. [FOGGING and BROKEN RECORD]

Son 2: You might scuff my glove up!

Son 1: I might, but you might scuff my mitt up, too. That didn't stop me from lending it to you. [FOGGING]

Son 2: Yours is an old one.

Son 1: It is, but I don't like to see it scuffed up any more than you like to see yours scuffed up. [FOGGING and SELF-DISCLOSURE]

Son 2: It's not fair.

Son 1: It probably isn't. But if you want to use my mitt, then I want to use your glove. Okay? [FOGGING and WORKABLE COMPROMISE]

Son 2: You will be careful with it?

Son 1: As careful as you are with mine. [WORKABLE COMPROMISE]

Son 2: Okay.

Son 1: Swell. Where is it?

Son 2: In the closet.

As you can see, this dialogue about baseball gloves is not about the gloves themselves, or who uses whose glove, but about self-respect, and working out a compromise by which each child gets something. The next dialogue is similar, but illustrates a situation that can be exasperating and infuriating. With this dialogue you can teach your child, as STAR and PLUS do, how to deal assertively with a sister or brother who takes things without asking.

DIALOGUE 76

Daughter Learns to Work Out a Compromise with Her Sister
About Personal Belongings
Age level: Seven through seventeen
Setting: Your daughter is dressing, and she can't find her new
blouse. She decides to ask her sister if she knows where it is.

DAUGHTER 1: Have you seen my new yellow blouse?

DAUGHTER 2: Which one?

DAUGHTER 1: The one you saw me buy last Saturday. With the lace trim?

DAUGHTER 2: Oh, that one.

DAUGHTER 1: Yes, that one. Have you seen it?

DAUGHTER 2: I wore it last night. I didn't think you would mind.

DAUGHTER 1: I do mind. Where is it? [SELF-DISCLOSURE]

DAUGHTER 2: I put it in the clothes hamper.

DAUGHTER 1: (Looking in the hamper) I don't see it.

DAUGHTER 2: It might have gotten pushed down.

DAUGHTER 1: Pushed down! It's right at the bottom and all wrinkled. And it's got ice-cream stains on the front!

DAUGHTER 2: I was going to wash it for you.

DAUGHTER 1: This makes me mad. I don't want you to wear anything of mine unless you ask me first. [SELF-DISCLOSURE and WORK-ABLE COMPROMISE]

DAUGHTER 2: It's no big deal. I'll wash it for you.

DAUGHTER 1: I'm sure you will. In fact I know you will, right now! But I don't want you to wear anything of mine from now on without asking me. [FOGGING and BROKEN RECORD]

DAUGHTER 2: What's the big deal? It will look fine once it's washed and pressed.

DAUGHTER 1: Perhaps, but I don't want you to wear anything of mine from now on without asking me. [FOGGING and BROKEN RE-CORD]

DAUGHTER 2: You wear my clothes sometimes.

DAUGHTER 1: You're right. I do. And it was dumb of me to do that, because it gave you the idea that you could wear something of mine without asking. [NEGATIVE ASSERTION]

DAUGHTER 2: Well, I had to wear it. Bill asked me out to the ice-cream shop last night.

DAUGHTER 1: I'm sure you felt that way, but I don't want you to wear anything of mine from now on without asking me. [FOGGING and BROKEN RECORD]

DAUGHTER 2: Then you can't wear anything of mine.

DAUGHTER 1: I didn't say you can't wear anything of mine. Just ask me first. I wanted to wear this new blouse today. Now I can't. That's why I want you to ask me first when you want to wear something of mine. [SELF-DISCLOSURE and WORKABLE COMPROMISE]

DAUGHTER 2: Okay, I'll ask you first.

DAUGHTER 1: Good. That makes me feel much better. Now, about washing this blouse . . . What's the best way to get ice-cream stains out? [SELF-DISCLOSURE]

DAUGHTER 2: I don't know. Let's ask mom.

DAUGHTER 1: (Handing sis the blouse) You ask her. I'm right behind you.

As you can see in the foregoing dialogue, the aim of the assertive child is to preserve her self-respect, not to set up a working arrangement of "What's mine is mine, and what's yours is negotiable!"

Using Assertive Problem Solving to Make Things Work Between Brothers and Sisters

In maintaining their self-respect, there are other things important to children besides personal possessions. If a child is manipulated into letting everyone else make decisions about even minor things, like what TV program to watch or what clothes to wear, that child's self-respect, as well as his or her ability to think independently, will be impaired. TV watching is trivial, of course, but the principle behind this dialogue practice is not. The goal is to help younger children gain experience in asserting themselves in many trivial areas as practice for more important situations.

In the next set of six dialogues, you can teach your child, as STAR and PLUS do, to be assertive with brothers or sisters in order to make relations between them more harmonious. These dialogues are learning examples for your child on how to preserve one's self-respect in social conflicts that are not as simple and clear-cut as the earlier ones we have looked at.

DIALOGUE 77

Younger Daughter Learns to Work Out a Compromise with a Brother About TV Watching
Age level: Seven through seventeen
Setting: Your daughter and an older brother are watching television. The older one always picks the program to watch. Your daughter decides to set up some arrangement whereby both can pick programs to watch.

DAUGHTER: Whenever we watch TV together, you pick the program we watch. I'd like to choose some too. [SELF-DISCLOSURE]

BROTHER: I do not! You pick some too!

DAUGHTER: I'm sure you feel that way. But how many programs have we watched tonight?

BROTHER: Three.

DAUGHTER: How many have you picked?

BROTHER: That doesn't matter. You wanted to watch them too!

DAUGHTER: I'm sure you felt that way, but I wanted to watch the nature program instead of the talking car. [FOGGING and SELF-DIS-CLOSURE]

BROTHER: You should have said something. The talking car is dumb anyway. I'd like to see it get totaled.

DAUGHTER: You're right. I should have. It was dumb of me not to. But if I say what I want to watch, will you trade? [NEGATIVE ASSER-TION and WORKABLE COMPROMISE]

BROTHER: You might pick something dumb.

DAUGHTER: I might—but then, you picked that dumb talking car. [FOGGING]

BROTHER: But you might pick something really dumb that nobody would want to watch.

DAUGHTER: Maybe, but I still want to trade off. You pick one, then I'll pick one. [FOGGING and WORKABLE COMPROMISE]

BROTHER: But what if two shows I like come on next to each other?

DAUGHTER: Then we can trade off so I can pick two shows that I like, too. [WORKABLE COMPROMISE]

BROTHER: You might like one of my choices and then I'd give it up for nothing.

DAUGHTER: You might like one of *my* choices and then I'd give it up for nothing. [WORKABLE COMPROMISE]

BROTHER: Only if you don't pick something really gross!

DAUGHTER: Okay, only if you don't pick something really gross. How about one veto apiece each evening? [WORKABLE COMPROMISE]

BROTHER: Okay.

DAUGHTER: Since you picked everything up to now, I'd like to pick the next one. [SELF-DISCLOSURE]

BROTHER: No way. That's not fair. We flip a coin to see who goes first.

SISTER: Okay. Heads or tails? [WORKABLE COMPROMISE]

The purpose of being assertive in a situation like this is not for the child to always see the show he or she likes—i.e, to always win. The purpose really has nothing to do with watching TV; it is, rather, to preserve the child's self-respect by raising his or her percentage of "wins." Make sure your child understands, however, that always trying to win is a sucker's play. If your child tries to win all the time, he or she will end up with very low self-respect, because always winning is an impossible goal to strive for.

In the next dialogue you can teach your child, as STAR and PLUS do, how to deal with an inconsiderate brother or sister.

DIALOGUE 78

Son Learns to Work Out a Compromise with His Sister About Being Noisy
Age level: Eleven through seventeen
Setting: Your son has a test tomorrow and wants to go to sleep.

His sister has some of her friends over and they are playing
records in her bedroom loudly enough to keep him awake. He
knocks on the door to her room to talk to her.

SISTER: (Opening door) What do you want? Can't you see I'm busy?
SON: I'm sure you are, but I want to get some sleep before my test
   tomorrow, so I'd appreciate if you would play your records quietly.
   [FOGGING and SELF-DISCLOSURE]
SISTER: If I played them quietly, it wouldn't be any fun.
SON: I'm sure it won't be as much fun, but I want to get some sleep
   before my test tomorrow, so I'd appreciate it if you would play your
   records quietly. [FOGGING and BROKEN RECORD]
SISTER: The record player isn't loud.
SON: I'm sure it doesn't sound loud if you're not trying to sleep, but I'd
   appreciate it if you would play your records quietly. [FOGGING and
   BROKEN RECORD]
SISTER: Why don't you stick some cotton in your ears!
SON: I could, but I want to get some sleep before my test tomorrow,
   so I'd appreciate it if you would play your records quietly. [FOG-
   GING and BROKEN RECORD]
SISTER: You are embarrassing me in front of my friends!
SON: I feel bad about that, but I want to get some sleep before my test
   tomorrow, so I'd appreciate it if you would play your records quietly.
   [SELF-DISCLOSURE and BROKEN RECORD]
SISTER: Well, I won't!
SON: When's the next time you have a test?
SISTER: On Monday. Why?
SON: If you turn your record player way down tonight, I won't play mine
   at all on Sunday night. How's that for a deal? [WORKABLE COM-
   PROMISE]
SISTER: Why should I care what you do on Sunday night?
SON: You have a test on Monday, the way I have a test tomorrow, and
   I'd like to get some sleep tonight the way you will Sunday night. Is
   it a deal? [WORKABLE COMPROMISE]
SISTER: We were having so much fun.
SON: You can have fun again Monday night after your test. [WORK-
   ABLE COMPROMISE]
SISTER: Okay.

SON: If I can't get to sleep because you are noisy tonight, you probably will be in the same boat on Sunday night. [WORKABLE COMPROMISE]

SISTER: I get the message. I'll keep the party quiet.

SON: Terrific. I appreciate a smart as well as a good-looking sister.

The dialogue above is a model for your son or daughter of three important parts of assertively dealing with an inconsiderate brother or sister. First is persistence. One does not deal with an inconsiderate person by just saying what one wants and walking away. Your son or daughter may have to go through this a half-dozen times in one night, in the example above, to get results. The real message this gives to the inconsiderate person is "If I can't sleep, you can't have any fun either."

The second important part is to point out that a compromise always exists in any situation—i.e., "One hand washes the other," or "Next week you may want the same consideration from me." This "personal" way of dealing with nuisances does not rely upon generalities like common decency, what every person should know, society's rules, etc., and is much more effective. Children as well as adults respond much more positively to personal requests than to those based on societal rules.

The third important aspect of dealing assertively with an inconsiderate person is to thank him or her for cooperating, since the request is a personal one, not one from the Big Book of Human Rules that we disobey at our peril.

In the next dialogue a daughter has to gain the cooperation of her sister in order to get to an appointment on time. The same assertive goals of cooperating with one another that were stressed in the previous dialogue apply here also.

DIALOGUE 79

Daughter Learns to Work Out a Compromise with a Sister About Getting Up and Out in the Morning
Age level: Eleven through seventeen
Setting: Your daughter has overslept a bit on Saturday morning.

She goes to the bathroom and her sister is there. Sis is notorious for dawdling in the morning, and daughter will be late for an appointment if she can't get sis to hurry up.

DAUGHTER 1: I did something dumb. I overslept. [NEGATIVE AS-SERTION]

DAUGHTER 2: So?

DAUGHTER 1: I feel bad about pushing you, but I'd appreciate it if you would speed things up—otherwise I'll be late for an appointment. [SELF-DISCLOSURE and WORKABLE COMPROMISE]

DAUGHTER 2: It's your fault, not mine.

DAUGHTER 1: Yes, it is, but I'd still appreciate it if you would speed things up so I'm not late. [NEGATIVE ASSERTION and BRO-KEN RECORD]

DAUGHTER 2: You should have thought of that before you overslept.

DAUGHTER 1: You're right, I should have, but I'd still appreciate it if you would speed things up so I'm not late. [FOGGING and BRO-KEN RECORD]

DAUGHTER 2: Well, I have a lot to do this morning. I have to take a bath, and wash my hair. Lots of things.

DAUGHTER 1: I'm sure you do, but I'd still appreciate it if you would speed things up so I'm not late. [FOGGING and BROKEN RE-CORD]

DAUGHTER 2: I have somewhere to go too.

DAUGHTER 1: I'm sure you do, but I'd still appreciate it if you would speed things up so I'm not late. [FOGGING and BROKEN RE-CORD]

DAUGHTER 2: Why should I?

DAUGHTER 1: You may have an important appointment next week or next month. If I'm in the bathroom first, I may feel like washing my hair then too. Is that what you want? [WORKABLE COMPRO-MISE]

DAUGHTER 2: Why don't you use the kitchen sink, or the one in the laundry?

DAUGHTER 1: It's not the sink I need to use first.

DAUGHTER 2: Why didn't you say so?

DAUGHTER 1: I should have, shouldn't I? [FOGGING]

DAUGHTER 2: I'll be in my bedroom. Let me know when you're finished.
DAUGHTER 1: I will.

The above dialogue points out that your child will very often have to be assertive in situations where there are no preset rules or structure to use as a guide. In these situations your child becomes a problem solver by getting rid of manipulation intended to block him or her from doing anything. Once manipulation is dealt with, problem solving usually works out a solution with little effort.

This problem-solving orientation used to make things work out between brothers and/or sisters is illustrated even more clearly in the next dialogue. Here, you can teach your child, as STAR and PLUS do, how to cope with a sister or brother in making agreements work in a detailed and practical way.

DIALOGUE 80

Daughter Works Out a Compromise with Her Sister on Sharing Clothes
Age level: Eleven through seventeen
Setting: Last Saturday your two daughters agreed to pool their money and buy outfits they both can wear. On Monday morning both sisters want to wear the same outfit.

DAUGHTER 1: I want to wear the blue outfit today.
DAUGHTER 2: I want to wear it too.
DAUGHTER 1: Well, we both can't wear it. First pick gets it.
DAUGHTER 2: I understand you want to wear it, but we haven't decided yet who gets to wear what and when. I want a better system.
DAUGHTER 1: It's simple. First to choose gets it.
DAUGHTER 2: I'm sure you would like it that way, since you said you wanted it first. But I want us to agree on a better system. [FOGGING and BROKEN RECORD]
DAUGHTER 1: What's wrong with first pick?
DAUGHTER 2: I don't like it. I want to set up a system so we both know where we stand. [SELF-DISCLOSURE and BROKEN RECORD]

DAUGHTER 1: One that gives you an advantage!

DAUGHTER 2: I'm sure you feel that way, but I want to set up a system so we both know where we stand. [FOGGING and BROKEN RECORD]

DAUGHTER 1: Like what?

DAUGHTER 2: How about rotating first pick? You one day and me the next? [WORKABLE COMPROMISE]

DAUGHTER 1: But what if I absolutely need to wear something on your day?

DAUGHTER 2: We can trade off. I give you one of my days and you give me one of yours. [WORKABLE COMPROMISE]

DAUGHTER 1: But what if you won't let me have first pick on one of your days?

DAUGHTER 2: What if you won't let me have first pick on one of *your* days?

DAUGHTER 1: It won't work.

DAUGHTER 2: It may not, but I'd like to try it. How about this? We write down our trade-offs on the inside of the closet door, and the one with the most trade-offs gets the pick if she wants it. [FOGGING and WORKABLE COMPROMISE]

DAUGHTER 1: How's that going to help me if I absolutely need to wear a particular outfit?

DAUGHTER 2: It may not always, but you can make sure if you are nice to me beforehand. [FOGGING and WORKABLE COMPROMISE]

DAUGHTER 2: Like how?

DAUGHTER 2: By saving up trade-offs before you need them. [WORKABLE COMPROMISE]

DAUGHTER 1: Okay, but how do we start today?

DAUGHTER 2: You start and I'll get one trade-off. [WORKABLE COMPROMISE]

DAUGHTER 1: No. You start and I'll get one trade-off.

DAUGHTER 2: Okay. I'll wear the blue outfit.

DAUGHTER 1: And I choose tomorrow?

DAUGHTER 2: Right. Let's mark down your trade-off on a sheet of paper on the back of the door.

In the next dialogue, as in the last one, problem solving between siblings is the whole purpose of the assertive practice. With this example you can teach your child, as STAR and PLUS do, how to assertively work out a compromise with a brother or sister that stresses mutual problem solving.

DIALOGUE 81

Son Learns to Work Out a Compromise with His Brother So They Can Help Each Other
Age level: Eleven through seventeen
Setting: Your two sons take turns cleaning up after dinner each weeknight. This week one son has Tuesday and Thursday night and his brother has Monday, Wednesday, and Friday. It is Monday night. On Thursday your son has to go back to school right after dinner to help with the school play. He talks to his brother as cleanup begins to see if something can be worked out to swap nights.

SON 1: Would you like me to clean up tonight?

SON 2: You want to do the dishes when you don't have to? What are you trying to get out of me?

SON 1: Not much. I just want to swap tonight for Thursday night.

SON 2: Why?

SON 1: I have to get back to school Thursday to help with the school play.

SON 2: How badly do you want to get off early Thursday?

SON 1: I don't understand.

SON 2: How much do you want to be able to get there on time?

SON 1: I would really appreciate it if you would swap tonight for Thursday night. [SELF-DISCLOSURE and WORKABLE COMPROMISE]

SON 2: You want a favor from me, right?

SON 1: Yes. I'd appreciate your helping me out. [SELF-DISCLOSURE]

SON 2: It will cost you.

Son 1: I don't understand. You want me to pay you to make the swap? [SELF-DISCLOSURE]

Son 2: No, just do something for me.

Son 1: What?

Son 2: Do tonight and Wednesday for Thursday.

Son 1: That makes me mad. It's not an even trade. [SELF-DISCLO-SURE]

Son 2: Take it or leave it.

Son 1: Well, I'll have to take it, but I'd like for us to help each other out the way we do now, instead of trying to take advantage when one of us gets in a jam. [SELF-DISCLOSURE and WORKABLE COMPROMISE]

Son 2: What do you mean?

Son 1: I was thinking of how I was helping you out with algebra without trying to take advantage of you. [WORKABLE COMPROMISE]

Son 2: You mean you won't help me with algebra if I don't swap nights even?

Son 1: No. If you want to always get something from me when you help me out, then I'll want something for helping you with your homework when you get stuck. [WORKABLE COMPROMISE]

Son 2: Like what?

Son 1: I don't know. I'll have to think of how to take advantage of you the way you're trying to take advantage of me. [SELF-DISCLO-SURE]

Son 2: That's not fair!

Son 1: It probably isn't, but you seem to want to do it that way. [FOGGING]

Son 2: I'd rather do it the way we always do.

Son 1: Will you swap tonight for Thursday? [WORKABLE COM-PROMISE]

Son 2: Okay.

This assertive problem-solving approach is continued in the next dialogue. With this example, you can teach your child, as STAR and PLUS do, how to deal with an older sister or brother in a situation that involves money and deciding how to use it.

DIALOGUE 82

*Younger Son Learns to Work Out a Compromise with His Sister
on Pooling Their Money and Agreeing How to Spend It*
Age level: Seven through seventeen
*Setting: Mom's birthday is coming up next week. Junior and his
sister have agreed that the best way to get a nice present for
mom's birthday is to pool their savings and buy one gift from
both of them. Now they have to agree on what to buy.*

SON: I think we ought to buy something for the house, like a vase.

SISTER: That's dumb!

SON: I don't understand. What is it about buying a vase that is dumb?
[NEGATIVE INQUIRY]

SISTER: It's not personal.

SON: I don't understand. What is it about buying something that's not
personal that's bad? [NEGATIVE INQUIRY]

SISTER: We should get her something really nice, like a new blouse.

SON: I don't understand. What is it about buying her a blouse that's
nicer? [NEGATIVE INQUIRY]

SISTER: I knew you wouldn't understand!

SON: You're right. I don't understand. What is it about buying her a
blouse that's better? [FOGGING and NEGATIVE INQUIRY]

SISTER: Women don't like things for the house as gifts.

SON: I really don't understand. What is it about buying her something
for the house that means she won't like it? [NEGATIVE INQUIRY]

SISTER: She can't wear a vase!

SON: You're right, she can't. What is it about buying her something for
the house that means she won't like it? [FOGGING and NEGA-
TIVE INQUIRY]

SISTER: You're impossible!

SON: I probably am, but what is it about buying mom something for the
house that means she won't like it? [FOGGING and NEGATIVE
INQUIRY]

SISTER: If we don't get something that I know how to pick out, like a
blouse, we will probably get something horrible, like a purple vase
with bubbles in it.

SON: It sounds to me like you want to choose mom's present. [SELF-DISCLOSURE]

SISTER: If I do, at least it will be something nice.

SON: If you pick out the present, I'm sure it will be something nice. But I want to buy something we both choose. [FOGGING and WORKABLE COMPROMISE]

SISTER: How?

SON: Let's look first. If we find a vase, or something for the house that we both like, we can put it on our list and then look for a blouse that we both like. Then we can flip a coin. [WORKABLE COMPROMISE]

SISTER: What if we can't find anything we both like?

SON: Then we still flip a coin. [WORKABLE COMPROMISE]

SISTER: Okay. But I still think a nice blouse would be best.

SON: Maybe you're right. But let's look first, okay? [WORKABLE COMPROMISE]

SISTER: Okay.

This particular dialogue is valuable in that it points out to your son that he does not have to be intimidated into doing what his sister wants (or vice versa) just because he does not have as much expertise as his sister does in women's clothing, or what women "really" like. To make this point clear to your children, give them the realistic, working definition of *expert:* An expert is anyone who knows just a little more than you do about a subject.

This chapter covers many examples of resolvable conflict between the children in your family that can be handled with assertive skills. The chapter's main aim has been to encourage you to teach your child how to deal assertively with degrading teasing and criticism, how to protect self-respect and decision-making choices, and how to use mutual problem solving in finding compromises based on two children helping each other.

Now let's turn to the next chapter and see how you can assert yourself to your children using the problem-solving option stressed above, as well as some new information for resolving several important conflicts between parents and children as they grow up.

CHAPTER EIGHT

Asserting Yourself to Your Child, Then Teaching Your Child How to Be Assertive to Mom and Dad

In my years of teaching seminars and workshops for teachers and parents in how to be assertive toward children, I am always asked one question: "How do I deal with a really pushy, stubborn kid who won't listen to me?" To answer that question, I ask another in return: "How did the kid get that way—pushy, stubborn, and insensitive to what you say?" After a few moments of dead silence, I answer my own question. "The reason the kid is so pushy and stubborn, perhaps even bratty, is that he or she has learned to be this way. He's been reinforced in the past for being pushy, stubborn, and bratty. But what has been learned can be unlearned. You have to retrain the kid to not be pushy, stubborn, or bratty in your presence!"

Most children test authorities to see if they mean what they say and whether there are any exceptions, limits, or loopholes in what they have told the children to do. This does not mean that there is anything wrong with these children. On the contrary, it is a sign that their natural intelligence is working. If you observe that one of your own children has learned to be stubborn, or if you are a teacher and one of your pupils makes life difficult for you, this observation means only that the child has gotten something—or gotten out of something—in the past for being stubborn.

Changing Chronic Negative Behavior

If you want to change chronic behavior—any kind of behavior—of your child or someone else you are often involved with, you must change your typical response to that behavior, and thereby eliminate any reward for it. In other words, you must be assertive, and teach the child that *you* are the authority who wants him or her to do something, not his or her school principal, the municipal authorities, God, or even your spouse, any or all of whom you may be tempted to cite in support of your demand. If you respond to your child's pushy, persistent "Why should I?" with manipulation based on external authorities like these, rather than your own personal, assertive authority, your child—like most —will automatically respond as dialectically as a graduate of Harvard Law School, giving you reasons why the school principal, God, or your spouse really doesn't want him or her to do what you want. Children do this only because it has worked for them in the past.

Parents and teachers faced with a guaranteed fight each time a child is asked to do something (or not do something) often find it easier to ignore the unwanted behavior and let the child have his or her way. Unfortunately, the option of ignoring unwanted behavior is usually seen as the lesser of two evils—the only other option being the role of a harsh, tyrannical dictator instead of a caring mother, father, or teacher. Happily, there is a further and more productive option: to be assertive to the children in your charge.

As you have seen in our practice dialogues, if you are assertive, you lessen the conflict by giving the child very little room to countermanipulate you. Also, since being assertive is far less work than being manipulative, you won't feel as exasperated by the child's stubbornness as you were in the past. Most important, when you are assertive to your child, you are also teaching your child to be assertive. We learn most of the important things in life by imitation of other people's behavior and self-correcting feedback. Thus, if you are assertive in dealing with your child, he or she will use your behavior as a model and also learn to be assertive in resolving problems. You are demonstrating for the child how to resolve conflicts in ways that are least costly to everyone in terms of hurt feelings, grudges, and loss of self-respect.

It is important to know how to be assertive to, and what to expect from, a child who is stubborn or uncooperative. In all likelihood you will have the same experience as the teachers and parents in the assertiveness seminars I talked about earlier. The first time you assert yourself to a stubborn child, it may take you a half-hour to get the child to listen to what you say and to realize that you mean it. The next time will typically be shorter, perhaps fifteen minutes; then ten minutes; then five minutes; and so on. Eventually the child will respond quickly to your request. The reason why assertive communication with children is so efficient is that repeated dialogues over a disputed behavior teach the child that you mean what you say and will not be manipulated into giving up. The child's repertoire of coping behaviors is just as efficient as yours. If a coping behavior that worked in the past no longer works, the child will abandon it.

The illustrative dialogue that follows points out that persistent Broken Record, Self-Disclosure, and other skills work to resolve parent-child conflicts as well as those with other people. This dialogue deals with a common problem parents have with younger children: getting them to leave the TV set and get ready for bed.

DIALOGUE 83

Getting Your Son Away from the TV and to Bed
Age level: Seven through ten
Setting: It is 10 p.m. and you find your son still sitting in front of the television set watching a movie.

YOU: I told you to get ready for bed.

SON: Huh? I didn't hear you.

YOU: Perhaps you didn't. But I want you to get up now, wash, and get into bed. [FOGGING and BROKEN RECORD]

SON: Just a couple of minutes more. The movie is getting to the good part.

YOU: I'm sure it is, but I want you to get ready for bed right now. [FOGGING and BROKEN RECORD]

SON: Five minutes more. I promise.

YOU: I'm sure you feel that way, but I want you to get ready for bed right now. [FOGGING and BROKEN RECORD]

SON: Watch this part coming up. It's really interesting.

YOU: I'm sure it is, but I want you to get ready for bed right now. [FOGGING and BROKEN RECORD]

SON: I've been waiting for a half-hour just to see this part.

YOU: I'm sure you have, but I want you to get ready for bed right now. [FOGGING and BROKEN RECORD]

SON: That's not fair!

YOU: You're right. It isn't. But I want you to get ready for bed right now. [FOGGING and BROKEN RECORD]

SON: You let Nancy stay up past her bedtime last week.

YOU: You're right. I did. That was dumb of me. But I want you to get ready for bed right now. [FOGGING, NEGATIVE ASSERTION, and BROKEN RECORD]

SON: You treat me like a little kid. All the rest of the guys my age can stay up and watch a movie.

YOU: I'm sure they can. And I know it upsets you when I make you go to bed. But I want you to get ready for bed right now. [FOGGING, SELF-DISCLOSURE, and BROKEN RECORD]

SON: My homework is done. I don't have to do it tomorrow morning.

YOU: I'm sure it is, but I want you to get ready for bed right now. [FOGGING and BROKEN RECORD]

SON: (Turning to other parent) Dad [or Mom], do I have to go to bed now?

YOU: I'm sure you would like to stay up with dad [or mom], but I want you to get ready for bed right now. [FOGGING and BROKEN RECORD]

SON: (Turning again to other parent) Dad [Mom]?

YOU: I'm sure you would like your father [mother] to help you out. But I want you to get ready for bed right now. [FOGGING and BROKEN RECORD]

SON: Aww . . . Dad [Mom]?

YOU: I'm sure you would like someone to say you can stay up, but I want you to get ready for bed right now. [FOGGING and BROKEN RECORD]

SON: This is rotten.

234 / *Manuel J. Smith*

YOU: It is rotten to take you away from a movie you like, but I want you to get ready for bed right now. [FOGGING and BROKEN RECORD]

SON: Aw, rats! It was just getting to the good part.

YOU: I'm sure it was, but I want you to get ready for bed right now. [FOGGING and BROKEN RECORD]

SON: I'm going. I'm going.

The key here is not to fall into the trap of requiring the child to *like* following the rules you set, such as going to bed on time. It isn't important that he or she like the house rules you lay down to preserve everyone's sanity, or even that he or she like *you* when you insist that they be followed. But it is important that you be as consistent as possible in enforcing them.

In the next dialogue a parent has to deal with a child who wants an exception to a rule: an advance on next week's allowance.

DIALOGUE 84

Saying No to Your Daughter's Request for an Advance on Her Allowance
Age level: Seven through thirteen
Setting: You are giving your younger daughter her weekly allowance, and she asks you to lend her some money.

DAUGHTER: Can I get next week's allowance now, too?

YOU: Why do you need next week's now?

DAUGHTER: That record I've always wanted—the one by the Runny Noses. It's on sale, but I don't have enough with just this week's allowance.

YOU: You know the rule. No loans. You can do anything you want with the allowance. It's yours. But you have to wait till next week to get more.

DAUGHTER: But the sale will be over by then.

YOU: I'm sure it will, but no advance loan. [FOGGING and BROKEN RECORD]

DAUGHTER: That's rotten!

YOU: I'm sure it is. But no loan. [FOGGING and BROKEN RECORD]

DAUGHTER: But this is an emergency.

YOU: I'm sure you feel that way, but no loan. [FOGGING and BROKEN RECORD]

DAUGHTER: Don't you care about me?

YOU: (Not letting yourself be baited into an argument about how much a parent should care) I'm sure it seems as though I don't care, but no loan. [FOGGING and BROKEN RECORD]

DAUGHTER: If you don't lend me the money, what can I do?

YOU: I don't know. What can you do? [SELF-DISCLOSURE]

DAUGHTER: If you weren't so rigid, you would lend me the money.

YOU: You're right. I am rigid about this, so no loan. [FOGGING and BROKEN RECORD]

DAUGHTER: It's not fair. Judy's mother lent her the money to get the record.

YOU: You're right. It's not fair that Judy's mom lent her the money and I won't. [FOGGING]

DAUGHTER: You're treating me like a little kid.

YOU: It must seem that way to you, doesn't it? [FOGGING]

DAUGHTER: How can I get anything I want if you are so rigid?

YOU: You certainly can't get that record if you need a loan from me. [FOGGING]

DAUGHTER: Just this once?

YOU: No loan. How come you didn't save last week's allowance so you could buy the record now?

DAUGHTER: I didn't know it was going to be on sale.

YOU: I don't like being the heavy pointing this out to you, but one of the reasons you get an allowance is to let you learn how to handle money. You could have saved a little bit from each allowance so that when sales came up, you would have the money to take advantage of them. That's what your father [mother] and I do.

DAUGHTER: That's no help to me now.

YOU: You're right. It isn't. But it can be next time you want to buy a record on sale. [FOGGING and WORKABLE COMPROMISE]

DAUGHTER: I thought you would help me.

YOU: I don't like saying no to you, but other than lending you the money, how else can I help you get the record? [SELF-DISCLO-SURE and WORKABLE COMPROMISE]

DAUGHTER: You could buy it yourself with your own money, and I could pay you back next week with my allowance.

YOU: That's just lending you the money. I said I won't do that. [BRO-KEN RECORD]

DAUGHTER: What else can I do?

YOU: Call up the record shop and see if you can get a rain check. Say you can't come in, and ask them to hold one of the records for you till next week. [WORKABLE COMPROMISE]

DAUGHTER: Do you think they will do that?

YOU: Maybe. I do it all the time at the department store.

DAUGHTER: Okay.

In the above dialogue the parent is consistent in trying to set things up so that the child's irresponsible behavior with respect to her allowance is not reinforced but the child is supported for thinking things out, as an adult would, to gain a wanted goal.

The simple and effective method used in the above dialogue is useful when a child's obeying you here and now is most important. Now let's look at an alternate way of dealing with problems between parents and children. This method, called "assertive problem solving," helps you to find out how your child's doing what you want is causing a problem for him or her that in turn interferes with your doing what you want.

In the next example you realize that it is taking longer and longer for Junior to come home from playing with the other boys, and this is holding up dinner. You have spoken to him before about his lateness and nothing has happened. This time you proceed on the assumption that behavior is always predictable: If Junior isn't coming home on time for dinner, either dinner is not as much fun as what he is doing, or there is a negative result of his coming home on time. You can use Negative Inquiry to see if you can identify this negative result and figure out how Junior could avoid or eliminate it, giving him a way to resolve his problem and still be home for dinner on time.

DIALOGUE 85

Finding Out Why Your Son Does Not Come Home for Dinner
Age level: Seven through thirteen
Setting: After dinner you tell Junior that you want to talk to him.

YOU: In the past week, you have been late for dinner four times. I want you to be here at six, when dinner's ready.

SON: It wasn't my fault. I couldn't leave on time.

YOU: I'm sure you felt that way or you would have come home for dinner on time. But I don't care whose fault it is, I just want you home on time for dinner. [FOGGING, SELF-DISCLOSURE, and BROKEN RECORD]

SON: Sure.

YOU: That's what you said last time I talked to you. I don't believe you when you say it like that. It sounds as if you're just trying to put me off. [SELF-DISCLOSURE]

SON: No. I'll be home.

YOU: If you had said that first instead of saying it wasn't your fault, I might believe you, but I don't. Let's talk about it. Tell me why you feel as if you can't come home for dinner on time. [WORKABLE COMPROMISE]

SON: It's no big deal.

YOU: It is to me. [SELF-DISCLOSURE]

SON: You wouldn't understand.

YOU: Maybe not, but I'll try. [NEGATIVE ASSERTION]

SON: If I have to go home before the other guys, I get embarrassed.

YOU: What is it about having to go home before the other guys that embarrasses you? [NEGATIVE INQUIRY]

SON: It makes me feel like a little kid when you call me.

YOU: What is it about my calling you that makes you feel like a little kid? [NEGATIVE INQUIRY]

SON: Their moms don't make them come home at six!

YOU: Don't they eat dinner?

SON: I don't know.

YOU: Either they eat dinner later than we do, or their moms don't care if they eat dinner. Which do you think it is?

Son: They eat dinner later than we do.

You: Okay, tomorrow, you be the last one to come home and see what the other guys say when they leave. [WORKABLE COMPROMISE]

Son: Why?

You: I want you to find out what time the other guys go home for dinner. [WORKABLE COMPROMISE]

Son: They may not go home until real late.

You: Don't you think they get hungry?

Son: Sure.

You: Do you think they go home when they get hungry?

Son: I guess.

You: Do you think they will stay there just because you're still there?

Son: You think they will get embarrassed too?

You: No, I think they will ask you if you're hungry, and why you aren't going home to dinner.

Son: Really?

You: Yes. Don't you get hungry before dinner?

Son: Sure.

You: Is being hungry something to be embarrassed about?

Son: No.

You: Then how about telling them you are hungry and going home to dinner, instead of waiting for me to call you? Would that make you feel like a little kid? [WORKABLE COMPROMISE]

Son: No, but sometimes I'm not hungry.

You: Then how about just saying you are going home to dinner? Would that make you feel like a little kid? [WORKABLE COMPROMISE]

Son: No.

You: Do you think you have to be the last one home tomorrow night?

Son: No.

Using the Trap Model of Behavior Change to Work Out Compromises with Your Children

To resolve behavior problems like the one above, you can often systematically figure out what is causing your child to disobey you by using the TRAP model of behavior change before you talk to the child.

TRAP WORKSHEET

Specify:

(in concrete, behavioral terms that affect you directly)

Trouble (Behavior) _____

_____

_____

_____

Result (Negative) _____

_____

_____

_____

Alternative (or Answer) _____

_____

_____

_____

Payoff (Positive or Negative) _____

_____

_____

_____

TRAP helps you organize your decision making and the best sequence of spelling out what you want changed, and why. TRAP is an acronym that stands for Trouble, Result, Alternative, Payoff, a sequence shown on the sample worksheet on page 239.

In many situations it's not simple to enforce the rules for a child, especially when he or she starts to mature. Sometimes a child does things you want done but upsets the household routine in the process. For instance, let's suppose that your older daughter has gotten into the habit of doing her homework just before she's supposed to go to bed each night, and this bothers you. It's not your daughter's studying or doing homework that bothers you, but when she decides to do it. You want her to begin studying earlier in the evening, but in previous discussions with her, she has complained that she can't study then because the other kids are too noisy and the TV's too loud.

The TRAP model helps you specifically identify what you want changed and why. Using TRAP, you may find out that what you want changed is not what you initially thought was bothering you, and that there is a more practical and useful alternative behavior that will solve the problem. For example, when you use TRAP, you may find that it's really not your child's studying late, but something else that happens when your child studies late that needs to be corrected. TRAP can help you figure out compromises with the child that work—i.e., positive behaviors are preserved and encouraged, and negative results of those behaviors are minimized.

The key concept of the TRAP method is *specify.* For TRAP to help you in communicating what you want, you must first specify, in concrete terms, what *trouble* the behavior in question causes you, what is the negative *result* of that behavior, what is the *alternative* behavior that will eliminate that *result,* and what is the *payoff* for changing. Oddly enough, most of us make the mistake of trying to eliminate a behavior that produces a negative result for us instead of eliminating the negative result. This distinction is important if the behavior itself, such as studying, is a positive behavior.

Use of the TRAP method of behavior change therefore frees you from having to be dogmatic with your children. Indeed, if you want your child to learn how to use his or her judgment effectively in handling important matters like studying, sex, or alcohol and drug use, it is important to get your child accustomed to being suspicious of dogmatic statements used to justify absolute rules that must be obeyed—e.g., "Everyone knows that children have to be in bed on time," or "Children always have to be home on time for dinner." Your child's peers can invent dogma just as well as you can, and you are not likely to approve of their dogma's effect upon your child.

Let's look at what TRAP has you do to resolve problems between you and your child. First, in order to communicate to your child (or anyone else, for that matter) what is bothering you, specify the *trouble* in concrete behavioral terms. To accomplish behavior change, you first have to present the child with evidence he or she cannot deny. This will avoid the problem you face when you say, "You're always late," or "You never get to bed on time," or "You always take too long doing your homework at night." If you answer your child or anyone else this way, I can guarantee you will hear a response such as "Not true, I got to bed on time last Thursday [or once in 1983]!" Avoid using the words *too, never,* and *always* in communicating with other people. They are imprecise and don't specify exactly what the trouble is. If you don't know specifically how often the unwanted behavior occurs, make a log of the behavior for a week or so. Then you can go to your child and say, "Last week you stayed up past ten P.M. three times, and this week once." When you use this type of explicit, concrete feedback, what you say cannot be denied, pooh-poohed, or ignored.

Second, specify the negative *result* that the troublesome behavior causes. If you can't think of any specific, concrete negative result that the unwanted behavior causes, don't worry—you have old friends available. Using Negative Inquiry on yourself will likely cause the *result, answer,* and *payoff* of the TRAP model to fall out and be identified. You can use the TRAP model by yourself beforehand to organize your thinking prior to talking to your child, or, as in the preceding dialogue, you can use TRAP while you are talking to the child, to identify the negative *result* that keeps Junior from coming home to dinner on time. In the present situation, if you are not sure why you get upset when your child does his or her homework right before going to bed, run something like the following minidialogue on yourself.

INQUIRY: What is it about daughter doing her homework late that is bad or upsets me? [NEGATIVE INQUIRY]

RESPONSE: Sometimes she doesn't get to bed on time because her homework is not finished by ten.

INQUIRY: What is it about her sometimes not getting to bed on time that upsets me? [NEGATIVE INQUIRY]

To that Negative Inquiry, you might give any of the following possible responses:

RESPONSE 1: When she doesn't go to bed on time, I can't get myself comfortable.

RESPONSE 2: She won't get enough sleep.

RESPONSE 3: When she doesn't go to bed on time, the other children complain.

Since none of these responses is specific enough to give your daughter realistic feedback on the problem she is causing, more inquiry on what troubles you personally is needed to get a concrete negative result of her behavior.

If you come up with the first response, you can follow it up with another Negative Inquiry to specify more clearly in your mind why doing homework late causes a negative result for you.

INQUIRY: What is it about daughter not going to bed on time that means I can't feel comfortable? [NEGATIVE INQUIRY]

RESPONSE: When daughter is up and about, that means my spouse and I can't relax, or chat, or fool around, or make love, or go to bed, or sleep.

This is a concrete negative result for you of her behavior. While you may not want to give this detailed, specific feedback to your daughter, you can tell her that you feel uncomfortable when she stays up late doing her homework, or that both mom and dad have trouble relaxing or sleeping if she is up and about. With this negative result, you know what will happen and do not have to speculate on what you are afraid *might* happen. What might happen is always subject to being pooh-poohed or denied.

If you gave the second response, "She won't get enough sleep," you can see that it does not spell out a concrete negative result for you.

It needs to be followed up to see if it actually is a personal, negative result.

INQUIRY: What is it about daughter not getting enough sleep that upsets me? [NEGATIVE INQUIRY]
RESPONSE: She may do badly in school.

This possible result might be a general worry of yours, but it, too, isn't specific or concrete enough for you to expect anyone to pay attention to it. Daughter may indeed do badly in school the next day, but she may also do very well in school despite the lack of sleep. The inquiry needs to be continued until a specific, concrete negative result for you is identified.

INQUIRY: What is it about daughter's not getting enough sleep that upsets me? [NEGATIVE INQUIRY]
RESPONSE: When she doesn't get enough sleep the night before, she comes home from school grouchy and grumpy and she's a real pain to deal with.

This is a specific, concrete negative result for you that can be used realistically in giving your daughter effective assertive feedback on her behavior.

The third response—complaints by other children in the family— is specific, but—as stated—it has nothing to do with any negative result for you. Children complain all the time, and it is unrealistic for you to ask one child to change his or her behavior just because other children complain about it. If they don't like their sister staying up late to do homework, tell them to complain to her directly instead of to you. Your job as a parent in a family system is not to make it work by getting everybody to please everybody else. More inquiry is needed.

INQUIRY: What is it about the other children's complaining that upsets me? [NEGATIVE INQUIRY]

RESPONSE: When the other children complain, I have trouble getting them to go to sleep, too.

This is a personal, negative result for you, and is concrete enough to be used as assertive feedback to get her to change.

As you can see, in using TRAP we are after a specific, concrete negative result that causes you a personal problem. If the first inquiry does not produce a specific, personal, concrete negative result, you continue with the inquiry until one falls out. If repeated Negative Inquiry does not produce a concrete result, you are very likely dealing with your own irrational worries and feelings of insecurity. Those irrational feelings may go something like "If I don't do everything I can to see that my daughter does things right, she may be a failure in life." You certainly don't want your daughter to be a failure, but it is a sucker's play to use that as a basis for trying to get her to change the time when she does her homework. I can guarantee that you will have little positive gain when you try to get other people, even your children, to reorder their lives to ease your personal worries.

The *alternative* and *payoff* parts of the TRAP model for changing behavior often automatically flow from specifically identifying the negative result. For example, if the main negative result of daughter's staying up late to study is coming home the next day grumpy, grouchy, and a pain to be around, the *alternative* behavior is not to be grouchy, grumpy, and a pain the next day. The *payoff* for not being grouchy, grumpy, and a pain will be permission for her to study late again in the future, if necessary.

If the negative result of studying late is that the other children don't go to sleep, the *alternative* would be for daughter to do it in a way that doesn't keep them awake or make your job of getting them to bed harder. The *payoff* would again be that daughter can continue to stay up late and study.

If the negative result of daughter's late studying is that it keeps you and your spouse awake, or makes you both nervous about engaging in private behavior, the *alternative* would be for daughter to remain in her room while studying after bedtime, having performed all her nightly ablutions prior to studying. She could then go directly to bed after finishing her work. Again the *payoff* for this alternative behavior would be that daughter could stay up late studying.

In the dialogue in which Junior was consistently late for dinner, if Junior were older, you might use negative inquiry to identify what the negative *result* was for you when your child showed up late. In all likelihood it would be problems in keeping dinner warm and everyone else from grumbling at you. The *alternative* for that situation would be to allow him to call you from a friend's house to say that he was going to be late for dinner and not to keep everyone waiting.

It is important to realize that the payoff for eliminating a behavior's negative result does not have to be a reward, a gold star, or a trip to Disneyland. It can be nothing more than permission to continue that behavior. It is also important to realize that the payoff for eliminating a negative behavior may be as simple as saying, "If you don't do that, I will be happy and will stop pestering you to change."

Now let's look at an illustrative dialogue wherein you use the information you gain from the TRAP model to work out an answer to the late-studying problem with your daughter.

DIALOGUE 86

Deciding If Your Daughter Can Stay Up Studying after Bedtime
Age level: Eleven through seventeen
Setting: It's 10 P.M. and you look into your daughter's room. She is supposed to be in bed, but is still doing today's homework. You enter to speak to her about this.

You: You are supposed to be in bed now.

DAUGHTER: This homework is really hard. It's taking longer than I thought.

You: I'm sure it is hard, but I've asked before that you get in bed by ten. [FOGGING and BROKEN RECORD]

DAUGHTER: It's only tonight. Besides, I'll just be a little longer.

You: One night is no big deal, but you have been doing your homework late every night. Last week you stayed up past your bedtime twice. Now again tonight. So I want to talk to you about it. [Specifying TROUBLE]

DAUGHTER: It's so noisy around here when the other kids are up that I can't think straight.

YOU: It is noisy, but your staying up causes me some problems, so I wanted to talk to you about it. [FOGGING and BROKEN RECORD]

DAUGHTER: What problems?

YOU: Three of them. When you study late, you come home grumpy the next afternoon. [Specific negative RESULT]

DAUGHTER: I am not a grump when I come home. You're just a sensitive person.

YOU: I probably am too sensitive, but if you want to stay up studying, I don't want to put up with a grump and a pain the next day. [FOGGING, SELF-DISCLOSURE, and specific negative RESULT, plus ALTERNATIVE and PAYOFF—i.e., WORKABLE COMPROMISE]

DAUGHTER: You mean last week. That was because Joanie gave me a bad time and I was upset.

YOU: Perhaps she did, but if you want to stay up studying, I don't want to put up with a grump and a pain when you come home from school tomorrow. [FOGGING and specific negative RESULT, plus ALTERNATIVE and PAYOFF—i.e., WORKABLE COMPROMISE]

DAUGHTER: I won't be a grump. I promise.

YOU: I don't care if Joanie or anyone else gives you a bad time, or if you are tired, or you feel grumpy, or whatever. If you act like a grump and a pain, no more staying up to finish your studying. You start it right after dinner. [SELF-DISCLOSURE and specific negative RESULT, plus ALTERNATIVE, and PAYOFF—i.e., WORKABLE COMPROMISE]

DAUGHTER: I promise.

YOU: The second thing. I get uncomfortable when you study late because you make noise that keeps your brother and sister awake. If you are really quiet, okay, but if you make noise that keeps them awake, no late studying. [SELF-DISCLOSURE and specific negative RESULT, plus ALTERNATIVE and PAYOFF—i.e., WORKABLE COMPROMISE]

DAUGHTER: It's impossible to be completely quiet.

YOU: I know it will be difficult for you, but if you make noise that keeps them awake, no late studying. [FOGGING and specific negative RESULT, plus ALTERNATIVE and PAYOFF—i.e., WORKABLE COMPROMISE]

DAUGHTER: Okay.

YOU: One more thing. When you study late, you keep me awake too. I feel I can't relax or go to sleep, because when you are finished, you wash and get ready for bed and then come in and say goodnight. If you want to study late, I want you to get ready for bed first and say goodnight so you don't keep us up until you are done. [SELF-DIS-CLOSURE and specific negative RESULT, plus ALTERNATIVE and PAYOFF—i.e., WORKABLE COMPROMISE]

DAUGHTER: That's not fair. The other kids don't have to wash and get into their pj's first.

YOU: You're right, but that's what I want you to do if you want to stay up late studying. If you want me to treat you more and more like an adult, I want you to take more responsibility for not upsetting things when you do what you want. [FOGGING and specific negative RESULT, plus ALTERNATIVE and PAYOFF—i.e., WORKABLE COMPROMISE]

DAUGHTER: Does this mean I can stay out later on dates on the weekend if I take responsibility for not upsetting you guys?

YOU: That's not a bad idea. I'd like that. But we'll talk about it later when we have more time. Okay? [SELF-DISCLOSURE and WORKABLE COMPROMISE]

DAUGHTER: Okay.

In the above dialogue, the concrete *trouble*, negative *result*, and the Workable Compromise spelled out beforehand by the *alternative* and *payoff* of TRAP help to communicate specifically that a problem exists and how the problem can be solved. But what do you do when your child asks for something before you have a chance to think about what is wanted? In such a case, you use your assertive skills to get the time you need to think about the problem and to use TRAP, if you choose, to clarify things. In the next dialogue you have to assertively deal with a daughter who is pressing you for a decision.

DIALOGUE 87

Deciding If Your Daughter Can See an R-rated Movie with Her Friends
Age level: Twelve through seventeen
Setting: You are at home and your daughter asks you if she can go to a movie with her friends on the weekend.

DAUGHTER: Is it okay if I go to the movies with Judy and the other guys on Saturday?

YOU: I don't understand. Why are you asking? You never asked permission before to go to the movies on Saturday. [SELF-DISCLOSURE]

DAUGHTER: We want to go to a sexy movie.

YOU: What do you mean, a "sexy movie"?

DAUGHTER: You know, an R-rated one.

YOU: An R-rated one? Which one?

DAUGHTER: *Sweat and Saliva.* It's an art picture, and it got real good reviews.

YOU: I'm sure it is, and did. But I'm not too sure you should. Besides, how are you going to get in? Don't you need an adult to accompany you? [FOGGING and SELF-DISCLOSURE]

DAUGHTER: Oh, we'll be taken in by Judy's older sister.

YOU: She's only three years older than you.

DAUGHTER: But she looks like twenty-one.

YOU: She isn't supposed to get in herself without an adult accompanying her!

DAUGHTER: Don't be a drag about this. I have to see this type of movie sometime!

YOU: I'm sure you do, but I don't feel very comfortable about your going there with Judy's sister.

DAUGHTER: Why not?

YOU: It just makes me uncomfortable—a bunch of young teenyboppers like you seeing that movie unescorted. I want to think more about it. [SELF-DISCLOSURE]

DAUGHTER: This isn't the Dark Ages, you know. All of us have had sex education at school. We're not going to see anything we haven't seen already!

You: I'm sure you won't, but it still makes me uncomfortable. So I want to think about it. [FOGGING, SELF-DISCLOSURE, and BROKEN RECORD]

DAUGHTER: What makes you uncomfortable about it?

You: I don't know. I'll have to think about why. [SELF-DISCLOSURE and BROKEN RECORD]

DAUGHTER: If you are afraid we'll meet some perverts, forget it! *Sweat and Saliva* is running at the Bijou. That's only ten blocks from here.

You: No, that's not it. I just don't know why. I want to think about it. [SELF-DISCLOSURE and BROKEN RECORD]

DAUGHTER: I could have gone anyway without telling you!

You: That's right, you could have. And I appreciate your asking me first. It gives me faith that you have a good head on your shoulders. [FOGGING and SELF-DISCLOSURE]

DAUGHTER: If I've got such a good head, how come you won't let me go?

You: I don't know yet. I want to think about it first. [SELF-DISCLOSURE and BROKEN RECORD]

DAUGHTER: Sure! And you'll take till next month to think about it. Thanks a lot!

You: I'm sure I've put you off like this in the past, and it was dumb of me to do that. But I really want to think about this. Let me think and we'll talk about it tonight. Okay? [NEGATIVE ASSERTION, SELF-DISCLOSURE, and WORKABLE COMPROMISE]

DAUGHTER: You promise?

You: I promise to talk to you tonight about it. I didn't say you could go. [WORKABLE COMPROMISE]

DAUGHTER: Okay.

Once some time is agreed to, allowing you to think about what your child wants, you can identify what it is that bothers you about your child's request and use TRAP to help in making your decision. In this situation involving the R-rated movie, you can use Negative Inquiry to identify the negative *result* of that behavior. For example:

INQUIRY: What is it about daughter seeing an R-rated movie with her teenage friends that bothers me? [NEGATIVE INQUIRY]

RESPONSE 1: It may prompt her to have premature sexual relations.

RESPONSE 2: It may make her think that sex is casual.

RESPONSE 3: It may give her some stupid ideas about what sex is.

RESPONSE 4: She may stop confiding in me, and turn to her friends for sexual information.

None of the first three responses is a specific, concrete, negative result of seeing an R-rated movie with friends, nor do they have any direct impact on you as a person or parent. Seeing an R-rated movie with her friends may prompt your daughter to have premature sexual relations, but on the other hand, it may not. In fact, the movie could be so gross as to put her off sex completely. In either case, the first response is purely speculative and therefore can not be effectively used as feedback.

As for the second response, seeing an R-rated movie with teenage friends may make your daughter think that sex is casual, but on the other hand, it may make her think that sex is quite profound. Like the first response, the second is also pure speculation.

The third response is pure speculation also. Your daughter, having no direct sexual experience, may already have a lot of dumb ideas about sex, and the movie may make no difference in her perceptions.

Most important, reasons 1 through 3 do not have any direct impact on you as a person or parent; they only speculate on what may or may not happen to your daughter.

In comparison, the fourth response gives you something to work with: Your daughter may not feel comfortable about confiding in you about sex if she sees an R-rated movie with only her inexperienced and not yet sophisticated friends. This response does identify a specific negative result that would have a direct bearing upon you, even if it is only a possible negative result. If your daughter were in the habit of going to R-rated movies regularly, and never talked to you about them afterward, or never asked your advice on how to place sex in perspective, you could talk specifically about how that negative result of her behavior bothered you. But since this is the first time the subject has come up, you have to deal with possible, specific negative results that affect you directly, and check them out with your daughter beforehand.

The *alternative(s)* and *payoff* (Workable Compromise) also emerge from this use of Negative Inquiry and the TRAP model. One compromise that would permit her to see an R-rated movie (which she is likely to see in any case, with or without your permission) is that she agree to talk about it with you afterward, especially if anything puzzles her. Another would be for her to see the movie with you, instead of with her inexperienced teenage friends. With this possible TRAP analysis of the problem, let's now proceed to the rest of the assertive dialogue.

Setting: That evening you talk to your daughter about your concerns regarding her seeing an R-rated movie with her friends.

You: I've had a chance to think about your going to the R-rated movie, and I know what's bothering me.

Daughter: Can I go?

You: Now that really upsets me! Aren't you interested in talking this out? [SELF-DISCLOSURE and WORKABLE COMPROMISE]

Daughter: Yes, sorry.

You: You and I seem to be able to talk about a lot of things. That's very important to me. If you have some problems, I feel much better if you talk them over with me. Maybe I can help, and maybe I can't. But when we talk things over, I don't feel left out. I like to know how you are and what's happening to you. [SELF-DISCLOSURE]

Daughter: What's that got to do with my going to see the movie?

You: I feel that one of the things daughters and mothers should talk about is sex. [SELF-DISCLOSURE]

Daughter: That's okay with me.

You: What bothers me is your seeing an R-rated movie with your friends and then not confiding in me about what you think. [SELF-DISCLOSURE and specific negative RESULT]

Daughter: You mean about what I see in the movie?

You: Yes. I'm worried that you might just take your friends' ideas about sex, instead of asking me what I think and how I feel about it. [SELF-DISCLOSURE and specific negative RESULT]

Daughter: You mean I can go if I tell you what I think about it afterward?

You: Yes, that's one way we can do it. [specific ALTERNATIVE, and PAYOFF—i.e., WORKABLE COMPROMISE]

Daughter: But it might be really gross!

You: It might be, and that's one reason I want to talk to you about how you feel about it. [FOGGING and SELF-DISCLOSURE]

252 / *Manuel J. Smith*

DAUGHTER: That would be embarrassing!
YOU: It might be. Another way would be for us to see it together. [FOGGING, and specific ALTERNATIVE, and PAYOFF—i.e., WORKABLE COMPROMISE]
DAUGHTER: That wouldn't be any fun. If it were horrible, I would really be embarrassed with you there!
YOU: It might be horrible, and then I'd be embarrassed too. [FOGGING and SELF-DISCLOSURE]
DAUGHTER: I'd rather go with the others and then talk to you afterward.
YOU: You understand what I'm concerned about? I'm worried that you might get an unrealistic picture of sex from the movie, and perhaps from your friends. If that happens, I'm afraid we might not share things anymore because you'd think I'm a rigid old fossil. [SELF-DISCLOSURE and specific negative RESULT]
DAUGHTER: Yes. Can I go with them?
YOU: If you promise you will talk to me about it afterward. (specific ALTERNATIVE, and PAYOFF—ie., WORKABLE COMPROMISE]
DAUGHTER: Okay. What if it's a really good picture the way they say?
YOU: You tell me about it. If I think it's good, maybe I'll go see it with Judy's mother. I know your father [stepfather, or mom's new boyfriend] won't go. [specific ALTERNATIVE, and PAYOFF—i.e., WORKABLE COMPROMISE]
DAUGHTER: I won't have to talk to *him* about it, will I? That would really be gross!
YOU: No, just me. [WORKABLE COMPROMISE]

TRAP is very helpful in working out compromises when your children start to mature and begin to challenge routine rules and your judgments on what you want them to do, what you want them to avoid, how you want them to dress, behave, etc. Research on the STAR program points out a number of situations in which children are likely to get into conflict with their parents. Following are some of the most common examples children reported to the STAR research staff.

· Mom wants daughter to dress in a particular style—for example, as a preppy—and daughter wants to dress more like her friends.

· Mom agrees to make cookies for the PTA, but waits to the last minute to ask for help, so there is a conflict because of a date, homework, or a test at school the next day.

· One parent has a favorite child, and at least one other child in the family becomes aware of it and accuses mom or dad of bias.

· Mom cooks to please dad, and is accused of being insensitive to the needs of a child with a weight problem.

· A daughter or son makes friends with someone mom or dad disapproves of, and mom or dad wants the child not to associate with that friend.

· Mom agrees to go to see her daughter in the school play, but at the last minute changes her mind.

· Dad teaches his son a hobby, and Junior becomes so expert that he starts to correct dad's mistakes.

· Dad agrees to host a weekend party for his son or daughter, and then is too busy or loses interest in it.

As your child matures, I can guarantee that conflicts like these will arise. There are two ways to handle such conflicts when they cannot be avoided. They can be dealt with straightforwardly and assertively, with less pain and hurt for both sides; or they can be dealt with under the table in a manipulative fashion. Coping better with conflicts such as these is one of the big pluses of teaching your child to be assertive as early as possible. If both parties in a conflict are assertive, the conflict is resolved much more quickly than usual, and with fewer hurt feelings. When one side or the other is called for a mistake or for being insensitive to the other, the assertive child or parent will waste little time on defending and denying and will spend more time trying to work out a realistic compromise that both sides can live with.

It is in your own best interest—and is much less effort and hassle in the long run—for you to teach your child how to be assertive to yourself, your spouse, and other adult members of the family. When both sides in a family conflict are assertive and straightforward, instead of accusatory or manipulative, and take a mutual problem-solving stance, problems that first seem impossible to resolve are rapidly reduced to practical, workable dimensions. Let's take a look at how you can teach your child, as STAR and PLUS do, to be more assertive in a problem-solving sense with you and other adult members of your family.

Teaching Your Child How to Cope with Errors that Make Parents Angry

One of the hardest but most necessary things for your child to learn is how to be assertive to you and your spouse. And even more difficult for your child is learning to remain calm and think clearly when he or she blunders and must face your initial angry reaction. It is a mistake for parents to inhibit their almost automatic angry reaction (nonphysical, of course) when their children do something stupid. Parents may try to do this, thinking that they are doing their children a favor by protecting them from one unpleasant aspect of human interaction and living together. But children have to learn to cope effectively with anger if they are to survive and prosper in this imperfect world of human beings who do get angry.

If you do not show your anger verbally when your child screws up and later temper it with love, your child may not learn how to cope with anger from someone close until his or her second marriage. I say *second* marriage because if this valuable lesson isn't learned, it may take at least one marriage for your child to learn that anger is just anger, nothing more. The fact that a parent or spouse is angry does not mean one is no longer loved.

You can use the following dialogue to teach your son or daughter, as STAR and PLUS do, a different way to cope with an angry loved one when a mistake or blunder is made.

DIALOGUE 88

Son Learns to Cope Assertively with a Blunder That Upsets Dad
Age level: Seven through seventeen
Setting: Your son and his father are eating lunch at home. Junior

is telling a story, and as he sweeps his hands out in a gesture, he knocks a glass of water into dad's lap.

SON: (Flabbergasted) Gosh!

FATHER: You idiot! Look what you've done!

SON: Gee! That was really clumsy of me. [NEGATIVE ASSERTION]

FATHER: I'll say! You're always doing something clumsy!

SON: You're right. But this takes the cake. I must be an idiot to do that. [FOGGING and NEGATIVE ASSERTION]

FATHER: I'm soaked to the skin!

SON: It sure looks like it. I feel really bad about doing that to you. [FOGGING and SELF-DISCLOSURE]

FATHER: Sometimes I feel like putting you in the backyard on a leash. But you'd probably do something stupid there, too.

SON: (With empathy) I don't blame you for feeling that way after I do something really clumsy like that. [SELF-DISCLOSURE]

FATHER: (Calming down) It looks worse than it is. Hand me a towel and maybe I can sponge most of it off.

SON: I really feel bad about spilling the water on you. [SELF-DISCLOSURE]

FATHER: Don't worry about it. Accidents happen. Just don't wave your arms around so much.

SON: Okay. I'll try to remember. [WORKABLE COMPROMISE]

In the next dialogue your son has to face Dad and report having done something really stupid. You can use this exercise to teach your child, as STAR and PLUS do, how to cope when money entrusted to him or her is lost.

DIALOGUE 89

Son Learns to Cope When He Loses the Money Given Him to Buy Mom a Present
Age level: Seven through seventeen
Setting: Yesterday Junior got a few dollars from dad to buy mom a birthday present. This morning he started out to go shopping and couldn't find the money. After searching everywhere, he has

*concluded that he must have lost the money. He decides to talk to
his father and tell him about the loss.*

SON: Dad, I really screwed up! [NEGATIVE ASSERTION]

FATHER: What did you do this time?

SON: I lost the five dollars you gave me for mom's present.

FATHER: You lost the money? Where did you lose it?

SON: I wish I knew. I've looked everywhere. [SELF-DISCLOSURE]

FATHER: Did you look in your pants pockets and your shirt pockets?

SON: Yes, dad. I've looked everywhere. [BROKEN RECORD]

FATHER: When's the last time you remember having the money?

SON: When you gave it to me, I put it in my pocket here. I've looked
everywhere. [BROKEN RECORD]

FATHER: Are those the same pants you had on then?

SON: Yes, dad. I've looked everywhere. [BROKEN RECORD]

FATHER: Did you look in the closet where you hung them up? On the
floor, and in the corner?

SON: Yes, dad. I've looked everywhere. [BROKEN RECORD]

FATHER: Did you go outside yesterday after I gave you the money?

SON: Yes. I went to the store with Jimmy. I looked along the street this
morning, and I asked the man behind the counter if anyone had
found five dollars yesterday.

FATHER: Well, that's it then. You lost it going to the store or in the
store. Nobody's going to give you the five dollars back.

SON: I guess you're right. It was a dumb thing not to take more care
of the five dollars, and I feel really stupid about it. [FOGGING,
NEGATIVE ASSERTION, and SELF-DISCLOSURE]

FATHER: What are you going to do now about your mother's present?

SON: I don't know. [SELF-DISCLOSURE]

FATHER: We're not made of money, you know. I work hard for it!

SON: I know. That's what makes me feel so bad. [SELF-DISCLO-
SURE]

FATHER: This is what happens when you are careless with money.

SON: I know. I feel really stupid. [SELF-DISCLOSURE]

FATHER: I'm willing to lend you another fiver, but you'll have to work
it off.

SON: Thanks, dad. I don't feel as dumb now. But what do you want me
to do? [SELF-DISCLOSURE and WORKABLE COMPROMISE]

FATHER: Mow the lawn and take out the trash for the next four weeks.

SON: (Not falling apart emotionally to the point where he's willing to do anything to make up for his mistake) That's a lot of work for five dollars.

FATHER: Ten dollars. The five you carelessly lost and this five.

SON: You didn't ask me to do the lawn when you gave me the first five.

FATHER: You are getting pretty pushy for someone who just screwed up.

SON: I guess so. But that's still a lot of work for five dollars. [FOGGING and BROKEN RECORD]

FATHER: How about three weeks? Agreed?

SON: Okay.

FATHER: I want the lawn mowed this afternoon when you come back from buying your mother's present.

SON: How about by tomorrow afternoon? [WORKABLE COMPROMISE]

FATHER: Okay, tomorrow afternoon.

Be sure to point out to your child with this practice dialogue that just because a mistake has been made, even with money, it does not mean the child has to make up for it forever, or feel so guilty about the mistake that he or she therefore must do anything to placate mom or dad. Make sure your child understands that negotiation is appropriate, even when he or she feels like a fool about doing something dumb.

If this training on how to cope with errors irks you a bit, it may be because your own parents did not place your mistakes in this perspective. But, keep in mind the purpose of assertiveness training: to give your child a lifetime advantage that you may not have had as a youngster. Also keep in mind that the main objective of this particular exercise is not to resolve a conflict between you and your child, but to enable your child to cope effectively with people other than yourself. You are just the "safe area" in which your child can practice and learn without getting hurt. This, too, is an advantage that your parents may not have known how to give you, so you had to learn the hard way.

Teaching Your Child How to Cope with Parental Errors

Amazingly enough, parents make mistakes too! Therefore children need to learn how to cope assertively in this situation as well. The key to enabling children to improve relations with parents is to teach children how to assertively negotiate workable compromises with their parents in a problem-solving rather than an angry, accusatory way. As a parent, if you are taking all this trouble to help your child to think, reason, and behave more effectively, then when you make a mistake that affects a child, you certainly deserve to have your child behave toward you in the manner illustrated by the following dialogue, rather than in the typical accusing, perhaps angry, and hurtful ways many preteens and teens use to confront their parents. You can use this dialogue to teach your child, as STAR and PLUS do, how to communicate straightforwardly and then negotiate with a parent who forgets something agreed to beforehand.

DIALOGUE 90

Daughter Learns How to Negotiate with Dad When He Forgets His Promise
Age level: Eleven through seventeen
Setting: Dad gets up from breakfast and says he will see everyone at dinner. He has evidently forgotten that he promised daughter a ride to school this morning so she could have more time before her first class to study for a test. Daughter reminds her father of this.

DAUGHTER: Dad?
FATHER: Yes?
DAUGHTER: You promised me a ride to school this morning, remember?
FATHER: I did?
DAUGHTER: Yes.
FATHER: Well, I'm really in a rush. It would be a lot of trouble to take you this morning. I'll take you tomorrow.
DAUGHTER: Thanks, but if you don't take me this morning, I won't be able to study before the test in my first class.
FATHER: Didn't you study for your test last night?
DAUGHTER: Yes, but the test is on history, with lots of dates and treaties. I would feel more comfortable if I could look at my book just before the test. That's why I asked you before. [SELF-DISCLOSURE]

FATHER: You're a good student. You don't need to cram at the last minute.

DAUGHTER: You may be right, dad, but I'd feel very uncomfortable if I didn't. That's why I asked you to drive me to school this morning. [FOGGING, SELF-DISCLOSURE, and BROKEN RECORD]

FATHER: I really am busy this morning. There's an early meeting I have to go to.

DAUGHTER: I'm sure you are busy, but I would feel really uncomfortable if I couldn't study right before the test. That's why I asked you before. [FOGGING, SELF-DISCLOSURE, and BROKEN RECORD]

FATHER: It would be impossible for me to make that meeting and drive you to school, too.

DAUGHTER: I'm sure it would be difficult, but I'd appreciate it if you could drive me to school as I asked you to. [FOGGING, SELF-DISCLOSURE, and BROKEN RECORD]

FATHER: You are really pushy, you know!

DAUGHTER: You're right, dad, I am pushy. But I'd sure appreciate a ride. [FOGGING, and BROKEN RECORD]

FATHER: It would look bad if I were late for that meeting.

DAUGHTER: It probably would. Could you phone the office now and leave a message that you might be a few minutes late? [FOGGING and WORKABLE COMPROMISE]

FATHER: You have all the answers, don't you?

DAUGHTER: I know I'm pushy, but I'd sure appreciate a ride. [FOGGING and BROKEN RECORD]

FATHER: Just like your mother.

DAUGHTER: I know. We give you a bad time, don't we? [NEGATIVE ASSERTION]

FATHER: Okay. Let me phone and let's get on the road.

DAUGHTER: (Giving dad a hug and a kiss) Thanks! I really like you. [SELF-DISCLOSURE]

FATHER: Don't waste time with this. Get your stuff in the car and wait for me.

DAUGHTER: Okay.

he above dialogue uses an example that is not very earth-shaking to teach your child to use a problem-solving rather than accusatory stance to negotiate with a parent. In the next dialogue the issues, feelings, and differences in wants between parents and child are not so simple and clear-cut. The problem is an emotional one, and a tough one: The child is coping with a traditional parent who sees a definite, well-defined role for the child in life and, with the best intentions, tries to help the child fit into it.

The major point here is to avoid asking if the parent is right and the child wrong, or vice versa. If you do that, you fall into the trap of the adversary model—i.e., "If I'm right, then you must be wrong and I have to prove it to you!" As we have noted, the adversary model has a poor track record in solving problems. In using the assertive-thinking-and-reasoning model, solutions to the problems are looked for and negotiated, instead of trying to get all sorts of external agencies—Mother Nature, genetics, or tradition—to prove that one side is right and the other is wrong. With this dialogue, you can teach your child, as STAR and PLUS do, to assertively negotiate with a parent who sets very dogmatic standards and is disappointed when they are not achieved.

DIALOGUE 91

Daughter Learns to Cope Assertively with a Parent's
Disappointment in Her Academic Performance
Age level: Thirteen through seventeen
Setting: Your daughter has just received her report card, and the marks she has gotten could be better. Part of the reason for these less than perfect marks is that your daughter is not very interested in the courses that her father insists she take. She decides to have a talk with him about her disappointing grades and his insistence that she take the courses she selects.

DAUGHTER: Dad, here's this quarter's report card.
FATHER: Hmmm . . . You didn't do as well as I thought you could.
DAUGHTER: You're right. I didn't. [NEGATIVE ASSERTION]
FATHER: These grades are not what I expected.
DAUGHTER: I'm sure they're not. [FOGGING]
FATHER: In fact, I'm very disappointed in you.
DAUGHTER: So am I, Dad. [NEGATIVE ASSERTION]
FATHER: Can't you try harder?

DAUGHTER: I guess I could, but I think I could do much better if I took some courses that I'm interested in. [FOGGING and SELF-DIS-CLOSURE]

FATHER: We talked about that before, and we both agreed that you should take courses that will get you somewhere in life.

DAUGHTER: You're right, I did agree. But I'm not too sure that was the right thing to do. [SELF-DISCLOSURE and NEGATIVE ASSER-TION]

FATHER: Don't you want to do anything worthwhile with your life?

DAUGHTER: I'm not too sure that what you feel is worthwhile is what I feel is worthwhile. [SELF-DISCLOSURE]

FATHER: What a thing to say!

DAUGHTER: I'm sure it upsets you for me to say that, but I would be more upset if we didn't talk about this. [FOGGING and SELF-DISCLOSURE]

FATHER: You've never heard me say no if you want to talk.

DAUGHTER: That's true. [FOGGING]

FATHER: The courses I thought you should take are ones you could benefit from, and I'm disappointed that you are not doing well in them.

DAUGHTER: I'm sure you feel that way, but I think I could do better if I took some courses that interest me. [FOGGING]

FATHER: Look at this—C in gourmet cooking. Don't you like to cook?

DAUGHTER: I'm sure I should like it, but it doesn't interest me as much as other courses I could take. [FOGGING and SELF-DISCLO-SURE]

FATHER: Like what?

DAUGHTER: Like Law and Politics. That really interests me. [SELF-DISCLOSURE]

FATHER: You also got a C in typing. That's a course that may help you get a job.

DAUGHTER: You may be right, but I would rather take computer pro-gramming. [FOGGING and BROKEN RECORD]

FATHER: How many girls take that course in high school?

DAUGHTER: You're right. Not very many. But what is it about my taking a course that not many girls take, like computer programming, that's bad? [FOGGING and NEGATIVE INQUIRY]

FATHER: That's for boys! The girls who take that are wasting their time.

DAUGHTER: I don't understand. What is it about my wasting my time on computer programming that's bad? [NEGATIVE INQUIRY]

FATHER: You will never be happy being a computer programmer, but you can get a good job as a typist.

DAUGHTER: What is it about my wanting to be a computer programmer that means I won't be happy? [NEGATIVE INQUIRY]

FATHER: It's unnatural.

DAUGHTER: I still don't understand. What is it about wanting to be a computer programmer that's unnatural? [NEGATIVE INQUIRY]

FATHER: You want to be a wife and a mother, don't you?

DAUGHTER: Maybe. I don't know. At least not right after I finish school. But I don't understand. What's wanting to be a computer programmer got to do with being a wife and a mother? [SELF-DISCLOSURE]

FATHER: It's natural for a girl to be a wife and a mother.

DAUGHTER: I suppose it is. But what is it about wanting to be a computer programmer that's unnatural? [FOGGING and NEGATIVE INQUIRY]

FATHER: Well, you can't be both and be happy. You have to choose.

DAUGHTER: I still don't understand. What is it about wanting to be a computer programmer that means I can't be a wife and a mother? [NEGATIVE INQUIRY]

FATHER: You won't have time. Both are full-time jobs.

DAUGHTER: Now I really don't understand. I can't see the difference between being a typist and a computer programmer. [SELF-DIS-CLOSURE]

FATHER: A typist's job is just a job. You can quit when you want to get married or have a baby. You can get that job back anytime. Anybody can get a typist's job. But you can't do that if you get a job as a programmer. You have to stick with it if you decide to have a career.

DAUGHTER: What is it about my sticking with a career as a computer programmer that's bad? [NEGATIVE INQUIRY]

FATHER: You won't have time to be a wife and mother. Well, maybe you could get married, but you sure won't have time to have children.

DAUGHTER: What is it about my not having children that's bad? [NEG-ATIVE INQUIRY]

FATHER: It's unnatural, as I said. Besides, your mother and I would like to have some grandchildren someday.

DAUGHTER: (Becoming aware of father's worries) It sounds like you're worried that I won't have any children if I have a career.

FATHER: Yes. And that's unnatural. Women are supposed to have children. Men can't have them.

DAUGHTER: You're right, Dad, men can't. But I would like to be a computer programmer. Look at my grades in math. Straight A's. [FOGGING and SELF-DISCLOSURE]

FATHER: Most men don't like women who are smarter than they are.

DAUGHTER: That may be true. So when I want to get married and have a child, I'll have to find a smart one. [FOGGING and WORKABLE COMPROMISE]

FATHER: If you wait until you have a successful career, only the weird ones will be left. I don't want a weird son-in-law.

DAUGHTER: I don't want to marry a weirdo either, but I would like to take courses in computer programming the way I did in junior high. [SELF-DISCLOSURE]

FATHER: Don't you trust my judgment about what's best for you?

DAUGHTER: I'm sure you feel you know what's best for me. But so far you haven't been very proud of my grades, have you? [FOGGING and NEGATIVE INQUIRY prompt]

FATHER: No.

DAUGHTER: I want very much to make you proud of me. If I can take courses in computer programming and get good grades, I think you would be proud of me. [SELF-DISCLOSURE and WORKABLE COMPROMISE]

FATHER: Yes, but it's unnatural for a woman to like those things.

DAUGHTER: Maybe, but that's what I want to do. [FOGGING and BROKEN RECORD]

FATHER: It's unnatural, but take some next term and we'll see how you do.

DAUGHTER: Thanks, Daddy. That makes me happy. I bet you will be proud of me. [SELF-DISCLOSURE]

FATHER: We'll see.

Although the above dialogue focuses on an issue that could have a major effect upon the child's life in terms of career and relationship goals, the principle behind the example can be applied by your child to deal with many situations, most of which are less important but no less emotional.

Most of us have unquestioned beliefs that automatically rule how we behave and think. Because these beliefs are so ingrained and we really don't examine them critically ourselves, they tend to have a large emotional component or as we say in the trade, a lot of emotional conditioning associated with them. Consequently, when anyone challenges these beliefs, or when we don't behave according to them ourselves, we tend to get upset; and the more emotionally rooted the belief is, the more upset we become. Because these beliefs are emotional, we automatically perceive them not just as beliefs, but as facts, or as statements of natural law. As such, these untestable beliefs about how we should live our lives can severely affect your child's ability to be his or her own judge of what is best to do.

There are many examples of this very human phenomenon. Girls often believe that learning to be sexy is more important than studying hard in certain academic subjects, because their peers, and perhaps their parents too, believe they don't have the brains or natural inclination for "hard" subjects. Boys often believe they have to behave unfeelingly because their peers, and often their fathers too, believe this is natural male macho, also dictated by Mother Nature. Many teenagers believe that using alcohol or drugs is part of becoming grown-up and acting like adults, because their peers do also. Many of us, children and adults, believe that tradition is always right because everyone has always done things that way, or that things have to be fair to work, or that justice and right will always prevail.

You will have to be sure your child understands that a belief held by classmates and friends has to be examined and tested to see if it works for him or her as an individual. Do the beliefs of your child's peers enrich your child's life and make it easier and better, or do they complicate individual interests and needs by making everyone conform rigidly in thinking and behavior?

If your child is to be his or her own judge, resisting pressure to accept their peers' decisions on what is right and what is wrong, one thing has to happen: Your child will have to face up to the fact that much of what other people, including peers, pressure him or her to do is based only upon their beliefs. Let's look at how one of these beliefs, taken as a natural law, is involved in the sexual molestation of children.

Conditions that Permit Sexual Molestation of Children, In and Out of the Family.

As unpleasant as sexual molestation is to talk about, I would be remiss if in teaching you how to train children to cope assertively with conflict situations, I did not deal with this phenomenon.

Even though we have no way of knowing how many children are sexually abused, one child's molestation is enough to greatly upset the vast majority of us. For this reason I will briefly discuss the factors that we do know underlie the sexual abuse of children, the primary causes of it in families and in the larger social group the child comes in contact with, and then what parents can do, in a very practical sense, to prevent it.

For our purposes here, there are two classes of child molestation to note: pedophilia, which involves the molestation of both boys and girls; and the use of prepubertal and pubertal girls for sexual purposes. I am not talking about cases of kidnapping, rape, and murder; these crimes are most often committed by people the youngster does not know, and the only means of prevention is to insist repeatedly that children never go anywhere with strangers. I am also not talking about children exploring their sexuality by playing "doctor" with each other. The most common form of child sexual molestation involves a man whom the child already knows. Clinical histories indicate that younger boys and girls are most often sexually molested by pedophiles outside the family but acquainted with the child and/or parents—friends of the parents, neighbors, neighborhood shopkeepers, teenagers, and even priests and ministers. These histories also indicate that child molestation within the family most often involves sexual intercourse with prepubertal and pubertal girls by stepfathers or live-in boyfriends. This account of the types of child molestation and those involved does not cover every case, but it gives us a fair picture of what happens most often.

There is no universal definition of what childhood sexual abuse is. Approved sexual behavior and activity of or with children varies from culture to culture and even among subgroups in our own society. *Abuse* simply means "misuse," and that's subjective, a judgment call. Most of us use whatever offends our own sensibilities as a definition. But while that may serve each of us personally, it neither spells out what the problem is nor tells us what can be done about it. A better working definition of *abuse* is "that which a child cannot, or doesn't know how to, protect himself or herself from, but which an adult can."

For example, if anyone tried to beat you up, you could protect yourself with means that are not available to a child, such as leaving for good, defending yourself physically, or obtaining the assistance of the law. If anyone tried to fondle or otherwise sexually molest you, you could fend him off with a variety of means that the typical child does not know about or know how to use, including ego and sexual-interest deflation such as "With you? Don't make me laugh!"

Children are sexually molested primarily for two reasons: The first is a general reason that applies to all sexual abuse. The second is more complex, applies within families, and can be specified with some degree of clinical certainty. We'll begin by discussing the first. The simple reason for sexual molestation is that children are typically not taught how to say no to sexual advances from adults, just as they are not taught to say no to what adults want in other areas. Children, particularly younger ones, see adults as authorities. If a pedophile insists that the child tolerate fondling, molestation, or intercourse, the child has no experience or life background with which to differentiate between the imposition of sexual demands and of the other demands adults place on the rest of his or her life.

If children were taught to say no persistently to sexual advances, most sexual molestation would not occur. Therefore, the best way to prevent sexual abuse of a child is to have the child practice saying no assertively to anyone who approaches him or her sexually, makes a sexual gesture, a sexual proposition, or touches or fondles the child inappropriately. There are two practice dialogues below. The first is for a younger child, age six through eight, who may not have the physical mobility to leave the presence of the potential molester as an older child would. The second dialogue is for a child age nine through twelve, who is more likely to have this mobility.

Practicing to say no to adults or older children who make sexual gestures toward your child can be done effectively just before the child enters school, and later reinforced at ages nine through twelve. For training a youngster to say no, all you need is Broken Record, lots of practice, and a neutral, unemotional explanation that no one older than the child, except you or a physician, should touch your child in the genital areas until he or she is grown up. Explain sexuality in the simplest way, stating that adults do engage in sexual love with each other, but that children are not physically ready for this yet, in the same way that adults can do lots of physical things that children can't. Add that some people have psychological problems that make it difficult for them to love other adults sexually, so they try to do sexual things with young children. (You can omit the word *psychological* if your very young child does not understand it.) Tell your younger child that if someone other than you or a physician touches him or her in a sensitive (erogenous) area —genitals, breasts, inner thighs, or buttocks—or near such an area, he or she should (a) say repeatedly, "No. I don't like that. Don't do it," in Broken Record fashion no matter what the person says; (b) leave the presence of that person as soon as possible; and (c) find you and tell you what happened as soon as possible.

Although the first practice dialogue sounds stereotyped and unresponsive, one of its purposes is to give the child a well-practiced "no" response that has a high probability of being used if the child is approached sexually. Its other objective is to make the potential molester back off and leave your child alone. It does not have to sound responsive or sophisticated in order to accomplish this. The first dialogue is much longer than any real-life incident is likely to be. Tell your children that the purpose of this lengthy training is to give them lots of practice in saying no to different things the person may say or do, but point out repeatedly that if they find themselves in such a situation, they should leave it as soon as they can. In the sample dialogue the molester is a neighbor, but it could be an older child, family friend, neighborhood shopkeeper, etc. This practice can be given at the same time you teach your child never to go anywhere with an adult outside the family unless he or she has your permission, or the adult is a police officer in uniform.

DIALOGUE 92

A Young Boy or Girl Says No to Molestation
Age level: Six through eight
Setting: Your child is in the presence of a neighbor, and the neighbor makes a sexual gesture.

NEIGHBOR: (Placing a hand on the child's thigh) Does that feel good?
CHILD: No. I don't like that. Don't do it. [BROKEN RECORD]
NEIGHBOR: Why not? Lots of children like it.
CHILD: No. I don't like that. Don't do it. [BROKEN RECORD]
NEIGHBOR: How about if I rubbed your back? Doesn't your mother do that for you?
CHILD: No. I don't like that. Don't do it. [BROKEN RECORD]
NEIGHBOR: Don't you like me? I'm your friend.
CHILD: (Child does not answer questions, but continues with Broken Record response.) I don't like that. Don't do it. [BROKEN RECORD]
NEIGHBOR: I like you.
CHILD: (No matter what is said, same response is used.) No. I don't like that. Don't do it. [BROKEN RECORD]
NEIGHBOR: Do you want some candy? I can get you some.
CHILD: (Same response as before) No. I don't like that. Don't do it. [BROKEN RECORD]
NEIGHBOR: Do you want to see some interesting pictures?
CHILD: No. I don't like that. Don't do it. [BROKEN RECORD]
NEIGHBOR: Come on. You'll like them.
CHILD: No. I don't like that. Don't do it. [BROKEN RECORD]
NEIGHBOR: Here, look at this picture.
CHILD: No. I don't like that. Don't do it. [BROKEN RECORD]
NEIGHBOR: (Taking child's hand) Do you like to hold hands?
CHILD: No. I don't like that. Don't do it. [BROKEN RECORD]
NEIGHBOR: I'll show you mine if you show me yours.
CHILD: (Removing hand, if possible) No. I don't like that. Don't do it. [BROKEN RECORD]
NEIGHBOR: (Indicating genital area) Would you like to touch me here?
CHILD: No. I don't like that. Don't do it. [BROKEN RECORD]
NEIGHBOR: We could keep it a secret. Nobody has to know.
CHILD: No. I don't like that. Don't do it. [BROKEN RECORD]
NEIGHBOR: Okay.
CHILD: (Leaves and finds you as soon as possible.)

The next dialogue, for the older child, has a twofold purpose: to convince the would-be molester that sexual advances will not be permitted and also that the child wants the molester to leave. Therefore the

Broken Record message your child uses stresses both goals. At this age level, if your child says that he or she wants to be left alone or will go to the police, that statement is believable and likely to be taken seriously by the potential molester. Again, for the purpose of practicing the Broken Record response to a variety of sexual advances, this dialogue is much longer than would occur in real life.

DIALOGUE 93

A Prepubescent Boy or Girl Says No to Molestation
Age level: Nine through twelve
Setting: The same as the dialogue above

NEIGHBOR: (Placing a hand on the child's thigh) Do you like that?
CHILD: No. Leave me alone or I will leave and go to the police. [BRO-KEN RECORD]
NEIGHBOR: Why not? Lots of children like it.
CHILD: No. Leave me alone or I will leave and go to the police. [BRO-KEN RECORD]
NEIGHBOR: How about if I rubbed your back? Don't you like that?
CHILD: No. Leave me alone or I will leave and go to the police. [BRO-KEN RECORD]
NEIGHBOR: Don't you like me? I'm your friend.
CHILD: No. Leave me alone or I will leave and go to the police. [BRO-KEN RECORD]
NEIGHBOR: I like you.
CHILD: No. Leave me alone or I will leave and go to the police. [BRO-KEN RECORD]
NEIGHBOR: Do you want something nice? I can get it for you.
CHILD: No. Leave me alone or I will leave and go to the police. [BRO-KEN RECORD]
NEIGHBOR: Look at this picture.
CHILD: No. Leave me alone or I will leave and go to the police. [BRO-KEN RECORD]
NEIGHBOR: Don't you like to look at sexy pictures?
CHILD: No. Leave me alone or I will leave and go to the police. [BRO-KEN RECORD]

NEIGHBOR: Come on. You'll like them.

CHILD: No. Leave me alone or I will leave and go to the police. [BROKEN RECORD]

NEIGHBOR: (Taking child's hand) Do you like to hold hands?

CHILD: (Removing hand) No. Leave me alone or I will leave and go to the police. [BROKEN RECORD]

NEIGHBOR: (Indicating breast, buttock, or genital area) Don't you like to touch yourself here?

CHILD: No. Leave me alone or I will leave and go to the police. [BROKEN RECORD]

NEIGHBOR: (Indicating genital area) Would you like to touch me here?

CHILD: No. Leave me alone or I will leave and go to the police. [BROKEN RECORD]

NEIGHBOR: We could keep it a secret. Nobody has to know.

CHILD: No. Leave me alone or I will leave and go to the police. [BROKEN RECORD]

NEIGHBOR: Okay.

This repetitive practice gives the child a simple, stereotyped response that will be remembered. Further, although there are no guarantees in life, this approach to sexual molestation by someone known to the child has the highest probability of success.

Again, your child should leave the presence of the molester at the first opportunity after he or she realizes that sexual gestures are being made, and should report the incident to you as soon as possible. When your child tells you of a sexual molestation attempt, do two things. First, calm down. In all likelihood your child has not been harmed and will suffer no great trauma unless you act as though something terrible has happened. If you give this message, because of the sexual context the child will almost automatically assume that the incident was really his or her fault. Second, after your anger subsides, and it will, I recommend that you not confront the molester yourself. Contact your local police department, ask to speak to the person who normally handles cases of child molestation, and then let professionals who know what they are doing follow up on the incident.

As indicated earlier, molestation within families is more complex. Clinical histories point out that sexual molestation and/or sexual intercourse involving prepubertal and pubertal girls sometimes occur within new families formed after a divorce or death of a spouse. In those cases on which psychologists, psychiatrists, or psychiatric social workers have consulted, there appears to be a particular factor that allows this molestation to take place. This factor has been identified as poor coping on the part of the natural mother, which is linked to her overriding belief that her personal identity is defined by her involvement in a long-term personal relationship. That relationship, therefore, is more important than the sexual molestation of her daughter.

Many traditionally reared divorcées and widows feel a loss of personal identity due to the potent belief that a woman is worthless without a man. This can prompt a woman to be less selective in her choice of a new mate. If that new mate is a man who wants to exploit her child sexually, the natural mother, getting a second chance to make a new relationship "work" and determined to keep it secure, may make it work at the expense of the child in many areas.

Clinical evidence shows that the mother of a child who was molested in a new relationship was usually aware of the sexual advances made to her daughter by her new husband or boyfriend, but did not confront him for fear of breaking up the relationship. When sexual molestation occurred and the daughter complained about the sexual interest of mom's new mate, the complaint was typically pooh-poohed with "Oh, you're exaggerating." In some cases, the daughter was directly told not to foul up this new relationship with her complaints—i.e., "If this relationship doesn't work, it's your fault!"

While this may seem bizarre reasoning to many of us, it is a bit more understandable if we realize how powerful is this mother's belief in the importance of having a stable relationship with a man. Without it she feels worthless as a person. To her, a stable relationship is part of the very nature of being female and a dictate of nature that she must obey.

In ignoring sexual gestures toward her daughter, the intent of the mother was for daughter to handle the problems on her own. If this worked, then mom could avoid raising an issue that had the potential to destroy her relationship. Unfortunately, without specific training in how to assertively handle this problem, most daughters faced the unpleasant options of either giving in to the sexual advances or leaving home. Given a situation with no negative payoff that would have cut off sexual molestation before it really started, the outcome was left to chance and the new mate's sexual ethics.

This deliberately ignored molestation can be psychologically devastating to a young girl, and its effects can last into adulthood. The negative effect is not caused by illicit sex per se, or an aversion to sex. It is caused by the daughter's feeling of abandonment and helplessness, of having no one on her side to whom she can turn. Years later, when mature enough to verbalize their feelings, women sexually molested as children will commonly say, "She chose him over me. I thought I counted, but I didn't." That sense of total rejection by someone who should have loved them affected their own close relationships as adults.

In hoping the problem will be resolved without her being involved, the natural mother mistakenly assumes that this problem is so emotional in nature that it cannot be worked out between her and her new mate. Experience has shown mental-health professionals that given a willingness to try and a nonaccusatory stance (being assertive but not punitive), there are few emotionally charged problems that are impossible to discuss and resolve. Becoming more mature and discriminating in one's sexual choice is not one of the impossibles.

If you are a divorced or widowed mother whose self-respect and primary personal identification depend heavily on being part of a long-term relationship, and you are beginning to build a new relationship, the first rule of being smart is to take your time. No matter how pressured you feel, remember that the only thing you absolutely have to do between now and next Tuesday is to keep breathing. Second, when you teach your child to be assertive, you are also teaching yourself. So when any problem is your new relationship comes up, remember that depending on how you talk about it, there is *nothing*—child rearing, sexual preferences, infidelity, choice of Chinese restaurants, etc.—that you can't discuss with your new mate. And if you can talk about it, the problem can be worked out without threatening or destroying the relationship.

To give your daughter experience in effectively saying no to unwanted sexual advances from anyone, have her practice being assertive in this situation, using the final dialogue. Before this practice in assertively saying no, make sure she knows how to determine whether a male is making a serious sexual advance or just trying to flatter her. If she cannot tell, instruct her to be quite straightforward in asking him why he is being so attentive and what he wants.

DIALOGUE 94

*A Preteen or Teenage Daughter Says No to Sexual Advances from
a Teenage Boyfriend or Older Male*
Age level: Twelve and older
*Setting: Your child is in the presence of a male teenager or an
older man. He begins to make sexual advances toward her, but she
does not want to be involved sexually with him.*

MALE: Do you know that you are very sexy?
DAUGHTER: (Innocently) Really?
MALE: Yes. I could go for you.
DAUGHTER: Are you serious?
MALE: Sure.
DAUGHTER: I'll take that as a compliment, but I'm not interested in
being sexy to you. [SELF-DISCLOSURE]
MALE: Why not?
DAUGHTER: Your putting the make on me makes me feel very uncom-
fortable. [SELF-DISCLOSURE]
MALE: Hey! You shouldn't feel that way.
DAUGHTER: Perhaps. But this makes me feel very uncomfortable.
[FOGGING and BROKEN RECORD]
MALE: Loosen up. This is no big deal.
DAUGHTER: I'm sure it isn't. But I'm not interested. [FOGGING and
BROKEN RECORD]
MALE: You're just uptight. I'll rub your neck to relax you.
DAUGHTER: I am uptight. But I'm not interested. [FOGGING and
BROKEN RECORD]
MALE: No big deal. I'm just trying to help you get rid of your neurotic
inhibitions.
DAUGHTER: I'm sure you are, but I'm not interested. [FOGGING and
BROKEN RECORD]
MALE: Don't give me that. You know you want this as much as I do.
DAUGHTER: I'm sure you feel that way, but I don't. [FOGGING and
SELF-DISCLOSURE]
MALE: (Putting his arms around her) Just relax. You'll like it.

DAUGHTER: (Removing his arms or walking away, if possible) I'm sure you feel that way, but I don't. [FOGGING and BROKEN RECORD]

MALE: What's the matter with you? I'm just trying to be friendly.

DAUGHTER: I'm sure you are, but I'm not interested. [FOGGING and BROKEN RECORD]

MALE: Nobody will find out. There's just the two of us here.

DAUGHTER: You're right. But I'm not interested. [FOGGING and BROKEN RECORD]

MALE: You're just a little tease. Getting me all hot and bothered this way and then chickening out.

DAUGHTER: I'm sure you feel that way, but I'm not interested. [FOGGING and BROKEN RECORD]

MALE: Well, I'll remember this when you want something from me.

DAUGHTER: (Not intimidated) I'm sure you will. But I'm not interested. [FOGGING and BROKEN RECORD]

As you can see from this dialogue, a calm, persistent, assertive response is effective in dealing with unwanted sexual advances from either a teenage boyfriend or an older male.

In this chapter we have talked about how you and your children can be more mutually assertive and straightforward with each other. The chapter also covered how you can work out, beforehand or on the spot, what you want from your children, and how to help them in sometimes complicated situations using the TRAP model of behavior change. Finally, we discussed the factors that permit sexual molestation of children, and how these factors can be minimized.

Let's turn now to the next chapter, where we will look at a routine, everyday method you can use to teach your child to be a competent person, one who has the thinking ability to make decisions about social rules, especially when automatically following them is not in your child's best interest.

CHAPTER NINE

Giving Your Child a Lifetime Advantage in the Late Twentieth and Early Twenty-First Centuries

This chapter is all about consequences of behavior—the payoffs your child receives for doing or not doing certain things—and the attitudes your child adopts because of the payoffs he or she routinely receives. It is an extension of the preceding chapters, since knowing the payoffs of behavior, or the lack of them, is the key in both asserting yourself to your child and teaching your child to think and reason about the consequences of his or her own behavior. As I have pointed out, you can assert yourself to your child until you are blue in the face and nothing will happen if your child sees no payoff for changing or improving—or if your child is always given childish payoffs and protected from any real-life consequences of misbehaving.

There are two rules of thumb in giving feedback that tells your child how well or poorly he or she is doing. The first rule is to lavishly heap positives for good behavior on your child. Always try to give your child a positive payoff when he or she does something well, or simply pleases you. It costs you nothing. You don't have to buy gold stars to paste on an achievement board, or extra cookies, or candy to pass out as rewards. Your telling your child that he or she is doing something well, that you are pleased, or even that you love him or her is reward enough.

This is particularly important when a younger child is learning something new. Praise for doing things properly will increase your child's self-confidence. This self-confidence means that as your child gets older, you won't have to pay as much attention to good behavior to positively reinforce it. This also means less work for you in child rearing later on. Think of it as paying your dues early so you can relax a bit afterward. With generous positive feedback, you are also preparing your child to be sensitive to the needs and feelings of others as an adult. How many times have you been disappointed because you did a good job on something and no one appreciated it? Even more important, how motivated were you to do a good job again after getting no positive social payoff?

Except for reminding you to remember their importance, giving your child positive payoffs is not something you have to be instructed in— you already know how to do it. But if you are like most parents, giving your child negative payoffs is a problem. Negative payoffs that are not well thought out are confusing, emotional, generally ineffective, and perhaps even counterproductive in helping your child to grow up successfully. Because you can count on your children to misbehave, make mistakes, and screw things up in learning what to do and not do, this chapter concentrates on how to use *appropriate* negative consequences in helping your child learn to think and reason competently instead of remaining a youngster who always needs your guiding hand to do things effectively and correctly.

Behavioral Feedback: Teaching Your Child the Rules of the Game and How and When to Obey Them

You can begin to teach your child how to be a competent person routinely, day by day, using the principle of behavioral feedback or behavioral payoff as soon as your child can talk and understand what you say. This behavioral-feedback method is based on the same psychological principle that makes the skills given in STAR, PLUS, and *When I Say No, I Feel Guilty* work so well in protecting the individual's self-respect and consequently his or her achievement motivation and general level of health. This method teaches children to be competent by compelling them to think about the consequences of their everyday actions.

Where you use behavioral feedback, you don't get into an argument with your child over what's right and what's wrong. Instead you expose him or her to the natural consequences of two alternatives, and let the child make the choice. For example, when your young son stubbornly refuses to take a bath, you give the following negative social feedback: "Then you will be smelly [grungy, dirty, sticky, stinky-poo, etc.] and I won't want to be near you until you wash!" You enlist the rest of the family to reinforce this feedback: "And we won't want to sit watching TV with you, will we?" And so on. You do this until the child decides he had better take a bath.

The point of using negative social feedback in this example of early learning is of course not simply to get the child to take a bath—you can do that easily with an insistent Broken Record. In using negative social feedback, you are teaching your child to think about the consequences of his or her behavior and to make decisions based on those consequences. In those cases where your child's not doing what you want done has no natural negative consequences, your feedback is a personal one, and not a dictate from on high: "I want you to do this because I like it when you do it!"

We will look at behavioral feedback in great detail, but first let's look briefly at the two complementary halves of learning to be a competent person: (1) learning the "rules of the game" and (2) learning how to decide when and how it is in one's best interest to follow the rules of the game and when it is not.

A major psychological aspect of your child's becoming competent is learning society's and our physical environment's rules of the game: what one does to be successful and avoid unnecessary work, trouble, injury, hurting other people emotionally, and so forth. These rules of the game, as I call them, guide our behavior without our having to think much about them. They are all learned rules, useful guidelines on how to behave routinely in the particular social and physical environment in which we are reared and live. We have them because they let us act without having to stop and think everything out first. They may not apply to other environments that have different motives, values, and payoffs, and they may not apply when our own social/physical environment radically changes—as our culture indeed has over the past thirty years.

These environmental rules are not based on instinct, natural law, basic human nature, or ancient wisdom, but they are so overlearned that it appears as if there are instinctual or natural reasons why we automatically obey them. We assume without thinking about it, for example, that women have to be sexy and men have to be macho. You can't go too far wrong in being a bit sexy or macho in today's society—our society will reward you for that—but it is a serious mistake to assume that your sexiness or macho quotient is laid out by nature and you can't vary it to suit the situation. If you do this, you start behaving as if what you do in life has been predetermined, and your belief that you are only following these dictates shuts off your thinking brain. As we've already seen, this makes you vulnerable to emotional manipulation: You react without thinking and asserting yourself in social conflict because you believe that you have been presented with imperatives that a decent, educated person like yourself has no choice but to obey.

To some extent our knowledge of these social and environmental rules allows us to behave effectively, productively, and almost effortlessly in our social and physical environment without much thought. For example, since you and I have learned the rules of the game beforehand, we know what can happen if we jaywalk, or drive through a red light. We don't have to think this rule out every time we come to an intersection —we stop automatically. It's not much use to us, however, in environments like rural Afganistan or Tibet, and that's when we need to think about these rules upon which we base our automatic behavior.

At the same time as your child learns these rules of the game, he or she can learn to think about how to use them. This is the second major psychological part of being a competent person, utilizing our ability to think for ourselves, if necessary, when society's or our particular environment's "rules" change or are no longer valid guidelines for us. If, for example, we are waiting for the light to change at an intersection and a pair of armed muggers comes up to us, it is in our own interest to judge for ourselves what is best to do: wait for the light to change as society wants us to do, or go like hell, dodging oncoming traffic. And when a friend wants your child to do something illegal, immoral, or fattening, it is in your child's best interest to exercise his or her ability to think and decide which is more appropriate—to always be nice to a friend, or to break this social rule by refusing to go along with what the friend wants.

How should you go about teaching your child to be a competent person, and how should your child behave? Child-rearing opinions vary, from the classical "Children should be seen and not heard" to the equally superficial notion that children should be protected from every hardship because they are only children once. Your common sense is your best tool for judging both folklore and expert advice. Forget how highly these have been praised. Common sense, for example, tells us that children are not going to learn very much about how to be competent adults if they are not allowed to interact with adults verbally and otherwise. Common sense tells us that if you want to learn how to cope with hardship, you have to experience at least a bit of it to practice coping with it, even if it causes difficulties, or sometimes hurts, or bruises your ego occasionally. Common sense should also tell you that as a parent, you have to decide for yourself what is the best way to rear your child. You really are your own judge in everything, including child rearing.

Children: Junior Adults in Training

The most practical way to view children is to see them as junior adults in training. If you want to save your child from having to learn painfully how to become competent after reaching adulthood, you can begin teaching your child how to think and behave appropriately long before that time. You can do this by making sure that the consequences of your child's behavior are at least a sample, a taste, of those an adult would receive. This, briefly, is the major principle used in teaching your child how to be competent.

This perspective of child rearing fits hand in glove with your child's learning to be his or her own judge. If children are to learn how to cope with and solve life's problems, then they must also learn the responsibilities that go along with being one's own judge and doing what one wants. The prime assertive right points this out explicitly: You are your own ultimate judge of your emotions, thinking, and behavior, and are responsible for the initiation and consequences of what you feel, think, and do.

As soon as children are old enough to understand you, you can teach them to make thinking for themselves routine. But before they start thinking for themselves, you have to teach them to discriminate—that is, give them something to make decisions about. Avoid rules that begin with "Always . . ." or "Never . . ." except where they pertain to obvious dangers, such as electrical wires, hot stoves, busy streets, or abandoned refrigerators. And to make sure your children see the worth of these rules of the game at the same time that they're learning to think and reason, don't teach blind obedience just because rules are made to be followed.

Instead, teach your children that the rules of the game are valuable because of their payoffs. The rules will help them avoid getting into trouble and will save them a lot of time and effort when they become adults.

Let me emphasize that the purpose of teaching your child the rules of the game is not to make your child more obedient and thereby make your life a bit easier. Nor is giving feedback to your child intended primarily to allow *you* to correct your child's behavior. Since children are children for only a few short years, and will be adults with adult problems for the rest of their lives, the major goal is to teach them how to think without you, so they can conduct their lives effectively, productively, and as happily as possible twenty years or more from now—i.e., in the twenty-first century.

Child rearing whose intent is to govern how the child shall behave under all circumstances—to make the child conform to a particular perception of what is "proper"—will probably limit the child's thinking and options in life. The child will also, unfortunately, have limited coping skills, having assumed that what was learned from mom and dad would cover all of life. It will not.

There are few people more devastated and angry than the adult who finally realizes that what dad and mom taught as gospel is only the accumulated personal preferences and prejudices of a number of past generations. More than 200 years ago, Thomas Paine, the eloquent American patriot, commented on our arrogant assumption that we know what is best for everyone, now and forever. Said Paine: "The vanity and presumption of governing beyond the grave is the most ridiculous and insolent of all tyrannies."

Each new generation needs the freedom to adapt its values and rules to the future environment in which it will live. Its members will have that necessary freedom to adapt successfully only if they know how to think for themselves in judging their own rules on how to live.

Protecting Your Younger Child from the Negative Consequences of Being a Child Learning to Be an Adult

How do you go about giving your child the freedom to think and the ability to use social rules as productive guidelines, and also make growing up as positive an experience as possible? First of all, protect your younger child from any really harsh consequences of making mistakes as he or she learns how to be a competent person. Remember, your child is just a child who is learning how to do the correct thing by thinking things out according to their consequences. A child is bound to make mistakes in learning what the rules are and how to think them out, and I can guarantee that your child will do very little thinking if heavy consequences are heaped upon him or her for doing the wrong thing.

I make this point because children are sometimes punished in ways that no adult in his right mind would put up with. When was the last time you were sent to your room without dinner when you did something wrong? If you want your child to learn how to think, avoid using contrived negative consequences that drastically complicate matters by telling your child he or she is an incompetent when things go wrong. It is much better to tell your child that his or her *behavior* is wrong than to tell the child that something is wrong with him or her personally. If your feedback to your child routinely says that he or she is incompetent, the child will eventually believe what you say, and may not try to do anything except avoid punishment and the possibility of being called an incompetent again. A clear message that he or she is incompetent is probably not what an adult would receive from you for a mistake or misbehavior. If you called another adult an incompetent, he or she would simply tell you to go to hell and ignore you.

Predictive Feedback: If You Did What Your Child Does, What Would Happen to You?

You can use predictive corrective feedback to shape your child's behavior into what is acceptable without saying, verbally or nonverbally, that your child is an incompetent and a disappointment. When you use predictive feedback, you give your child only a small sample of what would happen to you if you did the same thing your child has done. Predictive feedback is your best guess as to what will happen to your child as an adult when that particular misbehavior is engaged in. Misbehaviors and mistakes always have a natural negative cost in effort, time, emotional distress, money, etc. With predictive feedback, your child learns to foresee the realistic, practical consequences, or cost, of his or her misbehavior and mistakes, and to correct them in order to avoid these negative consequences. Let me point out that if a perceived misbehavior or mistake has no cost, then it is not misbehavior or a mistake—it is only a different way of doing things.

Let's look at a simple example of predictive feedback to see what it means, and then see how it can be applied generally in helping your child to develop a practical competence at being his or her own judge. Suppose you want your young son to learn the rules of the game about nudity, but also how to decide for himself when it is okay to be nude and when it is not. To accomplish this, you can teach your son that nudity per se is not wrong, but that in some circumstances it is inappropriate. Tell him that if as an adult he goes out in the street nude, people will be upset and he may well be hauled off to a psychiatric hospital for an examination. In short, teach your child that except in certain circumstances—such as sunbathing in the south of France, changing clothes in locker rooms, visiting nudist camps, taking part in political freedom-of-expression demonstrations, or within the family—public nudity as an adult will result in some definite negative consequences.

Since he is only a child, you don't arrange for him to experience the same negative consequences that would befall an adult. You don't have to get everyone in the neighborhood together and agree that the next time your child goes outside in the nude, everyone will scream and faint and he will be hauled off by the local mental-health team in a strait-jacket. Instead, give your child some negative feedback that is only a sample of what would happen to him as an adult. You could, for instance, tell your child in your best mock-serious voice that you are "shocked" at his indiscriminate behavior, running around outside nude! With this predictive sample of adult feedback, you give your child's primitive emotional and nervous system just a small foretaste of the negative consequences he would experience as an adult from people other than yourself. You give him no negatives for being nude in private. In short, you don't punish your child for being in the nude, or shout and scream at him, because that is not predictive; no reasonable person does that to an adult who goes nude in public.

This is probably not much different from what you would do, or have already done, in teaching your younger child other social rules. Predictive corrective feedback to teach a child what to do in a simple situation like nudity is not radical theory but practical common sense. In using predictive feedback you do not force your child to do one thing or another; you present the child with alternatives, and the natural consequences of each choice. When a child is stubborn, as younger ones and teenagers often are, you don't have to say yes or no to his or her behavior. Allow the child to make the choice and then experience the natural consequences of this choice.

My grandmother used this same kind of common sense to teach me the natural negative consequences of my actions when I was six years old and I threatened to run away. Grandma didn't laugh, put me down, or tell me not to be silly. She only said, "Then you'll need to take some food with you on your trip." She made me a bologna sandwich, wrapped it in a blue bandana tied to the end of a stick, and waved good-bye as I trooped out the kitchen door in my knickers and cap, my sandwich over my shoulder. Not knowing where to run away to, I sat down on the back stoop and ate my sandwich. When I came back an hour later, I told her it was a good sandwich, and I had decided to stay. Grandma just smiled.

You may be asking how predictive feedback works for other behaviors, less simple than nudity or threatening to run away when one is six years old. To answer that question, you have to look at why certain child-rearing practices work poorly—for example, the misuse of discipline to control a child's behavior.

Spanking: Will It Make a Child More Competent?

The purpose of disciplining a child is to help the child learn how to live in a consistent manner with other human beings. This aim is not very well understood by all parents. A typical parent's response to a child's misbehavior is "You broke the rules, so now you get it!" This perception by the parent assumes that there is some great set of rules laid down in ancient Mesopotamia that all children must obey lest they turn out to be slothful, indolent, unmotivated, perverted, and generally not very nice. It is not surprising therefore that discipline is used, and misused, to enforce these rules.

Under the guise of discipline, however, harsh consequences are sometimes used to punish or take revenge on a child more for upsetting a parent than for breaking a rule. In practice, so-called discipline is usually arbitrarily invoked to show the child "I'm the boss, and you disobeyed me!" rather than to help the child learn how to correct his or her behavior.

If you agree that the worthwhile intent of discipline is to help a child learn to live competently with others, should you discipline a child using spanking or other physical punishments for misbehavior or mistakes? Traditionalists tell you, "Spare the rod and spoil the child," claiming that more children today commit crimes and sass their parents because spanking has been largely abandoned. Antispankers argue that physical pain and punishment are inhumane and likely to cripple children psychologically for the rest of their lives.

Both these arguments are nonsense and completely miss the important question. Instead of trying to choose between conflicting but equally inflexible viewpoints such as the above, we should be asking ourselves what we want out of disciplining a child in the first place. The practical purpose of discipline is to teach the child how to regulate his or her own behavior—to discipline *oneself*. The purpose of predictive feedback is to make children aware of the consequences they will face for certain behaviors as adults and thus cause them to regulate their own behavior accordingly. Therefore, it's a waste of time to ask if disciplinary spanking is theoretically good for your child or not. There is a more important and practical question to ask: Is spanking predictive of what your child will experience for breaking the same rule as an adult, and will spanking make your child more competent?

Spanking has been used as a disciplinary method for a long time. Physical punishment of adults for misbehaving has also been used since ancient times. The two are related. Less than 300 years ago in Western society, people were routinely executed, burned, hanged, drowned, flogged, whipped, branded, beaten, or publicly humiliated for violating social codes. In order to survive, seventeenth-century children needed to be prepared for the fact that their world was harsh and cruel. Therefore, if you were rearing your child in that harsh society and, out of love and misguided thinking, refused to spank your child mildly as a sample of what to expect and try to avoid in adult life, your child rearing would have been idealistic to the point of negligence.

Survival: Where "Always" and "Never" Are Used

Today's equivalent of harsh seventeenth-century discipline is mildly slapping the hand of an infant to teach it that electrical wires are dangerous. The infant can't understand what you tell it, so you have to use very primitive means that the primitive brain can interpret to simulate what will happen if the child keeps pulling on the lamp and tele-phone wires. For the same reason, you spank your very young child for running out into the street without looking. When children are old enough to understand the danger, you simply tell them about it. But with young children, who have no abstract comprehension of streets and automobiles as dangerous things, you can mildly spank their bottoms (an attention-getting device, really) with the purpose of teaching them in the best way you can that streets are very dangerous for young children. If your child is really too young to understand that he or she may get hurt by running out into the street, you can at least demonstrate that you will get very angry when he or she does this. This very real negative consequence that the child will understand can be substituted for the abstract, yet very likely, negative consequence of being hurt by an automobile in the street.

As you can see from these two examples, mild physical negative consequences are used only to increase the chances of your child's survival when the child is too young to really understand the importance of what you are saying. These are also instances where you want to use the words *always* and *never* in teaching the rules to a young child. Where survival is concerned, you don't have to get fancy. Forget about possible negative psychological effects on the child's future development —if you don't use some physical feedback to teach the child what to expect, there may not be a future.

Punishment: An Invented Human Negative

It is important to note that physical means used to keep a child from being harmed are not intended as punishment. Punishment has little effect on behavior because it is artificial and usually so emotionally traumatic that its effects block any real learning. Punishment is an invented human negative, based on taking revenge for wrongdoing. No other species uses punishment. If you watch a cat discipline its kittens, you will observe mother cat, with claws retracted, whack a kitten that gets too aggressive and rambunctious with mom. That whack is a nega-tive consequence predictive of what other cats would do if the kitten did the same thing after it was fully grown. It is sufficient to teach the kitten not to get aggressive with adult cats. You do not see mother cat go up to the kitten and behave as if she had just said, "Okay, stupid! Now I'm going to beat the hell out of you because you got rough with your mother!"

Research and observation tell us that physical punishment is ineffective in changing behavior unless it is so severe that its use would be criminal, cruel, and inhumane in our society. Physical punishment is ineffective in child rearing because the child usually does not make the connection between the punishment and the behavior being punished. This point is made very clear by the joke about a father who decides to punish his two teenage sons for using swearwords casually. At Sunday dinner, dad asks older son what he wants to eat. His son replies, "A potato, broccoli, and I'll have some of that goddamned meat loaf." Without saying anything, dad clouts him on the ear, folding him over, unconscious, face down in the soup bowl. Then dad turns, smiles, and cordially asks his second son what he wants to eat. Younger son looks at his father, at his unconscious brother, and then back at dad, and says, "Uh, I don't know, but I sure don't want any of that goddamned meat loaf!"

If you use physical means routinely to regulate behaviors of your child, let me point out that we are not now living in a seventeenth-century society. We have radically changed our social standards over the past 300 years to the point where physical punishment of an adult is now totally forbidden, at least in cultures where the majority of the population is educated and values human life and dignity. Such being the case, to use physical punishment to correct childish errors and willfulness is to falsely predict to your child what to expect as an adult. Therefore, if you spank your child routinely, I would have to conclude that (a) you routinely and irrationally act out anger and need professional help, or (b) you expect your child to be associated in the future with a bunch of thugs who will do the same to your adult child as you do now.

Swearing: Teaching Your Child to Do It with Real Feeling

What do you do when your child begins to learn profanities from the other kids, and starts to use them in front of you? To take the best tack in dealing with this behavior, realize first that to be competent, your child has to know about swearing, and how to swear, but appropriately so. Like nudity, lying, and sex, swearing is a behavior about which a child has to use discrimination, deciding what is appropriate or inappropriate.

Your child must learn not only the appropriate use of swearing but what other people are trying to communicate when it is used. Although your own parents may have tried to stop you from using profanities as a child, you still know them, and probably use them occasionally because they serve a definite purpose in human communication.

Usually when you hear profanity from an adult, it is in the form of a single word expressed with feeling, or a string of angry, obscene words. We commonly describe this human behavior as "swearing," which means "taking an oath." Solemn or profane, an oath expresses how a person truly feels, and this is the psychological purpose of profanity: to communicate to others that something is seriously wrong and the person is very upset. You can observe for yourself that this is the usual way profanity is used, and the way we automatically interpret it. You can also observe that in hearing profanity, the majority of us seem more concerned with what is wrong than with the violation of manners. Profanity tells us very quickly that something out of the ordinary is happening: The other person is very upset, or needs help, or is so angry that he wants other people to stay away from him until he calms down.

Our acceptance of this use of profanity to communicate something emotionally important contrasts with our typical reaction of disgust or discomfort when we hear profanity used in a casual manner. My impression is that most of us react negatively to casual profanity, not because of the words themselves but because we don't approve of anyone taking a false or casual oath—i.e., using a perfectly good emotional communication device in a false way. You can check out your own reaction to casual profanity by comparing how you feel when a very young child repeatedly uses four-letter words to get a shock response from you and when a teenager casually uses the same words. You react to the young child almost with amusement, while your reaction to the teenager is quite negative. You very likely feel that the teenager is ignorant, or dumb, should know better by now, may not have been reared properly, or comes from a very low type of social environment.

With this information on the real payoff of profane swearing, how can you teach your child to use four-letter words appropriately? First of all, tell your younger child to be serious when he swears; that he should only use these words when something is really wrong and he means them. Then, if your child still uses them to shock you, don't use punishment, but predictive feedback. When adults swear casually, do you wash their mouths out with soap? No. Do you shake your finger at them? No. Do you threaten to tell their fathers? No. So when your child casually uses four-letter words, you don't do these things either. In all likelihood you would ignore the adult until the casual swearing stopped, while at the same time giving the usual nonverbal messages of disapproval—a questioning, lifted eyebrow; a slight smirk of contempt; a slightly negative downward shake of the head, etc. When your child starts to use four-letter words casually, that is the best natural, negative feedback to use.

If you physically punish your child with invented negatives such as soap in the mouth, spanking, or slapping, your child will likely develop a conditioned, negative emotional reaction to anyone else's profanity. And that doesn't make sense. Why in the world would you want your child to be emotionally conditioned to get upset when someone else swears? Predictive feedback does not have this unfortunate side effect. It doesn't punish swearing so that the child will be upset in the future when he or she even hears it. But without psychic trauma, it does teach your child to become discriminating about swearing in the presence of adults.

Lying and Misbehaving: Two Separate Problems

There is another advantage of using predictive feedback in teaching your child the rules of the game and how to place them in perspective. Predictive feedback does not take away your child's dignity or self-respect. For example, what can you do when your child, as most young, naïve children are wont to do, begins to lie as a coping method for avoiding the consequences of misbehavior?

In dealing with childish lies, most parents get their priorities backward: A child is often punished for telling the truth and gets off scot-free for lying successfully. If the child tells the truth when you insist upon it, and then catches hell from you, he or she soon learns that it's dumb to tell the truth. So in rearing your child, remember that misbehaving and lying are two separate behaviors, one of which is much more important than the other. If your child learns he or she has to lie routinely to avoid invented negative consequences, that will create many future problems, including the breakdown of essential communication between the two of you.

Given this dilemma, how do you keep communications open between you and your child, and still maintain order in your household? Again, your choice of feedback is the answer. If you use contrived negative consequences, like spanking or other unrealistic punishments, for doing something wrong, I can almost guarantee that your child will lie to you. The real negative result of contrived punishment for misbehavior is that your child's dignity and self-respect are threatened. A child will do almost anything not to feel and look like a fool, including lying to you. If you use predictive feedback—a taste of the natural negative consequences that the child would face as an adult for misbehaving—you avoid taking away your child's self-respect, and he or she is not likely to lie to you about misbehavior. Moreover, a taste of the adult consequences usually does the trick in getting the child to think twice about misbehaving again in the same way.

Adult mistakes and even adult misbehavior usually require only that the mistake be corrected or its negative results eliminated—that is, there is a cost to the person who misbehaves. Treat your children the same way. For example, if your daughter breaks your jar of hand cream after you told her not to play with it, she has to face your displeasure, clean up the mess, and pay for a replacement jar out of her next allowance. This addresses her misbehavior but does not take away her dignity and self-respect.

Also keep in mind that lying, like nudity, is not something you want to absolutely prohibit; rather, you want your child to learn to use discrimination in deciding when lying is appropriate. If you train your child never to lie, you are both going to be extremely embarrassed when your child tells a neighbor something not very complimentary that you said in private. Rules about lying are best taught with qualifications that make them subject to your child's thinking and judgment. You do want your child to have the ability to tell a boldfaced lie without flinching when the alternative is to hurt someone unnecessarily. If, for example, you ask your teenage daughter how old you look, do you really want the truth, or do you want to hear that you still look sexy and attractive?

Childhood Sexuality: Rules Set by Society, Not Parents

Another child-rearing subject in which the use of predictive feedback makes common sense is sexuality and sexual experimentation, with its presumed complications for character development and morality. Let me assure you that childhood sexuality and sexual response are natural. All children get sexually aroused from birth onward because such arousal is controlled by the fully active involuntary nervous system of the infant. Male infants are repeatedly observed to have spontaneous erections. Similar sexual arousal is presumed to occur in female infants, though in their case sexual arousal is not so readily observable. Some authorities theorize that childhood arousal of sexual responsiveness may even be necessary for proper development of the neurological connections between the primitive brain and the not yet fully developed thinking cortex of the growing child. So when you see your child showing sexual interest or arousal at any age, keep in mind that such behavior is natural, and may even be necessary for a happy sex life as an adult.

Nevertheless, some parents are so uncomfortable with any sign of sexuality in their offspring that they treat sexual development as something magical that is supposed to happen overnight just before adult mating, and they either repress everything concerning sex in their children or severely punish any sexual gestures. Even among the vast majority of parents in our society who are not anxious about sex and sexuality, we still observe clinically that most of their children are punished for doing anything sexual, such as exploring the genital area. They are taught that fondling oneself is either unnatural or animalistic and not what a person in their particular social class should do. So, no matter how the parents view sexuality, the result for the child is often the same. The child, unfortunately, doesn't know the reason for being chastised, except for the general charge of doing something "bad."

How then does one deal with the problem of sexual impulses in a child, and still let the child develop his or her own sexuality in a natural way? This question is best answered by asking another one, using the skill of Negative Inquiry and the TRAP model given in the last chapter: What is it about a child showing sexuality that is bad? If you use your imagination and list all the possible responses to this question using the TRAP model, you undoubtedly will come up with some possible negative results of childhood sexuality: for example, that the child may get to like sex too much and become promiscuous, or may not be able to control his or her sexuality.

I can assure you of two things with respect to worries like these. First, these worries are based on an assumption that the sex drive is something instinctual and automatic that people cannot control. This assumption has no basis in fact, and is on the same level of understanding and explaining behavior as "The devil made me do it." If that assumption were true—and it is not—there would be damned little anyone could do to control children's sexual behavior, and yet it is easily controlled. Second, there isn't a shred of scientific or clinical evidence indicating that innocuous sexual experience in childhood leads to sex getting out of control.

After going through all the possible negatives you might list using Negative Inquiry and the TRAP model, you will find only one that is quite specific, concrete, and affects you personally. Without any discrimination training for sexual behavior, your child is very likely to fondle himself or herself in front of guests or neighbors and embarrass you, your spouse, and other family members. This negative TRAP *result* is a practical one that you can work to eliminate without giving the child unnecessary sexual inhibitions.

In adult life, we are not punished for harmless forms of sexual expression. If you decide to demonstrate *Kama Sutra* sexual position number 78 to your neighbors on your front lawn, you will not be arrested, but only stopped from doing it in public and then referred by the police to the local mental-health clinic. Nevertheless, aside from exhibitionism, sexual expression in public is so rare as to be nonexistent for all practical purposes. As adults, we know the negative consequences that will befall us if we attempt public sex, so we avoid it. The TRAP *alternative*, therefore, is to teach your child, using predictive feedback, that sexual expression in adult life is usually a private affair.

When your child shows sexual interest, you can teach him or her that sex is not wrong but that sex is a private activity. Just as you teach your child when nudity will have negative consequences, so you can teach the child when sexual expression will have negative consequences, and when it will not. Most important, you can protect your child, who is simply a child learning about sex, from any invented negative consequences of expressing his or her sexuality as a child. For example, when your child can understand what you say, and begins fondling himself or herself in the presence of other family members, you can simply tell the child the same thing you or anyone else would tell an adult displaying sexual behavior: "Go somewhere else and do that, or stop." You can tell your child that he or she has a choice of continuing to do it in private, in the bedroom, or to remain watching TV with the family. Given the choice between watching TV or retreating to the bedroom to fondle himself or herself, your child will most likely confirm the observation that human beings are usually more interested in watching TV than in engaging in sexual activity. With repeated predictive and nonpunitive feedback like this, your child will learn that sexual exploration is okay in private, but not in public.

Some of my students, and others, have questioned this way of dealing with a growing child's sexuality. Sex, they argue, is one of the most natural human acts and should never be inhibited in any way, by any means, because of straitlaced, arbitrary pretensions. Why inhibit the child at all, they ask, even by setting up arbitrary social-discrimination training?

While I appreciate their sentiments, these questioners confuse the way one thinks things should be and the way they are. The children you teach today are going to have to deal with social restrictions on their sexuality twenty years from now. Perhaps there will be fewer restrictions then, but it's safe to assume that our sexual behavior will not be totally unrestricted. If our social structure were totally different and placed no restrictions on adult sexual expression, I would agree with their argument for teaching the child that "anything goes." Though such a world would be distasteful to me personally, only because it would be radically different from the one I was reared in, that would not be a valid reason to ignore its realities and fail to prepare the young child for adulthood in that world. But there is no expectation of sex on the sidewalks in the near future, so it would be very foolish to base your child's training on that kind of sexual freedom.

Child's Play: Training Ground for Adulthood

Like some others I have worked with, you may feel a bit uneasy about using predictive feedback to teach a child to be a competent person. You may be saying to yourself, "That seems like such a cold, mechanical way of rearing a child. It may be efficient, but can't the child and parent enjoy each other and have some fun, too? Does everything have to be part of training the kid to be an adult?"

To answer this question, you have to look at the reality of how children learn. The child's brain makes no distinction between what it learns when we say we are training the child and what it learns when we say we are having fun with the child, or showing love and caring for the child. Those are simply arbitrary labels we tack on for our own convenience. They have no neurological basis. Everything that happens to a child, everything that is introduced into the child's environment, is part of the child's learning of how to be a human being. When you cuddle your infant, for instance, you are teaching your child something important: that you are the best parent in the world and your child is highly thought of. When you chastise your child, you are teaching him something different. When you answer a cry from the crib, you are telling your child that he or she is not alone in life, and also that the child has some power over you.

When the child plays, he or she also learns the realities and characteristics of whatever is being played with, as well as the consequences of whatever is done. Playing with a puppy, your child learns that puppies are fun, cuddly, small, delicate and easily bruised, often leaky and wet, and with sharp teeth that hurt. Playing with blocks, your child learns that they are things to build bigger things with, that they don't bounce like rubber balls, and that they can hurt—for example, when you hit sister on the head with one. Playing with a friend, your child learns that other kids are fun, a pain, possessive, grabby, and sure to start a ruckus, which has to be resolved if play is to continue.

Children learn much of what they acquire in becoming human from their play activities through the trial-and-error experience of the consequences of those play behaviors. When we look at our children playing, we just see them having fun, but actually they are learning to deal with life. For this reason child psychologists use play activities as tools for diagnosing children's emotional and behavioral problems—such as anxiety and shyness, or poorly regulated aggressive coping—and play therapy is often used to retrain the child to cope better. Play therapy helps a child realize he or she is capable of making a positive impact upon things and people.

Children learn all sorts of things when they play together. Other young mammalian vertebrates—such as monkeys, cubs, and pups—prepare themselves for future coping as adult protectors, aggressors, and social beings by playing with each other. Human children do the same thing. A common mistake parents make is to protect a child from experiencing the consequences of rough-and-tumble play. If junior gets a bloody nose, instead of treating his injury and then sending him back into the fray to learn how to avoid getting a bloody nose, he is often isolated from the "riffraff," who are not yet civilized. The child who stays in such play, with all its ups and downs, learns a lesson that lasts into adulthood: how to cope and work things out when the world is not perfect. This child is much less likely to withdraw as an adult from difficult situations and get depressed, feeling helpless in the face of adversity and hard times.

The traditional practice of restricting female children to playing only with other females, and then limiting what they can play at to keep their experiences gentle and ladylike, is probably one reason why we see a much higher statistical incidence of depression in adult females than in adult males. This restriction of their personal practice environment as young children deprives girls of many profitable learning experiences in dealing with their environment and solving the problems it presents to them in later life. I suspect that tomboys who are allowed to experience and solve all sorts of youthful problems are much less likely to cope poorly as adults and experience less depression than the typical female child reared with traditional methods.

A successful treatment for children who get overly depressed, to the point of refusing to interact with other children, is to place them in a younger play group, where they can learn give-and-take coping as well as the problem-solving skills not learned earlier from an original peer group. So if you find your child playing with a younger group, or your son playing with girls, who are more forgiving, instead of with boys, this does not necessarily mean he or she needs a session with the local shrink. The child is only doing something predictable and valuable, in order to learn what he or she needs to cope socially, emotionally, and intellectually, if this was not learned from the peer group. At the same time, the child is protecting himself or herself from the negative consequences of being unprepared to play and cope with children of the same age or sex. When the child feels capable of interacting socially, he or she will rejoin the appropriate group.

This notion of giving your child realistic predictive feedback applies to children of all ages. As children start to mature, unless you want to follow them around bailing them out of trouble for the rest of your life, you have to allow them to experience more and more fully the natural negative consequences of not behaving as a competent person. This is where deciding things for oneself and taking responsibility for the consequences of ones decisions comes into play. Let's look now, in some detail, at how to foster maturity and competency, particularly in teens and preteens, by not bailing children out of the natural consequences of their behavior.

Teaching Children to Be Responsible for the Natural Negative Consequences of Their Behavior

Well-meaning parents often get into trouble because they feel compelled to protect their children from the natural negative consequences of not doing things in the most efficient and effective way. In talking to parents from all circumstances, I find it amazing how many problems this attitude generates for the family—and particularly for the mother, who most often believes that she is responsible for the child's behavior and its consequences. Most mothers I have known socially or counseled professionally place themselves in the role of being the "elastic" in the family. If anything puts a strain on the family organization, mom is the "elastic" that gives, in both meanings of that word. Mothers are prompted to do this by the erroneous assumption that if someone doesn't give, the family will fall apart, or some other horrible thing will happen. They also assume they have no choice in the face of irrational children who cannot be influenced except by extreme means that mothers hesitate to use.

Using Negative Social Consequences to Get Children to Clean Up Their Own Rooms

Mothers get into a bad habit by asking children to clean up their rooms when the children are still too young to be very competent at this task. Mom then gets into the pattern of asking, and then doing the job herself. As the child gets older, he or she takes it for granted that if he or she doesn't clean up the room, mom will eventually do it herself.

To change this chronic behavior pattern, you will need to suffer some minor discomfort. The point in having children clean up after themselves is not to teach them how to be maids or valets for someone else, but to teach them responsibility for their own actions. The best, and only, practical method I have seen used by mothers who have for years bailed their sons and daughters out of cleaning up after themselves is to use predictive negative feedback: Let the clothes, games, sheets, and blankets fall where they may; no matter what, the child cleans up and not mom. Mothers I have advised to try this method have reported that the time it typically takes for a child to go from complete slob to compulsive nitpicker ranges from a few days to a few weeks, depending mostly on how old the child is, and how sociable.

The success of this method is due mostly to the child's learning that a disorderly room is (a) more personal trouble than one that is orderly, and (b) a social negative. Being unable to wear a favorite T-shirt because it has not yet been fished out from under the bed and cleaned of its ice-cream stains, or finding no clean T-shirts at all, is a definite negative social consequence after a certain age. Cleaning up one's room is very much a socially responsive behavior. You may try unsuccessfully for years to get Junior to help clean the family car, and then suddenly one day he is asking you to get new seat covers so he can spiff it up for his first date.

In terms of room-cleaning responsibility, some mothers have put this negative social influence to work for them much earlier than puberty by inviting their children's friends over and then suggesting that they play in the child's messy room. They report good results.

Using Negative Social Consequences to Get Children to School on Time

Negative social consequences also play a big part in your child's behaviors related to school. A colleague of mine complained to me over coffee that the whole process of getting her two kids up, washed, dressed, fed, and then driven to school, had been growing longer and more trying each morning over the past several months. Curious as to why this problem was developing, I asked if her children were getting to school late. She said that in the past few weeks, no matter how much she'd prodded them to speed things up, they'd been late at least two days out of five.

Remembering how it was when I was their age—being late for class was a sin, with twenty-five pairs of eyes following my every step from door to teacher's desk and then to my seat—I asked her if she was doing anything to make them not feel so bad about being late.

"Oh," she replied, "I always take them into their class and make up an excuse for the teacher so they won't be embarrassed the way I was as a child."

Pointing out that her concern for her children's minor embarrassment might be the cause of her problems each morning, I suggested she think about which was more important: her kids' taking responsibility for getting to school on time, or their temporary embarrassment at being late without mom there to bail them out.

I saw my colleague again two weeks later. She told me that the morning after our chat, she let the kids dawdle as much as they wanted, didn't drive like a maniac to school, and then shooed them out of the car at the entrance and watched them walk slowly and reluctantly toward their classrooms. "The younger one even started to come back to the car from halfway across the playground and I had to tell him to get on with it," she told me. "The next morning the kids were up and dressed before I put the coffee on, and were pestering me to get rolling. They've not been late since."

My colleague had created this problem for herself by lovingly protecting her children from the natural consequences of their own behavior. When she let them experience the consequences of their tardiness, they made their own choice in favor of being on time. More important, she was also teaching her children how to think, make decisions, and plan ahead instead of relying on mom.

Children with Problems: Are They Sick, or Just Protected from the Natural Consequences of Their Behavior?

Natural consequences of behavior are particularly important in helping children to mature and become competent in taking responsibility for themselves. Unfortunately, some parents interpret lack of personal responsibility on the part of a child as a potentially serious and complex psychological defect needing treatment. In fact, however, this is more often the result of a child's being shielded by overprotective parents (like my colleague in the above example) from the natural negative consequences of not being responsible for oneself. Mistakenly attributing irresponsibility to deep psychic causes is more frequent in parents of teens and preteens than in parents of younger children, since at their age teens and preteens "should know better."

For instance, one mother I counseled lived with her husband and three teenage sons in a rural area where the two oldest boys drove their own car to high school and the youngest had to catch a school bus each morning to junior high. When I talked to this worried mother, she told me that in the last few weeks her youngest son had been getting up late and showing no interest in school and she was having to force him to go. I asked all the usual background questions about fights at school, problems with teachers, etc., but this mother could not come up with any negatives that might cause reluctance about going to school. She then revealed why she wanted to speak to me. "The only thing I can think is that he's developed a school phobia, so I'm thinking of sending him to the local shrink to straighten him out."

Some children do get very anxious about school and refuse to go, but this is very rare and caused by some prior trauma. There was no evidence of that here. I was puzzled, until I finally remembered to ask about consequences.

"How does your son get to school each morning if he misses the bus?" I asked.

"Why, I drive him there, to make sure he goes," she said.

That was the key to curing the mysterious "mental illness" with which her son was inflicted. If he was late in catching the school bus, his caring, loving, but overprotective mother drove him to school.

The morning after our little talk, when her son was finally dressed and ready to leave, mom told him he would have to get to school on his own since she was going in the opposite direction. He was an hour and a half late with no excuse note from mom when he finally got there. I talked again with this mother a month later, and she told me that he had not missed the bus once since she'd let him experience the negative consequences of his behavior. She'd recovered from the problem she had created for herself, and ended by saying, "He's a clone of his father. He has nothing to do with my side of the family."

Homework and Studying: How Much Native Intelligence Does Your Child Need?

If your child does not do as well in school as you think he or she should, or does not do homework regularly, or refuses to study, before you start to worry about your child's IQ or possible lack of motivation or something else, there are a few simple things you would be wise to check out first, including the natural negative consequences of not studying. This is much like being told that your child may be hyperactive and first checking to see if he has a heat rash and/or his undershorts are too small. Or like checking to see if the refrigerator's plugged in before you call a repairman.

When younger children do not do their assigned homework, it is usually because they do not understand what has to be done. This may happen because a child is not yet assertive enough to raise a hand in class when teacher says, "Does everyone understand that?" If this is the case with your child, you can run through some of the assertive training dialogue given earlier about how to ask for help from a teacher. It also may happen because some teachers, unfortunately, send children home with a mimeo or Xerox copy of their homework without much explanation of what it is all about. So before you do anything else, make sure your child understands the homework assignment.

If you find yourself doing some remedial teaching of your child at home, the best way to make sure that your child understands what to do is to explain what needs to be done and then have your child repeat this back to you. If your child cannot tell you what is supposed to be done, he or she does not yet understand. You may have to go through this process several times until your child can tell you what needs to be done in the homework exercise. This does not mean there is anything wrong with your child or that your child has a low IQ. It simply means that communication between the teacher and the child is not what it could be.

On the other hand, your child may have a conscientious teacher who really prepares him or her for doing homework. Or you may have a really bright child who rapidly understands what any teacher, even a mediocre one, teaches. In either case your child will very likely make the mistake of assuming that if he or she understands the principle to be learned in the homework exercise, that's all there is to it. You have to correct this mistaken notion. The reason for homework is to practice and remember what is taught.

Studying, learning, and understanding the important things in life takes a lot of hard work, even for a person of intelligence. So if your child is bright, he or she will find that lots of work, including homework, is still required. If your child is average, that only means he or she has to work a bit longer to learn the same things as a brighter child. Even the astronauts do not learn how to fly a spaceship by intuition, but by rote practice, over and over again, until what they do is automatic. The ability to practice something over and over again is something all of us have. High intelligence is a gift that has only very specialized uses, and few of them are practical, everyday ones. To live a very good life, how often do you have to casually discuss nuclear physics, Goethe, quantum mechanics, Nietzsche (the philosopher, not the football player), and relativity over a glass of wine, all in the same evening?

The old saying about success being one-tenth inspiration and nine-tenths perspiration still reliably describes human productivity and happiness. For that reason, every child, no matter how well taught or how bright, needs to practice developing good study habits. Eventually the average child is going to run into a poor teacher, and the bright child is going to run into a learning principle that tests the limit of the child's ability to intuitively understand something. The only way you can help your child prepare for these inevitable situations in school and in later life is to see that he or she develops a habit of studying anything new until it can be easily used.

What do you do when your child doesn't want to study? This is usually not a problem with younger children, but can become one as children near their teens. The real negative consequences of homework are readily apparent to anyone who has ever gone to school. Homework is mostly hard, boring work. For a child, homework has few positives to balance out its negatives. The only motivation for doing homework is in learning something new—sometimes—and dreading that one will be called upon in class the next day for an example from the homework.

You can positively reinforce your child's doing his or her homework with social praise when the child is younger, or even with homemade "green stamps," which your child can save up and cash in for some treat or toy. This method does work for younger children, but not for older ones. You can do lots of things with a younger child that you cannot do with older ones. Your older child is a bit more sophisticated and cannot be bribed with token rewards. You could try using the same reward system with a bigger payoff—a new convertible, which the child could earn through studying. But if you have that much money, your child is likely to think, correctly, that he or she will be given one anyway without studying. More important, it is not a terrific idea to get your child into the habit of depending on short-term external rewards for studying. That would not be smart, since academic achievement later in college cannot depend on your rewards for every term paper and quiz. Using predictive negative feedback—the consequences of *not* doing homework—is a safer bet with older children.

Predictive Negative Consequences: The Great Motivator for Homework and Studying

The TRAP model of behavior change can help you come up with realistic predictive feedback for use in solving this problem. To determine a specific, concrete, and personal negative TRAP *result* of your child's not studying, you can use Negative Inquiry: "What is it about my child not studying that is bad?" One answer would be "He won't get good grades." You can follow that response up with "What is it about his getting poor grades that is bad?" A likely response would be "He won't graduate from high school or go on to college." Again following up, you can ask, "What is it about his not graduating or not going on to college that is bad?" The likely response would be "If he doesn't go to college, he won't get a really good job, and if he doesn't even graduate from high school, he will have to do menial things to support himself." That is a likely negative consequence of a child's refusal to apply himself in academic learning.

At this point you have isolated a specific negative *result* of your child's not studying. However, it has very little connection to the here and now, or to the relationship between you and your child, both of which are essential in communicating what you want and why you want it. A concrete personal negative is still needed, and you can find it by using Negative Inquiry in a personal way: "What is it about my son's ending up as a low-level laborer that bothers me?"

The very likely answer is "It makes me mad! If he doesn't want to learn, then why in hell am I working so hard to give this kid an educational advantage? If he doesn't want to study, he can start now learning how to do the menial things he will be doing for the rest of his life: He can help us out doing chores, cleaning johns, housekeeping, labor, etc."

That response spells out not only a specific, negative *result* to you personally when your child does not apply himself academically (he is wasting your time and effort in trying to help him), but also a very likely and serious future negative consequence for him. This negative consequence is what you want to give your child a taste of, as well as indicating the TRAP *alternative* and *payoff* (Workable Compromise) to correct the problem (negative TRAP *result*) that your child causes for you.

When your child balks at studying and complains about doing homework, don't try to make his studying easier, but make the TRAP *alternative* even more negative than studying. The TRAP *payoff* is that he can continue to not study if he chooses to use the *alternative*. Tell your child that if he doesn't want to do his homework, so be it. But also assertively insist, in your best Broken Record manner, that he has a choice between homework and what he will experience as an adult for not doing homework: menial labor. Give him a choice of mowing, raking, and fertilizing the lawn; polishing and waxing the floors; beating the rugs and carpets; cleaning the johns; cleaning out the garage—or doing his homework.

Again, avoid taking the limited viewpoint that this negative feedback is punishment for not studying, or a way to express your disappointment and anger with your child. Using your anger as feedback may get your child to study for a short time, but what he or she does in the long run is what counts. Calmly tell your child of the negative *result* to you of his not studying, and then point out the *alternative* to studying. Parents who have used this predictive feedback find that children usually prefer homework to the more boring and distasteful alternatives presented to them.

Helping Your Teenager Become a Responsible Person

Older children, too, can benefit from being exposed to the natural negative consequences of not taking responsibility for their own behavior. Teenagers who seem irresponsible are particularly frustrating for parents to deal with, especially when no amount of talking seems to make any difference. In such cases it's a virtual certainty that you are protecting your teenager from the natural negative consequences of not cooperating with you, and from taking personal responsibility for the consequences of his or her behavior.

For example, one mother I counseled had a problem with her seventeen-year-old son. He regularly brought his soiled school clothes to her at ten o'clock on Sunday night. No matter what she said, he would not bring his bundle of clothes to her on friday night after dinner when she did the family washing. She even took an assertiveness-training class on how to communicate and it didn't help.

When I asked her if she washed her son's clothes at ten o'clock every Sunday night, she answered, "Of course. He needs clean clothes for school on Monday. If I didn't wash them, I would feel so guilty!" I pointed out to her that she had a choice: She could let him go to school in dirty, wrinkled clothes on Monday morning and experience the natural negative consequences of not taking responsibility for getting them washed; or she could continue to wash them on Sunday night.

Mom tried this out, fought back her feeling of guilt when her son went to school on Monday morning, and found him asking for help in washing his own clothes Monday evening. After that experience, his bundle was in place next Friday evening without her asking for it.

Predictive feedback is important because it teaches your child what to expect in becoming a competent person. It is an alternative to contrived negative methods of controlling a child's behavior, which not only don't work but have negative side effects that complicate things unnecessarily. In each of the above examples, the parents involved saw that allowing their children to experience the natural consequences of behavior changed things very quickly, without arguments, soul-searching confessionals and resolutions, spanking, incentives, punishments, or over threats of a child's turning into a worthless degenerate. The greatest advantage in using predictive feedback, however, is that it allows a child to make his or her own decision on what is best to do, rather than you always having to tell the child what to do, or, even more distasteful, having to argue with your child about what to do, and then seeing nothing happen.

The Key Sequence in Helping Your Teenager to Mature and Become Independent of You: Communication, then Consequence

In helping your child mature into a competent person, keep in mind that the optimal sequence in shaping your child's behavior and attitudes is always communication first, then consequence. There is no guaranty that talking to your child about the problems he or she has to solve will fix them, but it won't hurt, and very often helps, even if only in terms of moral support. Maggie, a good friend of mine, placed the situation in perspective when she told her almost-teenager, "When you were a little kid and you fell down and hurt your knee, you ran to me because I could take care of your problem. I could put a Band-Aid on it and kiss it to make it better. Now I can't always make things better for you. I wish I could, but I can't. You have to take care of all the hurts and rotten things you get into yourself. I'll try to help as much as I can, but it's really up to you now."

Being handed the responsibility for his or her own actions can be made less scary by assuring your child that even though mistakes that hurt are going to be made, one can learn from those mistakes to avoid them in the future. Tell your teenager or preteen that he or she can learn from things that go wrong, particularly in relationships with peers, boyfriends, and girlfriends. If anything in life can be guaranteed, you can guarantee your teenager that if he or she screws things up in a relationship, there will always be another relationship to do better in.

There was a tremendous increase in my own personal self-respect when I realized as a fourteen-year-old that practice and learning were more important than native physical ability not only in sports but in almost everything else, such as how I related to other people, including girls. In short, I could learn how to be a competent sociosexual being, and did. Things would have been a bit easier, however, if I had also known that I didn't have to try so hard to find a girlfriend. Teenage girls will subtly let a boy know that they are interested in him. In retrospect, I'm sure that lots of girls were interested in me then. Perhaps they were just a bit too subtle.

This type of perspective gained from your own experience can help your teenager, not only in maturing but in being a happier person. So don't hesitate to talk to your child, especially when he or she is emotionally upset because of mistakes due to inexperience.

If communication in these or other areas does not help your child mature, then you can always use predictive feedback, no matter how bad the situation seems to be. But when things get bad, you have to rely on your common sense rather than your emotions as the best guide on what to do, and when. If you listen to your gut instead of what predictive feedback and your own good judgment tell you, you may find yourself in the unfortunate position of two very caring and very nice people I counseled some years ago. Their son was fourteen when they asked for my advice. This lad had been picked up the night before by the police for auto theft, driving under the influence, and for hit-and-run of twenty-eight cars in the course of a four-block, low-speed chase. He wasn't a competent person, even in outrunning the cops.

His mother told me that she intended to refinance her home so she could get him out on bail, and then hire the best attorney she could find in Beverly Hills to defend him. When I asked if he had been in trouble before, the parents gave me a long list of incidents, a number of them involving the police. Mom's perspective on her son's chronic misbehavior was that she hadn't gotten him very good legal help before, and that F. Lee Bailey was the answer to straightening him out.

I asked her when she was going to stop bailing (literally and figuratively) her son out of the trouble he was making for himself. Not understanding what I was getting at, she said her son needed her protection. So I asked her, "When are you going to stop protecting him? After he murders somebody because he's never had to be responsible for his own misbehavior? How much good is a Beverly Hills lawyer going to be then?"

While mom was very upset with what I said, she saw the point. "If he has to stay in jail, will that straighten him out?" she asked.

"Has staying out of juvenile hall straightened him out yet?" I responded.

I gave her my best guess on what to do, having only secondhand information. "You're not going to be around forever. If he really wants to climb fool's hill, it's about time he learned how to find and use a public defender himself. As we say in the trade, why not give him some benign reality therapy?"

These very concerned and loving parents had to inhibit their natural impulses and refrain from doing as they had done in the past: lecture their son to be good, and then bail him out of the consequences of his actions. When he called them again from the lockup, they backed off emotionally as much as possible and placed the responsibility for his behavior directly on him. They began to treat him as an almost-adult by asking when visiting day was, so they could see him. They also asked how long he was going to be in jail before he came to trial, whether he had talked to a lawyer yet, and how long he thought his sentence would be for what he did.

After a few days of sweating things out, on both sides of the jailhouse wall, their son was released into their custody. On my recommendation, the three of them went into family counseling to see if they could communicate better with each other, behaviorally as well as verbally. At last report, Junior hadn't gotten into trouble with the law again, and had refrained from recreational use of drugs and alcohol.

In teaching your child how to become a competent person, how do you know when to begin to let go of him or her emotionally and judgmentally? As I have already pointed out, this process is best started early in the child's life. If you start early, your son or daughter doesn't have to make a radical change in thinking and behavior after puberty or graduation from high school. Even if children have been reared in a way that makes them dependent upon their parents instead of on themselves, it's never to late to begin. Communication, then benign consequences apply throughout life, not just in growing up.

Learning to trust your teenager to do the appropriate thing in general is no different from learning to trust your teenager to drive a car. You teach him or her to drive, practicing in an empty lot or in the country, and then coach from the passenger seat in traffic. When he or she seems competent to solo, you cross your fingers and let him or her get a license and drive. Of course, the best way to ensure that your teenager will get in trouble is to take away his or her confidence by revealing that you are worried. The same common sense applies when your teenager begins to expand his or her world outside the family. If your offspring has a history of making judgments that work, you bite your tongue and let him or her try out that decision-making ability in situations you have no direct control over.

One Last Observation

Most parents want their children to turn out to be somewhat like themselves: Daughters should be interested in the same things as mom, and sons interested in what dad thinks important. You cannot predict what sort of life your youngster will lead, what career he or she will choose, etc. But if your son or daughter gives no indication of becoming what you would like him or her to be, hang in there nevertheless. For me, at least, this was one result of being taught by my grandmother to be my own judge of everything, including what mom and dad wanted me to be.

As a teenager, I disappointed my family, especially my father, because I showed no enthusiastic interest in any academic subject, demonstrated no serious motivation for a career, and never appeared to be involved in anything worthwhile. I found out years later that some of the adults who knew me as a teenager felt certain I would turn out to be a ne'er-do-well. I didn't begin to apply myself to what I really wanted to do until I was twenty-two.

My ego likes me to tell myself that those were my basic learning years and I hadn't yet found anything challenging enough to really interest me. More objectively, I was not yet a real participant. I was a very naïve observer who didn't know his ear from his elbow, but knew he didn't. I was a skeptical, not a cynical, observer, and tried to find out about everything, including myself, before getting prematurely seduced into a career choice or a commitment because of a superficial attraction or because of what other people told me. This was one result of my family's teaching me to always do my own thinking. I think it helped much more than it hurt.

So when you teach your child to think for himself or herself, you also run the risk that your child will take his or her own sweet time in making the important decisions in life. These choices may or may not be the ones you would make for your child if you could, and you have no way of knowing where these choices will take him or her. But speaking from personal experience, they will eventually lead (more likely wander) to where your child really wants to be, and one can't realistically ask for much more than that.

Finally, no matter what your child accomplishes as a result of your teaching him or her to think independently, it won't be enough for you as a parent. My mother told me a few years ago, after my father had died, that he was proud of me as an innovative psychologist and would have been very proud of my success as an author of a widely read book that helped many people. "But," she added quickly, to make sure I had things in proper perspective, "he did expect you to win a Nobel Prize."

Appendix

A sample List of Criticisms for Helping a Child Practice Negative Assertion, Fogging, and Assertive Inquiry.

Your ·

- body is too skinny.
- eyes are not pretty.
- face is plain.
- hands are gross.
- bottom is big.
- legs are too short.
- nose sticks out.
- teeth are funny.
- mouth is like a frog's.
- eyes are too far apart.
- hair is too butch.
- clothes are too cheap.
- grades are too low.
- smile makes you look like a moron.
- nose makes you look like a clown.
- ears make you look like an elephant.
- legs make you look like a stork.
- legs make you look like a hippo.
- stomach makes you look like a basketball on toothpicks.
- hairy arms make you look like an ape.
- mouth makes you look like an orangutan.
- feet are too big.
- waist is too fat.
- fingers are bony.
- chest is flat.

Your ·

- legs are too big.
- eyebrows are too bushy.
- lips are too big.
- eyes are too close.
- hair looks funny.
- ears stick out.
- habits are sloppy.
- bicycle is too old.
- feet make you look like you're wearing swimfins.
- clothes make you look like a ratbag.
- shoes make you look like a bum.
- skirt makes you look like a tart.
- blouse makes you look like you are on welfare.
- sweater looks like you got it out of the Goodwill box.
- tennies look like the *Queen Mary*.

You act ·

- like a jerk.
- like an ass.
- like a dummy.
- like an egotist.
- like a boy.
- like a fool.
- like a tomboy.
- like an idiot.
- like a sissy.
- like a little kid.
- like a klutz.
- like a moron.
- like a girl.

You are ·

- stupid.
- thoughtless.
- useless.
- a boring person.
- gross.
- crude.
- supercilious.
- not cool.
- upsetting.
- clumsy.
- not good-looking.

You will ·

- make us look bad.
- make an ass of yourself.
- look stupid.
- look like a jerk.
- embarrass everybody.
- look ugly.
- look like a nerd.

What you want is ·

- cheap.
- selfish.
- not good.
- not normal.
- uncivilized.
- rebellious.
- perverse.
- mean.
- not logical.
- fattening.
- against human nature.
- tacky.
- too easy.

What you want is ·

- too slick.
- greedy.
- stupid.
- sickening.
- antisocial.
- thoughtless.
- old-fashioned.
- lousy.
- gross.
- immoral.
- worthless.
- unnatural.
- unclean.
- narrow-minded.
- destructive.
- unkind.
- bad for you.
- too hard.
- not the way we do things.

What you want will ·

- cost too much money.
- make you lose weight.

- upset your stomach.
- make you look ugly.
- make the boys avoid you.
- make you unfeminine.
- upset everybody.
- make others jealous.
- give you a headache.
- give you pimples.
- make you unpopular.
- make you look bad.

What you want ·

- doesn't make sense.
- can't be done.
- has never been done before.
- was tried last year.
- won't work.

You sound like ·

- a dope.
- a nerd.
- a jerk.
- a kindergartener.

Remind your child of the last time he or she did something foolish. Then criticize him or her using possible negative outcomes like the following, and have the child use Negative Assertion or Fogging to cope with your criticism.

If you hadn't opened your big mouth, we wouldn't be in trouble.

If you had done your homework, you wouldn't be asking me for help.

If you hadn't been daydreaming, we would have won the game.

If you had paid attention, I wouldn't have to tell you now.

If you hadn't overslept, we wouldn't be late.

If you hadn't been so clumsy, we wouldn't have to clean up.

When you _____, you could have hurt yourself.

When you _____, you could have hurt somebody.

When you _____, you could have caught a cold.

When you _____, you could have screwed everything up.

When you _____, you could have caused an accident.

When you _____, you could have ruined your sister's (brother's, father's, mother's) project (party, outing, date, afternoon, etc.).

Technical Readings

Austin, J., Ladouceur, P., and Toole, C. Unpublished report. "The California Drug Suppression in Schools Program: Program Description and Resource Guide." San Francisco: National Council on Crime and Delinquency, 1984.

Benn, W., ed. *STAR: Social Thinking and Reasoning.* Irvine, Calif.: Irvine Unified School District, 1981.

Benn, W., ed. *PLUS: Promoting Learning and Understanding of Self.* Irvine, Calif.: Irvine Unified School District, 1982.

Kearney, A. "Evaluation of the Effectiveness of a Drug Prevention Program." *Journal of Drug Education* 10 (2) 1980.

Peele, S. "Reductionism in the Psychology of the Eighties: Can Biochemistry Eliminate Addiction, Mental Illness, and Pain?" *American Psychologist* 36 (8) 1981.

Robbins, L., Davis, D., and Goodwin, D. "Drug Use by U.S. Army Enlisted Men in Vietnam: A Follow-up on Their Return Home." *American Journal of Epidemiology* 99 1974.

Skager, R., and Maddahian, E. Unpublished report. "Substance Use Survey for the Orange County Board of Supervisors, 1983–84." Orange County, Calif.: 1984.